A YEAR WITH RABBI JESUS

*Biblical and Wesleyan-Holiness
Lessons for Maturing
Disciples of Jesus*

Barry L. Callen

Steven Hoskins

A YEAR WITH RABBI JESUS:
Biblical and Wesleyan-Holiness Lessons for Maturing Disciples of Jesus

Copyright © 2021 by Barry L. Callen & Steven Hoskins
Printed in the United States of America on acid-free paper

All rights reserved. No part of this book may be reproduced or transmitted in any form or by any means, electronic or mechanical, including photocopying, recording, or by any information storage and retrieval system, without the written permission of the publisher, except where permitted by law. For per-mission to reproduce any part or form of the text, contact the publisher. www.emethpress.com., 7216 S. Ridgetop Ct., Dardenne Prairie, MO 63668

Library of Congress Cataloging-in-Publication Data

Names: Callen, Barry L, author. | Hoskins, Steven, author.
Title: A year with Rabbi Jesus : biblical and Wesleyan-holiness lessons for maturing disciples of Jesus / Barry L Callen, Steven Hoskins.
Description: Dardenne Prairie, MO : Emeth Press/Anderson University Press, [2021] | Includes bibliographical references. | Summary: "These pages are a personal invitation to join a life-changing journey. We will be giving attention to the whole biblical revelation while walking with Rabbi Jesus and listening humbly to his interpreting Spirit. Everyone has been accepted into the School of the Master! All costs are pre-paid for the year by the sheer grace of God. The perspective of this journey through the weeks of the year will be from the Wesleyan-Holiness tradition"-- Provided by publisher.
Identifiers: LCCN 2021037230 (print) | LCCN 2021037231 (ebook) | ISBN 9781609471767 (paperback) | ISBN 9781609471798 (kindle edition)
Subjects: LCSH: Church year--Prayers and devotions. | Bible--Meditations. | Jesus Christ--Teachings. | Wesleyan Church--Doctrines.
Classification: LCC BV30 .C28 2021 (print) | LCC BV30 (ebook) | DDC 242/.3--dc23
LC record available at https://lccn.loc.gov/2021037230
LC ebook record available at https://lccn.loc.gov/2021037231

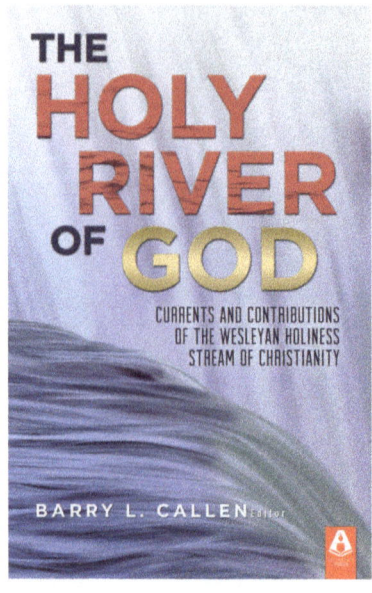

CONTENTS

Acknowledgments..vii
Introduction: Destination Emmaus..ix

WEEKS	SEASONS of the CHRISTIAN YEAR	THE LIFE LESSONS of our RABBI JESUS
	Season of Advent	
1	Advent 1	Joy in the Jumble
2	Advent 2	Anticipating is Not Enough
3	Advent 3	Don't Just "Put on a Happy Face"
4	Advent 4	Jerusalem? No, Bethlehem!
	Season of Christmas	
5	Christmas 1	We're Looking at God!
6	Christmas 2	Therefore, I Must Be ...
7	Christmas 3	Big Christ, Frail Church
	Season of Epiphany	
8	Epiphany 1	Finally, We Get it!
9	Epiphany 2	The Hinge of History
10	Epiphany 3	The Space Between
11	Epiphany 4	Rediscovering True Community
12	Epiphany 5	Who, Me? How?
13	Epiphany 6	It's Easier to Pluck Blackberries!
14	Epiphany 7	Turned on Its Head!
15	Epiphany 8	Now in Light of Then
16	Epiphany 9	Can You Hear It?
17	Epiphany 10	How Wide Is the Kingdom?
18	Transfiguration	What Time Is It?
	Season of Lent	
19	Lent 1	Landless People, Backwater Savior
20	Lent 2	Potholes in Salvation's Road
21	Lent 3	Stop Eating Bad Food!
22	Lent 4	Gilgal—Let's Roll!
23	Lent 5	Remember, Then Forget!
	Season of Easter	
24	Easter 1	I'm Still Creating
25	Easter 2	Dare To Risk
26	Easter 3	Human Walls Must Go
27	Easter 4	Words Must Walk

28	Easter 5	Multiple Visions, Single Message
29	Easter 6	Gone But Never Absent!
30	Easter 7	Look Both Ways!
	Season of Pentecost	
31	Pentecost	Building God's Tower
32	Trinity	The Wisest of Women
	Season of the Christian Life	
33	Christian Life 1	Sundays Should Be Special
34	Christian Life 2	Not Another Holy War!
35	Christian Life 3	Does God Control Everything?
36	Christian Life 4	The Power of Eminent Domain
37	Christian Life 5	God as Relational Love
38	Christian Life 6	When There Are No Rules
39	Christian Life 7	Nobodies Make a Big Difference
40	Christian Life 8	The Church Wall Is Crooked!
41	Christian Life 9	Don't Give Up on Words
42	Christian Life 10	Will the Real God Stand Up?
43	Christian Life 11	Keep Your Barns Under Control
44	Christian Life 12	Where Bankruptcy Is Impossible
45	Christian Life 13	Let's Start a Fire!
46	Christian Life 14	Lead Your Donkeys, I'll Lead Mine
47	Christian Life 15	I'll Do It My Way!
48	Christian Life 16	It's All An Open Book
49	Christian Life 17	Wash Me Clean, Lord
50	Christian Life 18	Learn from the Crooks?
51	Christian Life 19	Love All the Saints
	Season of Eternity	
52	Christ the King	The Dying God Is Eternal
(1)	**On to Another Advent**	

Appendix A—The Revealing Spirit of God 31
Appendix B—The Annual Cycle of the Christian Year....................................... 31
Appendix C—Contributors to This Volume... 31
Appendix D—Supplemental References.. 31

John Wesley & Charles Wesley
Asbury Theological Seminary

Annually the Wesleyan Theological Society selects an especially outstanding publication in the Wesleyan-Holiness tradition and grants the Smith-Wynkoop Book Award. Here are two recent recipients.

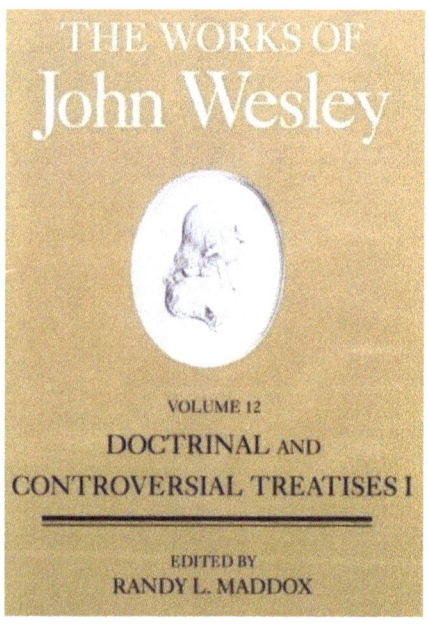

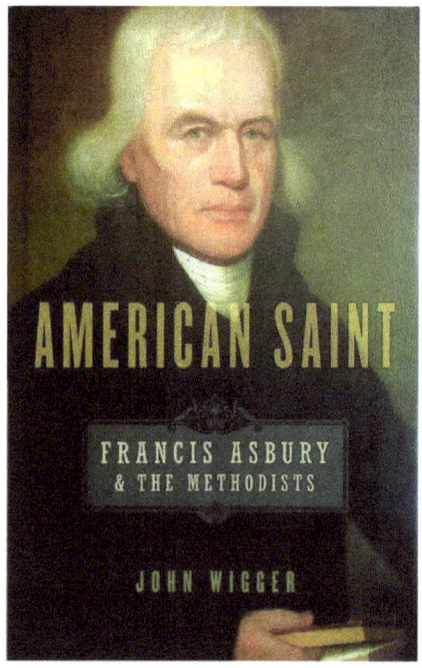

ACKNOWLEDGMENTS

These pages benefit greatly from the wisdom of a wide range of leaders of the Wesleyan-Holiness tradition. They come from past and current generations. Their names are listed under "Contributors" at the end of the book. Sources of the quotations from their published works are cited where used, with full publishing information for many available in the "Supplemental References." This is provided for those who may want to journey more deeply with Rabbi Jesus. The covers of many of these publications are featured throughout this book.

We have taken the liberty on occasion to do modest editing of punctuation, spelling, and capitalization of quotations. This is for the sake of clearer communication with the modern reader. We believe the original authors would want this done so that the truth they once sought to convey would shine through again without being unnecessarily hindered by passing writing styles of their older times.

Generally, we have been intentional in these pages about the use of inclusive language. However, for the most part the gender language of John and Charles Wesley has been left as in the originals. Particularly in the poetry of Charles, seeking to introduce inclusive language often awkwardly disrupts the integrity of the poetic flow. To balance this, we have included a generous number of the voices of outstanding women, something perfectly appropriate for the Wesleyan-Holiness tradition.

The quotes from John Wesley can be referenced to the 1978 reprint edition of *The Works of John Wesley* (14 volumes) issued by the Nazarene Publishing House, Kansas City, MO. Those volumes are a transcription, remarkably correct, of the 1872 edition of *Wesley's Works* (Jackson edition) by The Wesleyan Methodist Book Room, London.

The Charles Wesley hymns are listed only by title and include selections from the many verses of those Hymns. Many can be found in the classic *A Collection of Hymns, for the Use of the People Called Methodists* (7th ed. published in London by John Wesley) and can easily be accessed online.

Barry L. Callen, Anderson, Indiana
Steve Hoskins, Nashville, Tennessee

August, 2021

DESTINATION EMMAUS

These pages are your personal invitation to join a life-changing journey. We will be giving attention to the whole biblical revelation while walking with Rabbi Jesus and listening humbly to his interpreting Spirit. You've been accepted into the School of the Master! All costs are pre-paid for the year by the sheer grace of God.

Of course, one year won't be enough for your full maturing as a disciple. The first disciples of Jesus were privileged to be with him as select students for three years and they still distressed their Master teacher with how little they really understood. So much was new. So great was the heavenly vision. So demanding was the task to which they were being called. It just couldn't all be taken in that fast.

No matter. One year will be a really great beginning, and enrollment for year two is always a possibility. The complete maturing as disciples of Jesus will be incomplete in this earthly life. The call is to begin and continue learning from our wonderful Rabbi. His Spirit promises to eventually teach us all things, things even greater than those first disciples ever had a chance to grasp. Let's begin!

Rabbi Jesus: Our Guide on the Way

Nothing would be possible without one fundamental fact. God by nature is Self-revealing. We don't actually find the will and ways of God so much as they find us. The possibility of our learning rests on the fact that our Teacher chooses us to be students of the Divine. He is anxious for us to learn, grow, serve, and eventually graduate.

We now know that Jesus was more than a poor man horribly crucified. He also was raised from death and now reigns over all forevermore. Our Rabbi was much more than a man. He was God with us! Therefore, as we begin our study of the Scriptures and engage the fifty-two lessons from our Rabbi, here's the key to understanding. We must realize and celebrate the biggest truth of all. Our Teacher himself is the focus of all the revelation of God. These pages, therefore, assume the following:

> Jesus is the last word! Saint Paul wrote about the divine brightness that shines in our hearts "to give us the light of the knowledge of the glory of God in the face of Christ" (2 Cor. 4:6). In taking Jesus seriously as central for Christian faith, we should accept as authoritative what Jesus taught and, just as pivotal, who he *was* and who he still *is* through the ongoing life and ministry of the Spirit of Jesus.[1]

This grand foundation for judging truth and carrying on the Christian life means that really coming to know our Rabbi is the best way to know God and to shine true light back on the Old Testament and forward on the New. Beyond the many lessons themselves, critical will be your emerging relationship with our Teacher who is the ultimate revelation. Jesus is the school, the curriculum, and the way of life for now and forever.

Those first two men traveling to Emmaus, shocked and disheartened by the horrible crucifixion of Jesus, suddenly had a partner walking with them along their sorrowing way. They knew about the awful events in Jerusalem. They had put their faith in Jesus as God's true Messiah and now he was dead! Soon the tables began to turn. Though still unrecognized, Jesus slowly began dispersing their despair, "explaining to them what was said in all the Scriptures concerning himself" (Lk. 24:27).

Naturally they were surprised and soon overjoyed. Upon reaching their little village, they urged the stranger to stay the night. He did, their eyes were opened further, they finally recognized him, and he became their personal Rabbi—in fact, their Living Lord. Such a journey, so full of destiny, can we ours as well. God wants us to be able to worship in Spirit and truth, that is, grounded in the truth of Jesus and open to the Spirit who takes us more deeply into it (Jn. 4:24-25). "A theology that does not inquire after God's will for the present may be orthodox but is not really listening to God."[2]

You are invited to join those first needy disciples on the way to Emmaus. The mysterious friend who came to join them will do so again, now with us. As he does, we will have great advantages to enjoy (see below) and with them great opportunities and responsibilities to fulfill. May we hear well as we walk along, and may we come to embody for today the learnings we will be privileged to receive.

As we walk the Emmaus road with Rabbi Jesus, as did those first two learners (Lk. 24), we know at least this to begin. We never will find ourselves alone. The Risen Jesus, and now also the wisdom of God's actively ministering Spirit, will join and accompany us always. Thanks be to God!

An Enhanced Spiritual Curriculum

The Spirit of Jesus now brings to us a greatly enriched discipleship curriculum. First, however, a caution. Much has transpired over the centuries that is not dependable learning. So much "information" is now online that we will need instruction on which sites are dependable and which misleading dead-ends. We are especially blessed to have the full body of revealed Scripture to reflect on and be taught from.

Available now is the New Testament and not just the partial writings available to those first two confused disciples. We also have the accumulated wisdom of numerous past disciples of Rabbi Jesus. They, with the guidance of the Spirit, have studied the full Bible and been particularly successful in receiving and refining the church's increasing understanding.

While the following weekly lessons profit from the wisdom of many such Christian "saints," we will highlight in particular two of the Lord's leading disciples, John and Charles Wesley, and a wide range of the leaders of the rich Wesleyan-Holiness tradition that has followed their ministries. They heard Rabbi Jesus especially well and have shared with us in exceptional ways, both theologically and musically, theoretically and practically. See the graphic in *Appendix A* that pictures how the interpretive wisdom of the Wesleyan-Holiness tradition assists in understanding the teachings of Rabbi Jesus.

Emphasizing the Wesleyan-Holiness tradition is an inclusive rather than a narrowing stance. This tradition is a rich stream of several critical Christian traditions, including the Lutheran, Calvinist, Anabaptist, Pietist, and even Eastern Orthodox churches long separated from the Western Church. Holiness should be understood "as embracing all of the traditions of Christian spirituality. It is a both/and rather than an either/or tradition."[3]

For John Wesley, the Bible is the touchstone of authority on all matters of faith and practice. It is the lens through which he viewed all of reality. More than a compendium of doctrine, he understood the Bible to be the revealed narrative of salvation—the grand story of God in Christ through the Spirit for our restoration. Jesus, therefore, is the living lens through which we best understand the written lens, Scripture. Accordingly, in these pages we will listen to Rabbi Jesus teach us the meaning of Scripture, which in turn will be our authority for faith and practice.[4]

John Wesley taught his followers a "practical divinity," insights that inform many of the particulars of our daily lives of faith. His brother Charles was a poetic genius who composed thousands of the great hymns of Christian faith that have inspired generations. The rich spirituality that flows from their combined insights and ministries should not be seen in competition with other streams of Christian spirituality.[5] It's not *either* holiness *or* something else. The Wesleyan-Holiness stream of the faith is richly inclusive of the best of the evangelical, sacramental, contemplative, and activist emphases of Christian faith.[6]

Many thoughts and testimonies of Wesleyan-Holiness leaders will appear here as prime illustrations of the teachings of Rabbi Jesus.[7] His disciples strive to be as little captive of their times as possible, and yet as relevant to the present time as possible. With this in mind, we feature the Wesleyan-Holiness faith stream because . . .

> Wesleyans are a people who believe, experience, and practice scriptural holiness in both its personal and social dimensions. We are a people saved to serve in the turbulent times of the 21st century. Against the inevitable despair of a secular world and the dark pessimism of some theological traditions, Wesleyans are called to sing of grace and see God at work in human redemption until He himself declares the end.[8]

To better understand the Wesleyan-Holiness stream of Christian faith, see above for the book *The Holy River of God* (Callen, 2016).

An Annual Cycle

We have presented here a one-year plan for hearing well the full range of the teachings of Rabbi Jesus. It will assist you in becoming a well-informed and more mature disciple of the Master by reviewing the whole Bible through the life, teachings, and interpretative comments of Rabbi Jesus. This plan is sometimes called a "lectionary."[9] It covers the whole Bible, reflecting on the promises of the coming of Jesus, his actual first coming, and then on the resulting meanings of that coming as we live now and anticipate his assured coming again. See *Appendix B*.

The annual study plan begins with "Advent," our desperate hoping that Jesus will come. It proceeds through the earthly life as we walk along toward Emmaus and are guided by God's Spirit. We remember Bethlehem, birthplace of God actually among us, work our way toward the crucifixion, marvel at the resurrection, rejoice at the "Pentecost" of God's Spirit coming, and then proceed through the long "ordinary" times of our lives of faith in this troubled world.

Circling the Christian Year in this way gives us fifty-two large insights into the heart and mind of the Master, and into the goals and struggles of being true disciples of Rabbi Jesus today. Each week Jesus takes us back to the Scriptures he knew so well and explains their real meaning for us today. He also prepares us for related wisdom we now have from the Wesleyan-Holiness tradition of the faith.

This year's walk with Jesus will open the entire Bible and show how all of sacred Scripture is fulfilled in our wonderful Rabbi, and how it all joins to point our own way forward. Do join us for at least this year on a great spiritual adventure. It will be a rounded balance of Christian remembrance, celebration, and guidance. It will be thoroughly "catholic" spiritual journey in the sense that it proclaims and instructs concerning the entire biblical message in relation to the entire people of God. If life and opportunity allow, you can always make the journey again, continuing the endless circle! Rabbi Jesus assures us that his Spirit will remain with us and his Father is always faithful.

Another way to continue the journey is to sample the recent publications identified in the "Supplemental References," *Appendix D*. The covers of a few of them appear throughout these pages. These exceptional works would take you deeper into the theological foundations and current applications of the teachings of the Master.

Learning from the Master

Our spiritual journey and time with Rabbi Jesus will come down to three elementary questions and the best way to get at the best available answers. As we approach the Bible, the questions are: What is being said? Is it true? and What of it? How do we get to the answers, to the deepest meanings in life, to the best ways forward toward our God-intended destiny?

To get at the answers, we must embrace one great insight and life challenge. There's more to knowing than intellectual study will ever know. The deepest knowledge must be learned in the intimacy of relationship, from experience, and under a master. Therefore, our choice of masters is the most critical decision to be made. These pages choose Rabbi Jesus and embrace the following wisdom about him and our way of learning from him:

> He commands. And to those who obey him, whether they be wise or simple, He will reveal Himself in the toils, the conflicts, and the sufferings which they may pass through in His fellowship and, as an ineffable mystery, they shall learn in their own experience Who He is.[10]

As modern disciples of Jesus on our own ways to Emmaus, and to our best futures and intended destinies, we dare to walk with Jesus as our Rabbi, our wisdom Master.

We begin an annual cycle of lessons from our chosen teaching Master. As we go along, week by week listening carefully to the Spirit, we indeed will learn in our own experience who Jesus really is, and who we are to be in our own time and place. Note that Rabbi Jesus says the following in every entry of this book: "My Spirit is anxious to continue teaching you on my behalf." This is because of a central truth:

> The church that truly yearns for renewal will commit herself to one thing above all else. She will invite the Holy Spirit to come. And she will do so continuously until the Spirit shows up. The church is a charismatic community that is entirely dependent on the Holy Spirit for all she is and for all she has.[11]

Therefore, we gladly join Roger Green in issuing a challenge to the worldwide Christian community, one that first came from the International Spiritual Life Commission of the Salvation Army:

> We call for a restating and living out of the doctrine of holiness in all its dimensions—personal, relational, social and political—in the context of our cultures and in the idioms of our day, while allowing for and indeed prizing such diversity of experience and expression as is in accord with the Scriptures.[12]

Opening Prayers

Many of us often feel like we are "almost a Christian." We pray that our journey together with Jesus will move us from "almost" to being "altogether" a Christian. What will it take to move from almost to altogether? As we explore the 52 biblical lessons that follow, we must regularly offer this prayer to God's Spirit. "Fill my heart to overflowing with your love. Enable me to love my neighbor as I love myself. Let love be the test of my faith, O God."[13]

As we journey together with our Rabbi Jesus, here's another prayer, our prayer for you, ourselves, and the whole body of today's church:

> We pray for a revival of holiness in our day that creates authentic faith communities in which each person can be unleashed through the empowerment of the Spirit to fulfill God's intentions of redemption, new creation, love, and justice for all. May Rabbi Jesus and his Spirit come near and walk with us, opening the Scriptures and transforming our lives and witnesses to the glory of God.

---

1. James Earl Massey, quoted in Barry L. Callen, *Heart of the Matter*.
2. Clark H. Pinnock, *Flame of Love*.
3. Don Thorsen, in Thorsen and Callen, *Heart & Life*.
4. See Howard A. Snyder, *Yes in Christ*.
5. While Don Thorsen titles his 2013 work *Calvin vs. Wesley*, he notes that they agreed more than disagreed, and John Calvin is gratefully acknowledged as "undeniably one of the most influential Christian leaders of all time."
6. See Don Thorsen, in *The Holiness Manifesto*.
7. For a rather full accounting of this rich tradition of Christianity, its currents, contributions, and denominational representatives, see Barry L. Callen, author-editor, *The Holy River of God*.
8. David L. McKenna, *What a Time to Be Wesleyan!*
9. The annual biblical reading plan followed in these pages is basically the texts chosen for a year's preaching as identified in "Year C" of the Revised Common Lectionary.
10. Albert Schweitzer, in his classic *The Quest of the Historical Jesus*.
11. Jason Vickers, *Minding the Good Ground*.

12. Roger Green, in *The Holiness Manifesto*.
13. Paul Chilcote, *Praying in the Wesleyan Spirit*.

WEEK 1

First Sunday of Advent

JOY IN THE JUMBLE

There's never a good time. I can't marry yet—need my career first. Can't believe yet—still have unanswered questions and an unresolved past. Can't die yet—so many things still to get done. A would-be disciple said to Jesus, "I'll follow, *but not yet*. First, I have to get my kids raised and my parents buried." When used as excuses to avoid a hard decision, these are unacceptable delays in joining Rabbi Jesus in his world mission.

There never will be the perfect time for the really important things. If there's to be joy in this life, it will have to come right in the jumble of real life with all its fears and ragged edges and unfinished tasks. When called by God, we must dare to decide. Today's news is always bad if judged merely by media headlines. Instead, we are to look up and not down. Despite all, our salvation indeed is drawing nigh. Claim it. Proclaim it. Go *now*.

A. Prayer

Advent is the Christian season reminding us that God is able to reach into our chaotic circumstances and agendas and concerns to surprise and delight. Lord, give me the grace to be prepared for such a loving interruption, and then may I be willing to capitalize on it as you ask. Grant me the eyes to recognize when you intrude lovingly into the chaos of my life, and the wisdom and courage to follow you into the future that only you can give. I ask you to interrupt my status quo, Living God. Intervene, shake, dismantle, and renew me, I pray. Even if it hurts, Rabbi Jesus, teach me the truth and bring rest to my weariness and resolve to my future.

B. The Voice of Rabbi Jesus: Lk. 21:25-36

> You can make it. Help is on the way. What looks like cosmic chaos is actually the arena in which my Father is delivering your redemption. My Father is sovereign, even the worst of times and places. The arrival of God's kingdom is near at hand. Believe this and move on gratefully and boldly. Delay is unacceptable. The time is now, right in the jumble of your present lives. Be on guard. When the future starts happening, hold your heads high and stand firm. You are mine. Join me!

My disciples always will live in a kind of *in between*— aware of me, waiting for me, listening to me, and coming to know me in the midst of this unpredictable and tumultuous world. Here's my direction to you. Remember my first coming, be encouraged by belief in my coming again, and choose always to live *in the now*, inspired by what has been and what soon will surely be. You know the Bethlehem birth story telling of my already having come. Now long for that baby to return again as the triumphant adult to reign over all, including over your own tangled lives. Don't ever allow your longing for tomorrow to paralyze you in the present. Be hopeful and joyful always.

You are called to patience and faith in the space between the human now and the anticipated divine future. The parable of the fig tree and my warning to pay attention to the signs of my coming should remind you of what's really important. My Father is not absent or inactive in this awkward interim time of yours. He's persistently and powerfully at work in every present, even if you can't see it. Your lives of faith *right now* are privileged to proceed into God's future and be enlightened by that future *even before it arrives*. My Father enters your everyday struggles and draws you toward your soon-arriving destiny.

My Spirit is anxious to continue teaching you on my behalf. I'm providing you with select portions from the revealed Word of God and from a particular tradition of my church that has wisdom you need. Read carefully and continue listening closely to my Spirit, who will guide your minds and hearts to understand properly and apply effectively.

C. Light from the Revealed Word

1. Psalm 25:1-7. This psalm opens with the desperate prayer of someone waiting on God to forgive and rescue. Caught in the pain of life's injustices, the psalmist hopes to be taught from above. We are not God. Our salvation will never come from our own efforts, careers, economics, politics, or military prowess. Here is the only sane affirmation possible in a world in which we often trust other saviors and act like we ourselves can be the saviors of others.

Verse four might be paraphrased this way. "In the chaos of my present circumstances, help me God to really understand what I once learned in Sunday school. Only if I take Rabbi Jesus as the way, truth, and life will I be able to survive and even celebrate right in the jumble of life's harsh realities."

> Show me Thy ways, O Lord, Teach me your paths.
> Be my Master, Rabbi Jesus, guiding me into your truth.
> Since you are God, and clearly I am not,
> Please be my Guide as I wait expectantly.

2. Jeremiah 33:14–16. The Bible's prophetic literature points to the importance of waiting, anticipating, and trusting in a promised future that seems very removed from our current circumstances. By waiting in faith, we place ourselves in a posture of becoming partners with God in the advent of a new reality. Insignificant as we are, God is willing to covenant and partner with us—that's really love! The Advent season opens with a promise to Jeremiah that God will fulfill the divine promise of establishing his reign of love that will have no end.

With the world crumbling around him, Jeremiah pushes his people to see God's future, although it seemed laughable given the harsh circumstances. In Advent, the church anticipates the coming Christ, finding in him the fulfilling reality of all God's promises (2 Cor. 1:20). Jesus Christ brings God's reign to us in himself and through his Spirit.

We are to look around for signs of God's coming reign in Christ, and also be partners in planting signs of God's reign through how we live in Christ. Paul's word: "Brothers and sisters, do not be weary in doing what is right" (2 Thess. 3:13). We are given the personal assurance that, once we are active in Christ, regardless of circumstances, nothing in all creation "will be able to separate us from the love of God in Christ Jesus our Lord" (Rom. 8:39).

3. Thessalonians 3:9–13.

Here is a window on an early Christian congregation struggling to grasp the wonderful future inaugurated by the risen Christ. Paul looks forward to "the coming of our Lord Jesus" and urges believers to pursue lives of love and holiness. We must find joy in the awkward jumble of the here-and-now. God holds the future securely and is pulling us, even now, toward that future. We are to think and act like we really believe this.

Paul reminds us that we are living *in-between* times. One time is that Christ already has come and brought the gift of transformed life, even if the transformation is not yet complete. The other time is his promised coming again. Christianity is not a choice between now and then. It's forward-looking and forward-moving while in the process of revolutionizing the present by the power of God's Spirit. The "then" must be coming to initial reality in and through us *now*.

Like Jeremiah, Paul speaks of God's powerful working in the lives of believers, making love abound and strengthening hearts in their holiness quests. We already know what God's future looks like. It will be Jesus-like whatever the particulars. Therefore, we now must experience and express its first-fruits. Paul advocates neither hopelessness nor idle cloud watching. He urges living with the uneasy tension between serving lovingly in God's *present* while awaiting God's brilliant *someday*.

D. Reflections of Leaders of the Wesleyan-Holiness Tradition

Since no time is ideal, the best available time for real "salvation" is *now*. Writes a present poetess, "You aren't living the whole thing at once, that's what a minute said to an hour; without me you are nothing."[1] By salvation I mean not barely the vulgar notion of deliverance from hell or going to heaven, but a *present deliverance* from sin to a restoration of the soul to its original purity, the renewal of our souls in righteousness and true holiness, in justice, mercy, and truth.[2]

> Father, I stretch my hands to Thee,
> No other help I know;
> If Thou withdraw Thyself from me,
> Ah! whither shall I go?
> Surely Thou canst not let me die;
> O speak, and I shall live;
> And here I will unwearied lie,
> Till Thou Thy Spirit give.[3]

Recall Psalm 100:1-3 and then note this line of Charles Wesley in his "Love Divine, All Loves Excelling": "Joy of heaven to earth come down!" Here's something basic to every spiritual journey with Rabbi Jesus that's prepared to begin *now*:

> O God, I need a Master.
> Chain me back into freedom;
> Darken me back into light;
> Stab me back into wholeness;
> Quiet me back into singing;
> And erase me back into fullness.[4]

The early Christians were persons of joy (Acts 2:46). Christian joy is not something that solves all present problems. Joy is not necessarily something given to us but something we choose. Joy is an option; it is a choice instead of a gift. The attitude of joy will make an enormous difference in the ministry to which each of us has been assigned.[5]

It's time to go when God calls, regardless of the swirl of confusing events, unresolved issues, and unanswered questions that are all around us.

> Jesus calls o'er the tumult
> Of our life's wild, restless sea;
> Day by day I hear him saying,
> "Christian, come and follow me."
>
> In our joys and in our sorrows,
> Days of toil and hours of ease;
> Still he calls in cares and pleasures,
> "Christian, love me more than these."[6]

---

1. Naomi Shihab Nye.
2. John Wesley, *Farther Appeal to Men of Reason and Religion*.
3. Charles Wesley, "Father, I Stretch My Hands To Thee."
4. E. Stanley Jones, *Abundant Living*.
5. Dennis F. Kinlaw, *This Day with the Master*.
6. Cecil Frances Alexander, "Jesus Calls Us O'er the Tumult."

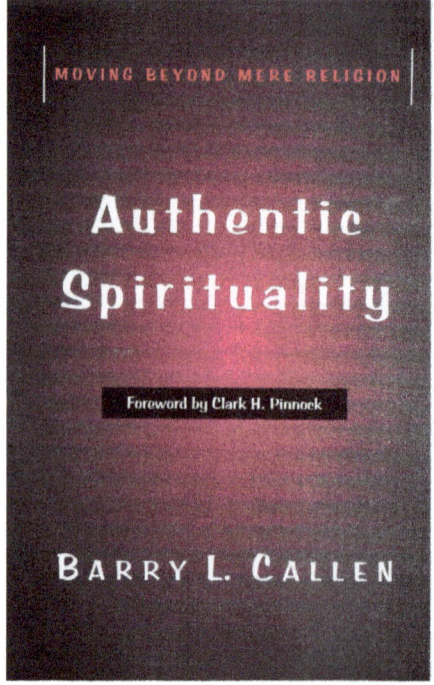

WEEK 2

ANTICIPATING IS NOT ENOUGH

God loves us enough to be angry with us when necessary. Football coaches at game halftimes often fume at their losing teams, even singling out particular under-performing players. Commented one player to an embarrassed teammate, "The Coach only yells at us because he loves us. All he wants is for us to be the best we can be. Let's forget the first half, make the needed adjustments, and go back out there and win!"

Once there sounded the voice of a strange preacher. He was yelling, "Messiah is coming, and is he ever angry!" When Jesus arrived at the River Jordan to be baptized by this preacher John, all he wanted was for God's people to be the best they could be, all that God wanted and was prepared to enable them to be.

The hard fact is simple enough. Beyond anticipation of God's coming, we must prepare, repent, and make ourselves ready to be made new. We dare not rush prematurely to Christmas and all the talk about glad tidings of great joy. First, God's deserved judgment must be faced and dealt with. Suffering is real in this human life, and so is the potential of singing right through it until the morning comes.

A. Prayer

Come, Lord Jesus, not only to fulfill my deep desire for you, but also to make possible your wonderful desire for me. Be truthful with me, even angry if necessary, and then give me the grace to repent, endure, and finally flourish in your truth. May God's glory actually begin to shine through me. Dear God, stop me from hurrying to the glitter and gladness of Christmas before my personal account with you has been cleared and I'm actually ready to rejoice and worthy to serve.

B. The Voice of Rabbi Jesus: Luke 3:1-6

> Playing the standard religious game will not get it done, my friends. I'm here to change the game! John the Baptist has pointed the way. Knowing that you are a sinner is the first part of receiving the coming good news. You've been told the truth about yourself. Now I'm telling you about my upset Father who expects repentance. Do that and his waiting love stands ready to forgive and restore. Anticipating my coming is not enough. You always must prepare properly to receive the graciousness of the soon-arriving God. Join me at the River Jordan. Go humbly into the water and look for the appearance of a heavenly dove.

How will the Messiah come? John said he would come not so much to comfort as to bring you to account. Messiah will start with a refiner's fire. This arriving won't be easy to receive. Anticipating God's arrival isn't enough. Required also is a realignment of hearts and lives so that they are in tune with my Father's agenda—repentance, restoration, and only then mission. An end must come to the distracting days of "cheap grace" when salvation is expected without the required repentance and forgiveness. Such things are costly. My Father is prepared to pay!

My church must seek the "blessing" of God's judgment, listening intently to that which purifies and never merely flatters. When my disciples accept God's upward calling, it will be good news for them and the world. Why? Because, when willing to bear God's refining, my disciples will be enabled to represent my Father's glory shining on his beloved creation. What lies beyond the words of judgment? The eternal faithfulness of God who will complete the loving work of creation with the needed re-creation.

My Spirit is anxious to continue teaching you on my behalf. I'm providing you with select portions from the revealed Word of God and from a particular tradition of my church that has wisdom you need. Read carefully and continue listening closely to my Spirit, who will guide your minds and hearts to understand properly and apply effectively.

C. Light from the Revealed Word

1. Psalm 16. Confession comes first. New life depends on having dealt with the old life. The cry is for God to save because there has been wrongdoing and open admission that apart from God "no good do I possess." Such confession is absolutely necessary as we wait on God's just response and gracious coming. When humbly repenting and patiently waiting, what happens? Finally, lines fall in pleasant places and there comes a goodly heritage (vs. 6).

We who would be changed by and then represent God must do more than anticipate the promised coming of divine goodness. We must clear the path of God's coming by dealing with the negatives of yesterday. Our confession and God's forgiveness form the only path to a wonderful new future that can bring joy even in the present.

2. Malachi 3:1–4. Many took advantage of Cyrus's edict. The Jews finally could go home from the long Exile and expect a blessed new beginning. They would rebuild the Temple and God would bring triumph and joy to them. "The treasures of all nations shall come in, and I will fill this house with splendor" (Hag. 2:7). However, what actually happened undermined this enthusiasm through the emergence of a wretched economy, high taxation, fiscal corruption, savage inequalities, and intermarriage with those who lived in the land prior to the exiles' return.

The high hopes soon cooled into disappointment and drifted into a frustrated carelessness. Malachi speaks harsh words of God's judgment on this religious decline. He addresses people who were wearing out God's ears with their questions and complaints. Their jumble had choked out all their joy. The prophet announced that someone was coming who would prepare the way for the Lord. Unfortunately, God's arrival rarely meets human expectations—typically it's sudden, surprising, and often comes with unwanted judgment.

Who can endure the day of God's coming? Who will be pure and blameless in the day of Christ? Who will prepare the way of the coming by repentance and forgiveness? These are the questions of the season of Advent, pointing to our unworthiness, unreadiness, and unwillingness for Christ's coming, at least on terms other than our own.

3. Philippians 1:3–11. At God's coming there will be a refiner's fire enabling renewed worship that is genuine and joyful. God is the power of new beginnings, and what God begins in us can be completed, but only if we allow it. Paul asks God for more love that produces more knowledge, that in turn produces a clearer sense of what is important and ultimately purifies we who believe and manage to prevail.

The goal is a sanctifying purity, love practiced in community that launches a chain of events which are the responsibilities of believers. These include growth in perception, life in unity, coping with anxiety, and living out a servant vocation. Popular culture says we are exactly who we are, and we should not be judged by others. Advent, to the contrary, is the time to realize our imperfections, admit our accountability, and long for God's purification.

How will purification be recognized? It will be lived out in active love in the Christian community, and then expressed by that community toward the whole world. The goal is captured in St. Paul's personal witness, "It is no longer I who live, but Christ who lives in me" (Gal. 2:20). Christ within is the source of joy in whatever present we find ourselves.

D. Reflections of Leaders of the Wesleyan-Holiness Tradition

Beyond merely anticipating the birth of our Lord, we must be preparing, "complying with," "panting for," becoming "thirsty for," and taking the initiative to come to the fountain where the blessings will be found. The high spiritual goal is "Christian perfection," a mature relationship with Jesus that radiates a true Christlikeness to the world. It's possible to see a great light even as we find ourselves waiting in the darkness.

What is, then, the perfection of which man is capable while he dwells in a corruptible body? It is the complying with, "My son, give me thy heart." It is "loving the Lord his God with all his heart, and with all his soul, and with all his mind." This is the sum of Christian perfection; it is all comprised in that one word, *love*. The first branch of it is the love of God; and he who loves God loves his brother also. "Thou shalt love every man as thy own soul, as Christ loved us." Here hang all the law and the prophets and the whole of Christian perfection.[1]

> Happy is the man forgiven,
> This let every sinner feel;
> Taste in Thee his present heaven,
> Pant for greater blessings still;
> O that all anew created,
> Might Thine image here retrieve;
> Then to paradise translated,
> In Thy glorious presence live![2]

Here are lyrics based on Isaiah 51 and the beatitudes of Rabbi Jesus:

> Ho! Everyone that is thirsty in spirit,
> Ho! Everyone that is weary and sad;
> Come to the fountain, there's fullness in Jesus,
> All that you're longing for, come and be glad!
>
> Child of the kingdom, be filled with the Spirit!
> Nothing but "fullness" thy longing can meet;
> 'Tis the enduement for life and for service;
> Thine is the promise, so certain, so sweet.[3]

I am called to be perfect even as God is perfect, to be absolutely Christlike in my life. This is a monumental claim upon my life. I will strive to open my life to the transforming power of God's perfecting love. The perfection to which I am called certainly does not mean that I will ever be free from ignorance or mistakes or infirmities or temptations, for only God's unconditional love is perfect in that sense. Rather, God calls me to develop such a close and loving relationship with Jesus that I would never want to do anything to separate myself from that love or withhold it from anyone else.[4]

It's possible to see a great light even when walking in darkness. It's possible to sing while suffering. Suffering can be seen as an invitation to surrender our lives to God, to open the heavy drapes to the morning light just outside. It tends to clear away clouds and reveal the stars that were there all the time. There are two words that sound the same when spoken but mean very different things. They are "mourning" and "morning." Can they ever go together? Yes! Mourn with those who mourn and a new morning will arrive (Matt. 5:7).[5]

---

1. John Wesley, *On Perfection*.
2. Charles Wesley, "Come, Thou Universal Blessing."
3. Lucy Rider Meyer, *Ho, Everyone Who Is Thirsty*.
4. Paul Chilcote, *Praying in the Wesleyan Spirit*.
5. Barry L. Callen, *The Jagged Journey*.

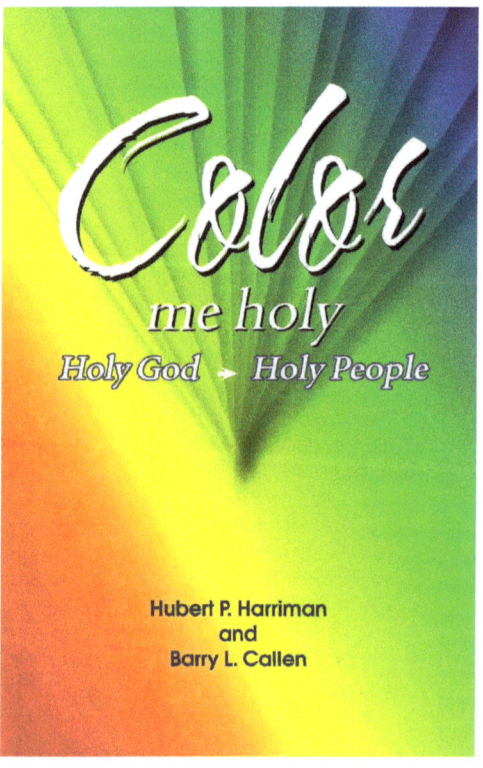

WEEK 3

DON'T JUST PUT ON A HAPPY FACE

There naturally is joy anticipated when it's believed that God will redeem and restore his people. The news of Messiah soon arriving in our troubled world floods our emotions. We're called to be joyful even while we wait. But our joy can't be senseless and giddy, only skin deep. There will be pain involved in the waiting and even in the coming. There will be ethical, moral, and political demands placed on the anticipating faithful. A shallow smile will not suffice.

Facial appearances can be very misleading. For instance, eye patches are assumed to have been worn by pirates to cover vacant sockets caused during gruesome skirmishes at sea. In fact, that was rarely the case. Patches were worn mostly because pirates often were adjusting one eye to darkness so they could transition more easily from sunlight to the darker conditions below deck.

People misread faces all the time. A child of God isn't to grin pleasantly just to make a good impression on the public. Even young kids easily see through such false faces. We who would follow Rabbi Jesus must find and experience a real joy that reflects the actual coming of God to our lives. The truly happy face comes from deep in a happy heart. People will be attracted to the authentic and mock the hypocrite.

A. Prayer

O God, put a smile on my face, but only one that has come to terms with your just judgment. Forgive me and then bless me with a smile that's more than surface and cheap. Make my face shine from deep within my grateful and joyful soul. As I await your coming, Lord, may I become a witness to genuine joy in this troubled world. May my new smile represent the fact that faith is a wonderful fulfillment and not a damper on life at its best. New creations naturally smile. Radiant Lord, make me new and shine through me.

B. The Voice of Rabbi Jesus: Lk. 3:7-18

> It's time to put out the trash to be burned. The fire will be my Spirit coming and cleansing. Don't rely on your being children of Abraham, heirs of his or any family or religious tradition. I can turn rocks into such traditional "religious" people. The real joy will come only from a restored relationship with my Father. Everything else is dead wood for the fire. That relationship must give evidence of more than conformity to any law. Obvious must be the fruit of life in my Spirit (Gal. 5:22-23).[1] That fruit is luscious indeed. It's life-sustaining and joy-producing.

The Romans allowed my people to practice their religion as long it was under the watchful eyes of Annas and Caiaphas and didn't upset the social status quo controlled from Rome. The prevailing oppressive power saw to it that nobody mixed religion with politics or dared to question the notion that Augustus Caesar and his representatives, Pontius Pilate assisted by Herod and backed up by Annas and Caiaphas, were the real power in Judea. That's the twisted world I knew firsthand.

John's message was rather simple and direct: "Messiah is coming!" Messiah, my friends, was thought to be both a religious and political designation for the coming leader who would confront the Romans, giving Israel an entirely different future. I did all that for my people, although not exactly as they expected or wanted. Herod Antipas finally imprisoned and cut off the head of John. But pity poor King Herod. He couldn't silence John's voice even when his head was gone! A wild conflagration flared up and eventually swept toward Jerusalem. You, my disciples, now are carriers of that holy fire.

People like Tiberius, Pilate, and Herod make world history, right? And yet, when it came time for God to make history, the divine Word came to none of them. The outcasts of society were selected to be the receivers and carriers of the good news of pure joy. I'm talking about those shepherds and now you. Receive my coming as it was and begin to change the world.

My Spirit is anxious to continue teaching you on my behalf. I'm providing you with select portions from the revealed Word of God and from a particular tradition of my church with wisdom you need. Read carefully and continue listening closely to my Spirit who will guide your minds and hearts to understand properly and apply effectively.

C. Light from the Revealed Word

1. Psalm 25:1-7. My head is held high, O God, and I'm looking straight at you. No sulking for me. I know that my cheeks should and can be reflections of your glory.

> None who wait on You, O Lord,
>   will need to be ashamed.
> Thy tender mercies to our minds recall,
>   redeem, Lord, from our troubles all.
> Shift the frowns of our sinfulness
>   to the brightness of your forgiveness.

Exiles always ask God, "Why us?" Disciples of Rabbi Jesus naturally ask, "Why did God allow the crucifixion of the Son?" The world's hurting people are full of unanswered questions. I'm one of them, Lord. I so want to do more than paste on a happy face while my insides shake in fear. Fill me with the joy of knowing your steadfast love and faithfulness. I wait on you, Lord. There is no other. Please come soon.

2. Zephaniah 3:14–20; Isaiah 12:2–6. Here are passages in which salvation gets the last word in spite of everything. Fear is replaced by trust and joy. Imperatives of praise pile up. Shout! Sing for joy! It's difficult to help the already comfortable understand what the promise of comfort means to the dispossessed and struggling who know firsthand lives fearful of economic collapse, neighborhood violence, undocumented status, and racial discrimination. It's also difficult for people of privilege to understand the deep joy of those who celebrate what little they have and relish with passion the promises of redemption.

The privileged are vain and foolish. They paint their faces and even have them surgically altered, trying to make themselves look young and happy. The Bible, however, speaks of a beauty that cannot be bought or faked. When God comes there will be no need for manufacturing a happy face. The joy will be spontaneous and attractive indeed.

3. Philippians 4:4–12. Paul was thinking of something much deeper than putting on a happy face as an artificial cover that misrepresents the inner reality. He knew that he was in prison; he knew there were big challenges facing the community of believers. Nevertheless, he had found in the gospel of Jesus the source of deep joy despite everything. He could sing from behind bars.

During the Advent season, Christians should give attention to the distinction between the material happiness that the commercial world promises and the abiding joy of Christian faith. That faith, while it cannot be bought, can be received freely and will sustain, come what may. Paul is calling disciples of Jesus to rejoice even when in prison. Joy that emerges from a real relationship with God is a far cry from the fleeting rush momentarily achieved through the Christmas season's latest toy or family dinner.

Christ's self-emptying had become Paul's abundance. "I have learned the secret of being well-fed and of going hungry, of having plenty and of being in need" (4:12). The joy of knowing Christ sustains in all circumstances. Believers are to rejoice in the Lord, let their gentleness be known, and not worry about anything. There may be hard times, of course, but believers never should live as though things are out of control or the bottom line is in doubt. The promise is that the shalom of God will stand guard at our heart's door.

D. Reflections of Leaders of the Wesleyan-Holiness Tradition

There's plenty of reason to smile! Jesus is coming to accomplish all that we need. Joy is arriving on earth. The resulting holiness potential is truly beautiful. The Christmas smile comes when we can sing from the heart the Christian's "theme song."

These things must necessarily go together in our justification: upon God's part, His great mercy and grace: upon Christ's part, the satisfaction of God's justice; and on our part, faith in the merits of Christ.[2]

> Love Divine, all love excelling,
> Joy of heav'n, to earth come down;
> Fix in us Thy humble dwelling,
> All Thy faithful mercies crown.
> Jesus, Thou art all compassion;
> Pure, unbounded love Thou art;
> Visit us with Thy salvation,
> Enter every trembling heart.[3]

I once was talking on the subject of religion with an intelligent agnostic. He said, "Well, madam, all I have to say is this. If you Christians want to make us agnostics inclined to look into your religion, you must try to be more comfortable in the possession of it yourselves. The Christians I meet seem to me to be the very most uncomfortable people anywhere around. They seem to carry their religion as a man carries a headache. He does not want to get rid of his head, but at the same time it is very uncomfortable to have it. And I for one do not care to have that sort of religion." This was a lesson I have never forgotten, and it is the primary cause of my writing this book.[4]

Christians need to rediscover the beauty of holiness—the brilliant, splendorous, glorious, delightful, restorative color of God. Only then will we know the sheer joy of having it poured out on us like rain on a dry and thirsty land. It was this and only this that could cause the early disciples of Jesus to "consider it all joy" when they encountered various trials (James 1:2). They could embrace suffering as a kind of glory (Phi-lippians 3:10) and even sing in the darkness (Acts 16:25). *Joy to the World* should be more than a popular Christmas carol. It's the Christian's theme song![5]

---

1. John Wesley "repeatedly insisted that the essence of sanctification is outward conformity to law but the renewal of our affections (hearts) thro participation in the Divine nature" (Randy L. Maddox, *Responsible Grace*).
2. John Wesley, *The Lord Our Righteousness*.
3. Charles Wesley, "Love Divine, All Loves Excelling."
4. Hannah Whitall Smith, *The God of All Comfort*.
5. Hubert P. Harriman and Barry L. Callen, *Color Me Holy: Holy God, Holy People*.

WEEK 4

JERUSALEM? NO, BETHLEHEM!

The Advent season is like the broccoli of the Christian's annual banquet. It's what has to be gotten through before digging into the sweet treats of Christmas and Easter. It's what we need most and want least. Today's biblical texts point to God's promises of redemption. They breathe confidence that God can be trusted to keep these promises. They focus, however, and quite surprisingly, on Bethlehem and not Jerusalem. That's not where people expected or wanted the good things.

Bethlehem, the necessary broccoli, was a little nowhere place in contrast to the everything of Jerusalem just a few miles away. Do we really wish to come to know God and become part of his wonderful future? Then apparently we must start at the bottom, the only place available, where we're currently stuck, where God chooses for Jesus to be born.

An occupied little town full of refugees, Bethlehem was a bit disgusting, a powerless nowhere, surely not the location of God's arriving future in the birth of the only Son. That's where the coming Christ would be born, however. Like Bethlehem, Jesus would begin his earthly sojourn as an apparent nobody and eventually grow to be a "suffering servant" rather than a parading prince. That lowly example sets the path we also are to walk.

A. Prayer

I long, dear God, for the luscious banquet of your arrival in power and triumph. But so far my table is filled with so much food that is soured and spoiled. Come to me, Lord Jesus. If you come in a way and place I don't expect and find hard to accept, mend my mind and reshape my heart so that I can take in the real You. I've preferred to lease a nice apartment in downtown Jerusalem as my religious headquarters. If finding you requires moving to some little room on a Bethlehem back alley, I'll do it. Show me the way to your birthplace. I really need to find you, the real you, and start understanding and living the unusual ways of God.

B. The Voice of Rabbi Jesus: Luke 1:39–45 (46–55)

> My Father is not to be found parading about in the capital city as the king everyone wants and loves. I, the Son of God, was born in a little town in the country, not among arrogant kings but with the humble and faithful who seek to serve and not rule, love rather than dominate others. I grew and now have revealed my Father's true heart by accepting the Cross on your behalf. You must go into the world and live cross-like lives in my name. My banquet table looks quite different from the feast settings of the world's privileged. That should be the case for you as well. Feast on the real Bread of Life and you will be satisfied indeed.

I realize that the scene was a little absurd. My coming as the Messiah to redeem Israel was proclaimed not by archangels or high priests or emperors or even ordained preachers. Rather, two marginalized, pregnant women—one young, poor, and unwed, the other far beyond the age to conceive—met in the hill country of Judea to celebrate and possibly commiserate about their pregnancies. The picture was of an upside-down world being set right-side up and threatening those in power. If you are faithful, it will be the same for you.

Mary was told that she would have a baby by the Holy Spirit. After getting over the shock, she broke into song. It was less a lullaby and more a battle song. Through Mary and her coming son, both misunderstood and threatened nobodies in the world's eyes, my Father was planning world change. Those in power are to be cast down. The lowly and oppressed are to be lifted up. The great transfer of power was beginning in little Bethlehem, not in the gleaming Temple in Jerusalem.

With Mary's song comes the question for you, my disciples. Will you sing with her? The church should echo my mother's song, soon to be called the "Magnificat." The music is so sweet that you may miss the great message. My Father is scattering the proud, dethroning the powerful, and banishing the rich into impoverished emptiness.

My Spirit is anxious to continue teaching you on my behalf. I'm providing you with select portions from the revealed Word of God and from a particular tradition of my church with wisdom you need. Read carefully and continue listening closely to my Spirit who will guide your minds and hearts to understand properly and apply effectively.

C. Light from the Revealed Word

1. Psalm 80:1–7. Here's the voice of an imperiled people, a frantic prayer uttered under siege. God once provided water from a rock, but now God's people drink only their own tears. If there's a Christmas spirit to come, the people are lacking the spiritual, physical, and financial resources to join the party. For those who have lost a loved one or a job, who have become disabled or depressed, who wonder if war will ever end, Psalm 80 speaks a word of patience, faithfulness, and hope.

Eventually the world will see the children of God not as beaten persons in retreat but as ones obviously loved and blessed by God despite their circumstances. For now, however, God's people sometimes must endure laughing enemies. The big-shots in Jerusalem haven't the time of day for nobodies born in Bethlehem and reared in Nazareth.

The last verse of the beloved "O Little Town of Bethlehem" is hardly sentimental. It conveys the longing felt by those praying Psalm 80. If we dare to invite the Lord to "come to us, abide with us," we can be grateful that he does come with both justice and mercy, and to lowly little Bethlehem places where most of us actually live. Come and breathe life into our lungs, dear baby Jesus, so that we may understand who you really are and shout your joy!

> Shepherd of Israel, come and gather your scattered sheep.
> No longer be a sleeping volcano while we live on a diet of tears.
> Come, and soon, please! Smile on us with rays of your salvation.

2. Micah 5:2–5a. Rather than an approving reference to the royal line of David in Jerusalem, the prophet's hope is precisely the opposite. It's a rejection and a going back to the drawing board on Judean kingship. In Micah's day, the central authorities in Jerusalem responded to Assyrian threats with force rather than diplomacy. The people were exhausted and angry. Micah goes back to Bethlehem and finds another royal line, one that will not resort so easily to violence. As a prophet from a village devastated by war, he calls for a ruler who trusts more in God than in military might.

Micah announces that a new and different kind of ruler is on the way. The new leader will come not from Jerusalem, the city of David the king, but from Bethlehem, the rural village where David the peasant was born of humble origins. There will be a reversal away from the powerful establishment of Jerusalem. The poor will have a champion, one of their own who has nothing and yet will hold in his hands the future itself. Judah's harvest center, little Bethlehem ("house of bread"), would one day place a shepherd king in the very center of God's redemptive plan.

Jesus would be a new beginning, a Messiah unlike the one people expected or to whom they would willingly resign themselves. With the birth of Jesus, God would confront the powers of the world by setting up his rule in the face of human pride. It would happen in the obscurity of Bethlehem and by the weakness of a terrible cross. Unthinkable. Amazing. God at work God's way.

3. Hebrews 10:5–10. The incarnate Christ speaks in the words of Psalm 40, declaring that God did not desire "sacrifice and offering."

We are not to be artificially "religious" and act "piously," as though we are especially important people. The contrast between continual animal offerings and the single offering of Christ is to remain central and constant. The new covenant in Christ is the will and way of God. The prior practices of sacrifice were never intended to be permanent or capable of accomplishing full redemption. That comes only through the sacrifice of Christ, the Bethlehem baby yielding his life so that we might live eternally.

Someone is sitting in church and lost. Someone is filled with guilt and shame. Someone is hurting and hoping for an infusion of the restoring love of God. From whence will it come? Not from the world's rich and powerful, or even from the church's elite. The saving story of God's acting for our salvation is one of voluntary suffering and sacrifice, once for all, and not with animal blood. God's love has bled for all of us and is gently calling to a new creation in Christ. The terrible price already has been paid by a little baby, one born in Bethlehem of all places.

D. Reflections of Leaders of the Wesleyan-Holiness Tradition

Note John Wesley's "in the meantime." Things for us often aren't the big and glistening Jerusalems but the dull little Bethlehems of everyday life. God knows our "low state" and has plans for our "sorrows to flee away." Jesus is coming not to the Temple in Jerusalem but to the humble temples of our hearts where we actually live. Come Lord Jesus! As you come, help us recognize that your light of saving grace shines on all, even on those we consider the least among us.

God is pleased to give his angels charge over us, namely that he may endear us and them to each other; and that by the increase of our love and gratitude we may find an increase of happiness when we meet in our Father's kingdom. *In the meantime*, may we imitate the angels in all holiness, suiting our lives to the prayer our Lord himself has taught us, laboring to do his will on earth as angels do it in heaven.[1]

> My soul extols the mighty Lord,
> In God the Savior joys my heart:
> *Thou hast not my low state abhorr'd*;
> Now know I, Thou my Savior art.

> Sorrow and sighs are fled away,
> Peace now I feel, and joy and rest:
> Renew'd, I hail the festal day,
> Henceforth by endless ages blest.[2]

May I never rest till I have the witness of the Spirit that my heart is the temple of the indwelling God, and have the full confidence that Christ reigns supreme on the throne of my affections, bringing every thought into obedience with himself.[3]

God's prevenient grace and providence become a preparation for the proclamation of the gospel of Christ. They keep open the possibility that all people can be drawn to God. It is the purpose of the Spirit to direct all people to the person of Christ, and it is the responsibility of Christians to seek to enable this to happen.[4]

---

1. John Wesley, *Of Good Angels*.
2. Charles Wesley, "The Magnificat." Emphasis added.
3. Phoebe Palmer, *The Way of Holiness*.
4. Philip R. Meadows, in Callen-Thorsen, *Heart & Life*.

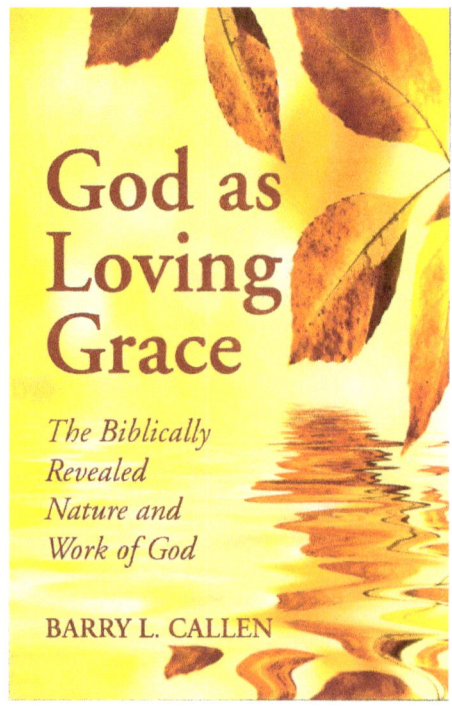

WEEK 5

CHRISTMAS DAY

WE'RE LOOKING AT GOD!

The word is "theophany," a divine appearance. It refers to the rare times when we see God appear. When this does happen, usually it's surprising and other than what we would have expected. Who expected to see a vulnerable little baby in a smelly Bethlehem barn as the appearance of God? Who expected the glory of God to be announced first to dirty shepherds not welcome in the sacred halls of the Jerusalem Temple? Who is God anyway? Go to Bethlehem and take a look!

The prophet Isaiah says, "The LORD has proclaimed to the end of the earth: Say to daughter Zion, 'See, your salvation comes." The psalmist says, "All the peoples behold God's glory" (97:6). The angel tells the shepherds that the Messiah's birth is for "all people." Paul's letter to Titus says, "the goodness and loving kindness of God our Savior appeared" when Christ came.

Too often, claiming to have seen God is mere delusion. In the Christmas season, however, we celebrate a direct and amazing sighting of God without delusion. If we can realize what we are seeing there and respond appropriately, we finally can start to live. Theophany. Come and see the Divine appearance, and rejoice!

A. Prayer

People so often are deluded, seeing what they want to see, claiming to have seen what wasn't there. Human eyes are dim and often fooled. Open my eyes, Lord, and allow me to see what is real and normally well beyond my sight ability. Let me see the Bethlehem baby for who he really is. Then give me the humility and courage to allow him to be my Rabbi, my Teacher, my Savior. If his lessons turn out to be hard, send his Spirit to me to interpret for me the life meanings of the Master's teaching. I want to see what's really real. Take me to Bethlehem and open my eyes to an emerging new world.

B. The Voice of Rabbi Jesus: Luke 2:1-20

> Some came to my humble little birthplace and saw just another very ordinary baby. When looking at me as that newborn in Bethlehem, they couldn't see what was right in front of them. That's not surprising. I looked like any other baby of poor parents. What they should have seen was none other than God coming to be with them—and with you! Some early visitors from far away came to visit. They had no stake in the local politics and did manage to really see me and understand far more than the others. Human preoccupations tend to blind eyes. If you're going to represent me as disciples, you'll have to have your eyes wide open to the amazing reality of God's arrival in my birth. My Spirit will be with you and is a wonderful eye-opener.

To know me as the Savior yet to come in obvious glory, you first must know me as having already come in fragile flesh. Granted, you don't know the details about the eventual future, but you do know something very important. Never forget this critical fact. The future will be stamped with my face. Know me now and you already will know the essence of what is to come.

Your five senses often fail to catch the fullness of reality. I once asked my Father to put his glory on display (Jn. 12:27-29). When he granted my wish, most in the crowd thought they heard nothing but thunder. A few sensed a message from heaven. They were right. My Father had spoken. You now are seeing me. Open the eyes of your hearts, my disciples, to see my Father active in your midst. My church always must believe that the vulnerable infant of Bethlehem is the very One who presides over the affairs of the universe and one day will implement judgment and justice for all. I, the Bethlehem baby and now your Rabbi Jesus, was present at the time of creation (Jn. 1) and will preside at creation's ending (Rev. 1:4-8).

Note what one special disciple of mine concluded. "However strange or terrifying or unlikely it may seem, I have to accept the view that He [Rabbi Jesus] was and is *God*. God has landed on this enemy-occupied world in human form."[1] I am here now and promise always to be with you.

My Spirit is anxious to continue teaching you on my behalf. I'm providing you with select portions from the revealed Word of God and from a particular tradition of my church with wisdom you need. Read carefully and continue listening closely to my Spirit who will guide your minds and hearts to understand properly and apply effectively.

C. Light from the Revealed Word

1. Psalm 97. May we sing excitedly with the ancient Hebrew about a dramatic sighting of God.

> Jehovah reigns, let the earth be glad!
> Dark clouds surround God,
> And on justice rests his throne.
> Fire goes before him and
> His foes burn up all around.
> His lightening bursts illumine the whole world,
> Enabling the earth to finally see God.

I long to get to the very end of these words of the psalmist. While I want to be glad, I'm too often overwhelmed with the dark clouds that surround God. I'm inclined to reflect the prophet's observation that God hides himself (Isa. 45:14-15). I want to see the divine lightening bursts that will illumine my world. Only then will I finally see God and truly rejoice. Lead me to Bethlehem and help me understand who that little baby really is. Let me learn that even God's judgmental fire is really his hot, passionate, saving love in action, the beauty of his glory (vss. 6-9).

2. Isaiah 62:6–12. God had promised restoration and now the Jews were back home in Jerusalem after the awful Exile. The place was in ruins. Isaiah looks to a future when the rubble-ruined highway has been cleared, salvation has arrived, and Zion knows that it's "not forsaken." The wait was frustrating, even embarrassing. Hope was still alive but stuck in the shadows of God's "until" (vs. 1).

The noisy clamor from sentinels on Jerusalem's walls (v. 6) reminds modern Christians of all the sounds and bustle of the weeks before Christmas. We angle for spots in crowded parking lots, jostle with crowds in stores, and scurry to get a tree up and decorated in our homes. In the midst of all this, Isaiah reveals a deep need of God's salvation and a trust in God's promised presence. We must not lose God's quiet voice of promise amid the loaded agendas of the Christmas season.

In his last sermon, on the eve of his assassination, Martin Luther King, Jr, commented on the threats of violence he had received. "We've got some difficult days ahead." He affirmed that God "allowed me to go up to the mountain. And I've looked over. And I've seen the promised land. I may not get there with you, but I want you to know tonight that we, as a people, will get to the promised land. Mine eyes have seen the glory of the coming of the Lord!"

Christmas is God's actual coming. Just another baby born in impoverished circumstances? No! When seeing little Jesus, we're looking at none other than *God with us!*

3. Titus 3:4–7. The arrival of God is not what we deserve. It's a free gift from God. The birth of Jesus came solely from the amazing love of God for us wayward humans. The manner of the baby's conception and birth insists that it was not the routine result of human action. Jesus was "conceived by the Holy Ghost." It was God deliberately appearing, God's loving initiative for our salvation.

Titus was ministering in tough territory. The residents were notoriously lazy, self-indulgent, gluttonous, and cruel. They lived with an attitude of, "If it feels good, do it, there won't be consequences." But it must not be so for those who follow the child of Bethlehem. His appearing teaches us to say "No!" to such arrogant living. By the Spirit's power active in us, we can be level-headed, self-controlled, and in our right minds, with our eyes seeing things as they really are. We must keep our eyes on Jesus.

It's not enough to celebrate Christ's birth once a year. We dare not walk away from the manger unchanged. We have a beautiful gospel story to tell the nations, and we tell it best when we lead lives of self-control and love for others. Win one sense, we cannot make the Christmas season last all year long. We can, however, allow Christ and his appearing to remain with us our entire lives. The grace of God has appeared to help us avoid ungodliness so we can witness to the One who is "the reason for the season."

D. Reflections of Leaders of the Wesleyan-Holiness Tradition

The Wesley brothers properly identify the true identity of Jesus—amazing! If the "offspring of the Virgin's womb" is actually "Christ the everlasting Lord," then his church today is to be reflecting him to the world so that others also can see. But how can this be done when the church is so very frail?

Jesus is God over all, blessed forever. He was with God, with God the Father, from the beginning, from eternity, and *was God*. He and the Father are one; consequently, he thought it not robbery to be equal with God. Accordingly, the inspired writers give him all the titles of the most high God. They call him over and over by the incommunicable name Jehovah, never given to any creature. They ascribe to him all the attributes and all the works of God. We need not hesitate to pronounce him God of God, Light of Light, very God of very God: in glory equal with the Father, in majesty co-eternal.[2]

> Veiled in flesh the Godhead see,
> Hail the incarnate Deity,
> Pleased as man with man to dwell,
> Jesus, our Emmanuel.
> Hark, the Herald Angels sing,
> Glory to the newborn King![3]

Did you ever have a moment or an hour in which you were lost in fellowship with the Lord, having no thought of time or space, in which experiences were wrought in you, emotions swept through you, purity and love and power and comfort and assurance were imparted to you, that you have never been able fully to explain or express in words? Oh, how invaluable is such an experience to a soul, especially in a time of fierce temptation! It sweeps away forever the intellectual and moral and spiritual fogs and uncertainties that becloud the mind and heart. It fixes a man's theology. It settles for him the fact that he himself is a living soul, morally and spiritually responsible to God. He feels the breath of eternity in him.[4]

---

1. C. S. Lewis, *The Case for Christianity*
2. John Wesley, *Spiritual Worship.*
3. Charles Wesley, "Hark, How All the Welkin Rings."
4. Samuel Logan Brengle, *Love Slaves.*

WEEK 6

THEREFORE, I MUST BE . . .

Knowing who Jesus really is comes first, and not always easily. His parents struggled with his identity. Who he actually is admittedly stretches our imaginations almost to the breaking point. We are trying to grasp an stunning affirmation. The claim is that the man born among us is the One who is before and above all, including all time, and yet the One who has come to us as an innocent baby of a poor family immediately under threat by local authorities. This One encompasses the full A to Z of all reality!

This Jesus is a great paradox come from a wondrous God. The paradox goes like this. The God of the eternities took on our flesh, our fragile humanity, so that we might partake of the Divine life. The God of all ages desired to be with us at great cost. So, what must we now be and do in response to such amazing love? There are things we must and now can become. We can be restored to creation's original intention.

A. Prayer

You are not easily found, O God, although the coming of Jesus has made a great difference. Who would have thought of looking for you in a Bethlehem barn? One time the parents couldn't find Jesus among the travelers, and later two women couldn't locate him in a graveyard. Guide me into true worship because of who you really are. In Jesus, your Son, you've enabled me to see the real you. Bring me to new life in your resurrected presence and by your resurrection power. Point me toward that which I now must be in light of who you are.

B. The Voice of Rabbi Jesus: Luke 2:41-52

> At first my own parents had no idea who I was or what I was sent to do. I understand your difficulty. As my disciples, you must learn the truth about me and then be inspired by that knowledge to become new persons and serve your world accordingly. I know these lessons I am sharing with you are very big, but the stakes also are very high. You must become fresh creations truly alive in my Spirit. My Father both wishes this and is making it possible.

You likely want to come into the Christian life fully formed, all growth pains avoided, all knowledge readily at hand. Sorry. The life of faith may begin at the celebration at your baptism, but much spiritual growth must follow that. If you are to have a matured relationship with my Father and the ministry he intends for you then, like me, you must grow "in stature and favor with the LORD." Sadly, many of my future disciples will have a limited understanding of the faith. Many will stop growing in their faith when they are barely new-born disciples. This will be a great threat to my church.

I once said to my earthly parents, "Why have you been searching for me? Didn't you know that I must be in my Father's house?" Later, two women were searching for my missing corpse and I said to them, "Why do you search for the living among the dead?" Now I say to you, my dear disciples, that if you ever are to be all my Father has in mind for you, you must search diligently for me and learn about me. I gladly will make myself available to you. I will be with you always in the richness of worship, in the glory of resurrection, and in the humility of selfless service. Since my Father is lovingly reaching for you, when you reach, you will be found.

My Spirit is anxious to continue teaching you on my behalf. I'm providing you with select portions from the revealed Word of God and from a particular tradition of my church with wisdom you need. Read carefully and continue listening closely to my Spirit who will guide your minds and hearts to understand properly and apply effectively.

C. Light from the Revealed Word

1. Psalm 148. The call goes out to all creation to praise God, from the highest heavens to the deepest seas and everything in between. There are no exclusions or excuses. Everything must praise God because God created everything and deeply loves it all and is the essential resource for all good within it. God said the word and the world was established. Now the creation has something it should be saying in response to God. Psalm 148 begins and ends with the phrase "Praise the Lord!" Sandwiched in between is everything that should be doing that. As children of God, we must come to see everything and everyone in light of God having come lovingly to us in Jesus Christ.

God's ultimate Self-revelation could have come through overwhelming displays of shocking power. Instead, the almighty Creator of the universe came as a vulnerable child, displaying both the majesty and mystery of this all-powerful and all-loving God. The same God who set the stars in their courses has become fully present with us to set things right. God was birthed in a stable and soon would be hung on a cross for our salvation. It would be a stunning Christmas condescension to our lost condition. Now we must be praising and representing this wondrous God.

2. 1 Samuel 2:18–26. The prophet Samuel was dedicated to ministry at a young age. He grew up in God's service and lived in the Temple. As reported in Luke's Gospel, the childhood of Jesus mirrors that of Samuel. He also was at home in the Temple. Like Samuel, Jesus grew in divine and human favor. Samuel was instrumental in the reorganization of Israel from tribal confederacy to monarchy, Jesus was instrumental in the reconstitution of God's people from the old to a new covenant. In this season of Christmas, our waiting is over, the Savior has come, and now we are invited to join him in making all things new.

In between Christmas and Easter we will watch Jesus grow. We will follow him to Egypt where he will live as a refugee, and go with him to the Temple where he will amaze all who hear him. As we recall these formative times in his earthly life, we now have some parenting work of our own. Like Hannah and Mary, in the name of Jesus we must birth justice in the world of our time, nurture hope in all surrounding despair, assist in the growth of the kingdom of God, and display a new manner of living. Now that Christmas is past, who must we be? We must become *Christ in us for the world*.

3. Colossians 3:12–17. Jesus of Nazareth is the "cosmic Christ." In his resurrection and return to his Father's right hand, he has become Head of the church, his body, while continuing to be Master of the whole universe. He is the full image of God who is calling his followers to a new way of life rooted in and inspired by him. These lines of instruction to the Colossian believers form one of the classic "sanctification" passages in the New Testament. They speak of the new life that the Holy Spirit seeks to birth in us.

The "peace of Christ" is to "rule in your hearts," and the "word of Christ" is to "dwell in you richly." All false teachings are to be swept aside. All harsh ascetic practices and all fear of unseen powers are to be abandoned. Their replacements are to be a vivid portrait of what it looks like to be formed in the image of Christ and to live as one clothed entirely in the Christ who is "all in all."

D. Reflections of Leaders of the Wesleyan-Holiness Tradition

Here is John Wesley's classic prayer of complete Christian commitment. The problem is that we must be confident of who Jesus really is or we will never dare giving ourselves fully to him. The lyrics of John's brother Charles affirms that Jesus "came from above," giving us an inheritance that can never perish. That inheritance must be shared with all who suffer.

> I am no longer my own, but Thine.
> Put me to what Thou wilt, rank me with whom Thou wilt.
> Put me to doing, put me to suffering.
> Let me be employed by Thee or laid aside by Thee,
> Exalted for Thee or brought low for Thee.
> Let me be full, let me be empty.
> Let me have all things, let me have nothing.
> I freely and heartily yield all things to Thy pleasure and disposal.
> And now, O glorious and blessed God,
> Father, Son, and Holy Spirit,
> Thou art mine, and I am Thine. So be it.
> And the covenant which I have made on earth,
> Let it be ratified in heaven. Amen.[1]
>
> O Thou Who camest from above,
> The pure celestial fire to impart,
> Kindle a flame of sacred love
> On the altar of my heart.
>
> There let it for Thy glory burn
> With inextinguishable blaze,
> And trembling to its source return,
> In humble prayer and fervent praise.[2]

Note this classic holiness hymn from the Camp Meeting movement of the late 1800s. Once we know that Jesus really is the one "coming down from the Father above," wonderful peace can sweep over our spirits forever!

> Peace, peace, wonderful peace,
> Coming down from the Father above!
> Sweep over my spirit forever, I pray,
> In fathomless billows of love![3]

The world is full of refugees, orphans, and other struggling persons. People do not feel accepted, do not belong, are disconnected and therefore experiencing life as aliens and strangers. People often find themselves lonely even in a crowd. They are unsatisfied in spite of indulging in fascinating and expensive things. Biblical revelation is not intended as more condemnation of those already suffering, but as love extended and true family offered. Peter writes to "God's elect, strangers in the world who have been chosen and given new birth and an inheritance that can never perish" (1Peter 1:1-4).[4]

---

1. John Wesley, *Wesleyan Covenant Prayer*.
2. Charles Wesley, "O Thou Who Camest From Above."
3. Warren Cornell, "Wonderful Peace."
4. Barry L. Callen, *Authentic Spirituality*.

WEEK 7

BIG CHRIST—FRAIL CHURCH

Jesus is the *incarnation*, that is, God present in flesh with us and for us. The church of Jesus is called in its flesh to be what it never can be on its own. The coming of Jesus is now to be extended into the whole world through the fellowship and witness of his disciples. We have recalled the vulnerable little baby, God with us in Bethlehem. Now we must realize who are to be *in Christ,* physical expressions of Christ's continuing spiritual presence in the world.

The Bethlehem baby was little and vulnerable, and the church surely is very frail in many ways. Nonetheless, we are called to be God's light in the world, the very hands and feet of Jesus. We are to represent Christ even while knowing ourselves to be weak human vessels hardly able to present well such amazing good news. Our reliance must be on the ministry and gifting of the Spirit of Christ. An effectively witnessing church must be one that, despite its human frailties and diversities, has found a unity in love by the grace of God.

A. Prayer

Almighty God, although we humans didn't know how to come to you, we now realize with joy that your love brought you to us. You've entered our world and made all the difference. Therefore, I now come into your presence knowing that I also am called to make appearances in the world on your behalf. While you expect this of me as your child, and of us believers together as your church, you know we are not ready for the task. Help me. Help us. May the brightness of you glory find ways to shine through your church regardless of its frailty. Teach us and gift us as only you can.

B. The Voice of Rabbi Jesus: John 1:10-18

> The big truth is that I am here to make God as plain as day to you, my disciples. Open the eyes of your hearts, my dear friends. Let my Father show you the grand plan that you now are privileged to join in fulfilling. Don't let your obvious limitations stop you. Go forward in the wisdom and strength of my Spirit. Your human limitations will always exist. No matter. My Spirit understands this and will compensate as necessary.
>
> The Divine has broken into your world. God's glory has become tangible and available for your receiving and sharing. The curtain in front of the Holy has been pulled back. In my coming, the very kingdom of God has drawn near. The richness of my Father's Word has become transforming grace for all who will receive.

I am God now present to you. My Father is not separate from the difficulties of fleshly existence, but intimately aware of them and present with you in them. Your material existence, my Father's original creation, truly matters and can be redeemed. I have shared in the fullness of the human experience, except for sin. I understand human suffering, having known the most gruesome of human deaths. Therefore, in all that you experience, God is as close as your next breath. My Father bears the pain you bear and celebrates the joys you often will know in my service. You will never be alone.

My future disciples will come from a long line of sojourners, refugees, and nomads. No wonder you should practice hospitality toward immigrants. The borders of nations artificially define people's interactions with each other. In a world where nationalism and racism are commonplace, you are to live as people called to serve a God whose love and grace transcend all human borders.

The Spirit of my Father is anxious to continue teaching you on my behalf. I'm providing you with select portions from the revealed Word of God and from a particular tradition of my church with wisdom you need. Read carefully and continue listening closely to my Spirit who will guide your minds and hearts to understand properly and apply effectively.

C. Light from the Revealed Word

1. Psalm 147:12–20. The psalmist affirms God's commitment to the people of Israel. God's word is the divine order that is apparent in God's control of nature (vss. 15, 18). This order gives the community of faith a manner of living that will promote it—right relationships among the people and the people righty related to their living environment. We should be anxious to offer praise to God because God con-tinues lovingly to order and reorder the world. It's now being done through the person and work of Jesus Christ and his church by the power of his Spirit.

We pray that the church's borders will be made secure with bread on her tables and peace at her gates. How else can we ever be God's people successfully doing all that we are called to do in this world? God strengthens the bars of the church's gates (vs. 13). And God does something else to sustain a frail church. God invests in the church's future by nurturing the young within its borders (vs. 13). And still more, God works to make peace among the faithful (vs. 14).

How frail and needy are God's people, and yet how blessed we can be if we will be open to God's gracious working in and through us.

2. Jeremiah 31:7–14. God's salvation is announced with gladness. Why the party? What are we celebrating? For the prophet Jeremiah, and now for the church of Jesus, we are to join the song of gladness, and do more than sing it. We must accept the divine assessment of our faults and failings. We must receive gratefully God's healing balm of mercy and restoration.

Jeremiah, often in tears because of the serious failures of God's people, is also a prophet who can smile. Why? Because God remains in love with his people despite everything, and God promises to provide for those who are so loved.

3. Ephesians 1:3–14. A major purpose of Paul's letter to the Ephesians is to instruct non-Jewish readers about what it means to be Christian. Through the saving work of Jesus Christ, they, and now we, have been chosen as children of God since before the creation itself. It's part of God's grand plan to "gather up all things in him."

The privilege of the church is to be involved in something far greater than its tiny gatherings for worship, prayer, and singing. The church is invited to live in hope and envision more than what's immediately experienced. While the mystery of God's will is not yet completely revealed, the disciples of Jesus can cherish the daily blessings of forgiveness and wisdom, while trusting God's pledge for an even greater future.

God has designated Christ "the head over all things for the church." This same Christ has granted power to believers, reminding us that we are to be the living embodiment of Christ in today's world, an extension of the incarnation of Jesus celebrated in the Christmas season. For such a mission, the church is small and frail, granted, although its Lord is large and without limitations.

D. Reflections of Leaders of the Wesleyan-Holiness Tradition

Adequacy in the Christian life will come only from our joining John Wesley in having our hearts "strangely warmed." It also comes only from our agreeing with John's brother Charles that the truly happy heart is the one in which Christ is born. Such adequacy leads to "Masterful" living. What must there be about the church that will make it significant in the eyes of the world? Members must be united with Christ and active in his love.

In the evening I went very unwillingly to a society in Aldersgate Street where one was reading Luther's preface to the Epistle to the Romans. About a quarter before nine, while he was describing the change which God works in the heart through faith in Christ, I felt my heart strangely warmed. I felt I did trust in Christ, Christ alone, for salvation; and an assurance was given me that He had taken away my sins, even mine, and saved me from the law of sin and death.[1]

> Happy the place, but happier still
> The heart where Christ is born:
> The heart which He vouchsafes to fill
> Need neither sin nor mourn;
> No city could with Bethlehem share
> The honor of His birth,
> But every soul by faith may bear
> The Lord of heaven and earth.[2]

This is the time of the year when we recall that the gospel of Jesus Christ is what transforms the impossible into the possible. Indeed, it is the incarnation and the resurrection of Jesus Christ which totally reframe the world and all of human history. It is these two great singularities, incarnation and resurrection, which reframe a world of despair and cynicism into the larger frame of hope and promise.[3]

Holiness is nothing more than living full of the Master who is holy. It is the convening center that begins with the Master and extends outward in your life. It creates healing and wholeness in a way that integrates who you are inside with what you do in your behavior. And who better to provide that center than God, whose very nature in holiness. God is the Master who becomes visible in you.[4]

The church must show the world that the kingdom of God has come. There must be something in the church that is beyond culture, nationality, race, class, education, and other such things. The church falls down when she becomes too strongly tied to a particular culture. That is why I oppose the creation of white churches or black churches. There is nothing mysterious about a church made of people who look alike and act alike. Such a church says nothing very significant to the world, especially if the world feels unwelcome there. There must be something in the church that cannot be explained except by the fact that *God lives in his people*.[5]

The best indicator that one belongs to Christ and is a part of his body is union with Christ through a faith which is active in love.[6]

The unity of the church is a unity in love. Structures of the church will vary from time to time and must not be allowed to limit love. Love binds everything to-gether (Col. 3:14). The molecules of the body of Christ cannot be bound together by coercion. Unity must not be seen exclusively in structural terms, but in the networking of God's people in loving relationships for the evangelism of the lost. The Christian church exists both to be one and to participate in God's work of making all one.[7]

---

1. John Wesley, *Journal*, 1738.
2. Charles Wesley, "Jesus was Born in Bethlehem."
3. Timothy Tennant, TimothyTennant.com (2018).
4. Kevin Mannoia, *Masterful Living*.
5. Samuel G. Hines, in Barry Callen, *The Wisdom of the Saints*.
6. Kenneth J. Collins, *Soul Care*.
7. David L. Cubie, in the *Wesleyan Theological Journal*, 1998.

WEEK 8

Epiphany of the Lord

FINALLY, WE GET IT!

Our Christian faith rests on "Epiphany," the Greek word meaning appearance or manifestation. What has appeared? It's God's willingness to be seen and understood by mere humans. Because of a great love for us, God has made obvious his own very nature, ways, and expectations of those who come to see and are willing to follow. key fact is that we don't find this gracious divine revelation so much as *it has found us*! We are able to come to God primarily because God has first come to us. God wants not only to create but also *communicate*. "And God said . . ." permeates the Bible's revelation.

In the life, teachings, work, death, and resurrection of Jesus Christ we see as much of God as we can see or ever need to see. Epiphany! Love has appeared and been made obvious. The baby in Bethlehem opens our eyes and we begin to understand. If the Advent season was about waiting for the arrival of God's promised Messiah, the Epiphany season now is about the grand expectations of what will be revealed to us after Jesus has arrived and departed back to his Father. God wants to make more and more manifest the meanings of Jesus having been here. This desire to communicate is the ongoing ministry of God's Spirit.

A. Prayer

Dear Father, like the Magi who followed the star, I come seeking increasing understanding. Please let your divine light, the source of all true understanding, shine on me and guide me by your Spirit. In turn, may I then be faithful in guiding others to the Light of the world, helping them understand who has come, Jesus, who is now here, the Spirit of Jesus, and what difference they make in what we understand about life's new potential. Thank you, Father, for Self-revealing. In my thinking and teaching and living, may I never distort what you have revealed

B. The Voice of Rabbi Jesus: Matthew 2:1–12

> **Wise ones from the East came to see about my birth and then to avoid danger had to return another way. Soon my own family had to flee the country with me as a little child. My very existence and mission of love threatened those in power. Following me won't always be easy, friends. Be prepared. Know at least this. With my help, you'll always be able to manage. What you will need to understand will keep being clarified as necessary. If you stay close to my revealing Spirit, you will know all that you need to know and be able to do all that you are called to do.**

Even in my infancy, I was here for all humanity, not only for the chosen few of my own Jewish people. I came to draw people together, wise men from the East, Syrians from the north, Egyptians from the south, Romans from the west, humanity in general. Everyone is invited to God's saving grace, even those who have been traveling radically different paths in search of their true spiritual home.

When you gather to worship as my disciples, you are to be in the company of people from all nations. Unfortunately, that will not be readily apparent in many congregations functioning in my name. Sometimes they will be some of the *least diverse* institutions in terms of race and socio-economic standing. That will not represent me well. The challenge is for my disciples to end the waiting time of Advent darkness and the mystery time of Christmas dawning and march forward into the brilliance of Epiphany's bright and broad day.

The Magi's prominent place in Matthew's narrative of my life underscores the importance of what they symbolize. They were outsiders—they came *to me* and now you must go *to them*. Matthew colors his whole Gospel with a revolutionary hue. The world cannot remain the same once I, the Messiah, have entered the picture. King Herod saw that much of the truth. Rather than bend his knee to God's anointed, he chose terror, as tyrants always do. My love is very threatening to those with worldly power.

My Spirit is anxious to continue teaching you on my behalf. I'm providing you with select portions from the revealed Word of God and from a particular tradition of my church with wisdom you need. Read carefully and continue listening closely to my Spirit who will guide your minds and hearts to understand properly and apply effectively.

C. Light from the Revealed Word

1. Psalm 72:1–14. The picture drawn in this psalm is a sad one. The righteous kingship intended by God was never realized in Israel. Only a handful of kings began to approach the intended standards of justice and righteousness. Since the vision of kingship remained an elusive ideal, future expectation was always needed. God alone is King, in contrast to all arrogant humans who claim ultimate authority on earth. When will people finally get this obvious truth? The psalmist prays that God will give the new king the power and will to do acts of justice. Otherwise there will be no *shalom*, no peace and well-being for the people of God.

In Jesus Christ, we see the king who finally enacts God's justice and displays God's love. He is the Prince of Peace whose power of love extends throughout the world. Jesus illumines the darkness and draws nations together. He delivers the poor and heals the needy. He redeems those who are lost and oppressed. Rabbi Jesus is the Messiah, the ideal king finally come.

A core conviction must become apparent to the Christian community. Jesus truly understood, enacted, and embodied the will of God in a ministry that now is *also ours*. Jesus might well have sat as the model for Shakespeare in *The Merchant of Venice*: "The quality of mercy is not strained. It droppeth as the gentle rain from heaven, upon the place beneath." And it now has really happened. God has settled down upon us as a baby to redeem us in love and place a spotlight on the paths we now are to walk.

2. Isaiah 60:1–6. Christ's ministry would be a revelation to his own people and to the larger non-Jewish world. The "wise men" would come from the East following a star and finding a child. A key theme of central importance in the Hebrew Bible (Old Testament) suddenly crystalized in this baby. We finally could understand differently God's Self-revelation in the history of Israel, and we could anticipate properly God's coming reign.[1]

Here's the clarified understanding. The light that would come to Israel would not be for Israel alone. "Nations shall come to your light, and kings to the brightness of your dawn." Throughout the Old Testament, God used foreigners, outsiders, women, even the least expected and sometimes most unsavory of non-Jewish characters to fulfill the divine will.

Although God's people often missed this crucial truth, God always has been the universal and loving sovereign over all humanity. From the beginning, God has intended to bless all the families of earth through the covenant made with Abraham. Epiphany! This great truth now has come to light for all to see.

3. Ephesians 3:1–12. Finally, we get it! God's "eternal purpose" can now be "seen" in ways previously unimagined. This "mystery" is news even to the heavenly hosts. There is something of a Copernican revolution underway. The entire universe of God's providence has been revised in our understanding. The Gentiles (non-Jews) were thought of as outsiders, and now that understanding has been shattered. Jesus made clear, "epiphany," that there is "one God and Father of *all*, who is above *all* and through *all* and in *all*."

This change of understanding is like what happened at the 1787 Constitutional Convention of the young United States. It was agreed there that each African-American slave would count as three-fifths of a person. To Jewish eyes, the Gentiles came up short in the alleged divine apportionment scheme. One Gentile was not equal to one Jew. No wonder, then, the shock over the Apostle Paul's insistence that in Christ the "others" are no longer strangers and aliens, only part-persons, but now *fellow heirs*, full and equal members of the same body, sharers in the one grand promise of God.

We who now belong to Christ are participants in the greatest of all universal stories. We are being empowered to share this wonderful story with all others. Like Paul, we are prisoners of Christ Jesus for the sake of all, Jew and Gentile alike. This is the big truth that's now been made apparent—epiphany!

D. Reflections of Leaders of the Wesleyan-Holiness Tradition

Finally we get it. We see God as more than the heavenly Priest who pronounces our forgiveness. God also is the heavenly Prophet, the source of all wisdom. He is the King who eventually will subdue and reign over all things. We should crown him in our own hearts this very day!

We may dwell upon God bearing "the iniquities of us all," as "wounded for our transgressions" and "bruised for our iniquities," that "by his stripes we might be healed." But we should not preach Christ if we were wholly to confine ourselves to this. We are not clear before God unless we proclaim him in all his offices, not only as the great High Priest "reconciling us to God by blood," and "ever living to make intercession for us," but likewise as the Prophet "who is made unto us wisdom," yea and as King forever, giving laws to all whom he has bought with his blood, restoring those to the image of God, and reigning in all believing hearts until he has "subdued all things to himself."[2]

> Rejoicing, in hope, and patient in grief,
> To Thee I look up for certain relief;
> I fear no denial, no danger I fear,

Nor start from the trial, while Jesus is near.
Yet God is above men, devils, and sin,
My Jesus's love the battle shall win,
So terribly glorious His coming shall be,
His love all victorious shall conquer for me[3]

Jesus is not only Savior, Sanctifier, Physician, Advocate, and Judge, but He is also King—King of kings, Lord of lords. This is mightily magnified all through the New Testament. We crown Him King in our hearts and in our lives today, and rejoice that the time is nearing when He is to be King, not only in our hearts, but acknowledged King over all the earth.[4]

---

1. For a full discussion of the relationship between the "Old" and "New" Testaments, see Barry L. Callen, *Beneath the Surface: Reclaiming the Old Testament for Today's Christians* (2012).
2. John Wesley, *The Law Established Through Faith, II.*
3. Charles Wesley, "Omnipotent Lord, My Savior and King."
4. Martin Wells Knapp, *Jesus Only: A Full Salvation Yearbook.*

WEEK 9

Baptism, the Lord's and Our's

THE HINGE OF HISTORY

It's "pivot" time on the Christian calendar. Things were one way and now they're going to be another. Why? Because God is truly sovereign over history's events and it was time for a major pivotal event. Jesus finally emerged in full public view. The great agent of world change was about to launch his public ministry.

The hinge event was Jesus' baptism. People were wondering if John the Baptist might be the Christ, but John let them know the truth. One far more wonderful than he was coming soon. The Messiah would present himself for baptism. Because of this pivotal event, people would begin to realize who Jesus really was.

Disciples faithful to Jesus soon would experience "epiphany" by coming to understand what was announced at the Master's baptism. He was a full human being and also the long-awaited Messiah. He was and remains the greatest of all paradoxes, being simultaneously fully human and fully *God with us*.

Beginning on that hinge day at the Jordan River, Jesus redefined humanity and its understanding of divinity. Believers could no longer think of either without thinking of Jesus. God Almighty had become present in this young Jew from Nazareth. Never again should anyone say that God is distant or unloving, not after the coming of Jesus, the Son so present with us and so self-giving for us.

A. Prayer

Lord Jesus, you came to us as one unknown. When we finally realized who you really were, all our expectations and understandings were overturned. We are slowly realizing through you who God actually is and who humanity is supposed to be. Give me the grace not only to understand who you are, but also to gladly receive you into my life. Now that I know you, may your gracious presence be with me so obviously that others may also know. You offered yourself for baptism, though without sin. I want to do the same because of my sin and your now-available salvation. Erase in my head all wrong notions of your Father. Become in and through me whatever you wish to enable, and help me to follow wherever you lead. Keep revealing yourself to me as you truly are, Lord, ending who I would have you be.

B. The Voice of Rabbi Jesus: Luke 3: 15-22

> It took my Father's Spirit to reveal that it wasn't John but me who was the ultimate One coming from God, the one fully revealing the Father. In me, God is with and for all who will believe. My friends, receive this pivotal revelation. Believe it and be changed. I am my Father's presence with you and for you. I am the hinge on which all human history swings.

It's critical that people come to realize who I really am and how expansive my mission truly is. My time at the Jordan River with John involved the opening of heaven and a declaration from my Father about my identity and role in changing the world. Likewise, you, my precious disciples, are to embody and promote the arriving reign of God. The first step is knowing who you now are in relation to me and because of me. You are beneficiaries of the salvation I bring. When in me the divine Word became flesh, it became possible that all "who received me, who believed in my name, I gave power to become children of God" (Jn. 1:12).

My baptism signaled my willingness to be a part—the crucial part—of the new world order my Father pledges to enact. In turn, for you my disciples, the waters of baptism are to wash over you with God's love and announce your incorporation into the new fellowship of the redeemed. In those waters of baptism, God witnesses that "you are my child and I am well pleased" (Lk. 3:22). Rising from those waters, you are to know who I am, whose you are, and what is the role of the church in my ongoing ministry. Baptism is hinge time in your personal history.

My Spirit is anxious to continue teaching you on my behalf. I'm providing you with select portions from the revealed Word of God and from a particular tradition of my church with wisdom you need. Read carefully and continue listening closely to my Spirit who will guide your minds and hearts to understand properly and apply effectively.

C. Light from the Revealed Word

1. Psalm 29. Here's what we humans finally know. What we cannot do for ourselves, God is able and prepared to do for us. Therefore, we must hear the voice of the LORD thundering over the waters, full of holy splendor and majesty, and we must ascribe to the LORD the honor due his name. We finally know that God creates out of chaos and pain and rides even on the floods. No matter the many negatives of those ancient Bethlehem and River Jordan scenes of the birth and baptism of Jesus. The key fact is that angels were singing, "Glory to God!"

God comes to form a chosen people who are to be loving examples of the arriving righteous reign of God. Let each of us humbly pray, "Include me among the chosen, Lord, and help me act in ways that fit being one of your chosen creators of a new day." We should fall to our knees and cry out, "Glory!" God gives strength to his people and blesses them with peace. Oh that we all might come to know that blessing and peace, and actively be about our special mission as the chosen and sent of God. Jesus has come, allowing all to be new.

2. Isaiah 43:1–7. "Do not be afraid." These are welcome words from God. Expressionist painter Edvard Munch, most famous for his painting "The Scream," captures the angst that fear produces. Big fears today include the concern that life may be meaningless and war will alienate all humanity from itself, unless first we destroy our own living environment altogether. The screams of a threatened humanity are being heard on all hands.

The prophet begins with this dramatic pivot: "But now" (43:1). Isaiah is announcing that things used to be one way and now are changing. What used to be was Judah's captivity in Babylon. What has changed is that God has ended the captivity, brought the exiles home, and restored the community. What had caused the exile was that God's people were "deaf" and "blind" to the ways of God. God judges severely. "But now," proclaims Isaiah, it's time to "restore." Now there is a Savior on the scene!

Redemption occurred not because Israel suddenly had come to her senses. Rather, it emerged from the loving character and initiative of God despite human failure. God is the original Creator and the One creating again. The salvation of the people was coming not because they first loved God, but because God first and always loved them. "You are precious in my sight, and honored, and I love you" (43:4). God will bring his people home to rebuild the community of faith. Eventually, God will even send his Son.

3. Acts 8:14–17. Philip baptized "in the name of the Lord Jesus." This phrase is used in Acts to distinguish the church's baptism from all others, including that of John the Baptist. John's baptism was about repentance and forgiveness (Lk. 3:3), but Christian baptism "in the name of Lord Jesus" is that and much more.

Christian baptism proclaims that the recipient is now in a serious relationship with Jesus. Through this relationship Luke associates the church's baptism with forgiveness of sins, reception of the Spirit, entrance into the church's fellowship, and engagement with God's mission in this world. In short, Christian baptism represents a major life turnaround that is prepared to assist with the world's turn-around.

D. Reflections of Leaders of the Wesleyan-Holiness Tradition

John Wesley makes clear what Christian baptism is to mean. But what about the baptism of Jesus? It revealed his true identity and mission. Now our task—and privilege—is to gladly receive the presence of Jesus with us and the loving seal of his Spirit on us. This seal inclines us toward a key biblical theme, God's special caring for the poor. The presence of Jesus inclines us to a freedom and openness that allows respect for others, including non-Christians.

By baptism we enter into covenant with God, into that everlasting covenant which God hath commanded forever (Ps. 111:9), that new covenant which he promised to make with the spiritual Israel, even to "give them a new heart and a new spirit, to sprinkle clean water upon them and to remember their sins and iniquities no more," in a word, *to be their God*.[1]

> We now Thy promis'd presence claim,
> Sent to disciple all mankind,
> Sent to baptize into Thy name,
> We now Thy promis'd presence find.
> Oh! That the souls baptiz'd herein,
> May now Thy truth and mercy feel,
> May rise, and wash away their sin—
> Come, Holy Ghost, their pardon seal.[2]

It took me a long time to realize that the Spirit whom Jesus gave to his disciples was not just the third person of the Trinity; it was the Spirit who had empowered Jesus' own life and ministry. The secret to Jesus' life was the Spirit, and the Spirit is anxious to be the secret of your life and mine. The Spirit was the one who initiated Christ's conception. It was he who anointed Jesus at his baptism. The Spirit was the source of Jesus' power over the demonic, and the Spirit enabled him to endure the Cross. It was the Spirit who, with the Father, raised Jesus from the dead.[3]

One of the most important themes of contemporary theology is the growing claim that God's mercy contains a "divine partiality" as an integral dimension of the biblical witness. This claim is that God has a "preferential option for the poor." I remember when the holiness insistence on "plain dress" was required as a central mission intention of the movement—to welcome the poor. We dressed down to go to church so that the poor would not feel uncomfortable in our midst.[4]

David Bundy writes extensively about E. Stanley Jones who, representing the Wesleyan-Holiness movement, was "perhaps the best-known of the thousands of Anglo-Saxon missionaries active in India in modern times." In 1938 *Time* magazine called Jones "the world's greatest missionary evangelist." In India he experienced a major reorientation of his theological stance. The change released him to his unusually productive ministry. At first his theology had been neatly "tied up with a blue ribbon" and defensive. But he placed the securities of his faith on the altar and became "free to explore, to appropriate any good, any truth found anywhere." This allowed him to love rather than pity India.[5]

---

1. John Wesley, *A Treatise on Baptism*.
2. Charles Wesley, "The Magnificat."
3. Dennis Kinlaw, *This Day with the Master*.
4. Donald W. Dayton, in the *Wesleyan Theological Journal*, 1991.
5. David Bundy, in the *Wesleyan Theological Journal*, 1988.

WEEK 10

THE SPACE BETWEEN

The Epiphany season is the time to recognize the dramatic appearance of God's plan in Jesus and look forward to God's ongoing action through the Spirit's ongoing ministry among us. For believers, this time is the space between our baptisms and God's "eschaton," that is, between our faith beginnings and God's eventual coming again to make all things right and take us home.

Along the tough road between now and then, we are in danger of frustration, impatience, and trivializing the good news from God, reducing Jesus to a means to our own ends. We forget that he is Lord, not ourselves. While very present to us, Jesus will not be contained or managed by us. Therefore, we pray that God will keep transforming our compromised lives and churches into living signs of God's arriving glory, bringing us and others face-to-face with nothing less than the very presence of the living God.

Jesus first arrived on the scene of our troubled lives in a majesty wrapped in mystery. Whenever he arrived, even at a wedding reception, unexpected glory broke forth. In the presence of Jesus, needs were met and people became reconciled to God. As we disciples of Rabbi Jesus now go forth, living and serving in the space between his first and last comings, we must remember this. The glory comes not because of who we are or what we do. It comes only because of who Jesus is and what his Spirit is graciously prepared to do through us.

A. Prayer

O Fountain of Life, I have rejoiced in the coming of your Son and sought to drink deeply of your living water. Still, I know that the challenges before me are yet many. Brace me now for the difficult faith journey yet ahead. I anxiously await your final triumph but fear that somehow I will falter along the way, fail in the space between now and then. Forgive me, Lord, for the ways in which I am tempted to use you for my private purposes rather than allow you to use me for your great work. Help me go forward loving others as you have come and so wonderfully loved me. Forgive me when I foolishly try to manipulate you. Help me to share new life, the eternal life which you have freely provided me.

B. The Voice of Rabbi Jesus: John 2:1–11

> I was thought of as ordinary at best until that wedding day in Cana. Soon I would be on my way to a personal "eschaton," death on the Cross, supposedly the end of me. That violent ending, and the following resurrection, now should make clear to you that there was nothing ordinary about God's work through me for your salvation. Implementing that finished work now belongs to you. You live between my comings. You came alive because of my first and will reign with me forever after my last coming. In between the two, learn to begin living the eternal life, the very life of my Father, until I come again to take you home.

The first of my "signs" came at a wedding in the little town of Cana. It there made clear how and why I, the arriving Messiah, would become known to the broader world. In times of crisis, I would be present and meet real human needs. My Father's intervention was needed in Cana and I was there and ready to deliver. Such signs would be evidence in action of the opening claim of John's Gospel: "The Word became flesh and lived among us, and we have seen his glory" (1:14).

This Cana story is not ultimately about a wedding, miraculously produced wine, or obedience to a mother's command. It's intended to elevate awareness of my status as God's Messiah. My action was not simply to save the wedding party from embarrassment, but to offer a sign that points to something well beyond the miracle itself. It points to my being God's agent who acts on God's behalf in addressing human need. Later I would pray to my Father, "The glory that you have given me I have given them, so that they may be one, as we are one" (Jn. 17:22). You, my disciples, are to be unified in me, now acting by my side and together as agents of God in this world.

My Spirit is anxious to continue teaching you on my behalf. I'm providing you with select portions from the revealed Word of God and from a particular tradition of my church with wisdom you need. Read carefully and continue listening closely to my Spirit who will guide your minds and hearts to understand properly and apply effectively.

C. Light from the Revealed Word

1. Psalm 36:5–10. "For with you is the fountain of life; in your light we see light" (v. 9). These magnificent words depict the central message of this psalm, and even of the Bible as a whole. Humanity's depend-ence is on God. Like the Moon, we frail humans are called to receive and then reflect the warm, life-giving light of the Sun (Son). Let us pause and give thanks for the glorious grandeur of and our personal proximity to the grace-giving God, the fountain of life itself. Verse 8 can be trans-lated, "Give us to drink from the rivers of your Gardens of Eden."

The struggle is in the *space between*, the trouble-filled time between now and then, our immediate problems and God's eventual solutions. The hope is our belief that God cannot be untrue to his own nature of constant and loving faithfulness. Therefore, no matter what, in life or death, God's steadfast love will accompany those of us who know and love him. So we pray this in the "meantimes" of our lives. "Keep showing us your love, O God, for without it we are without hope" (vs. 10).

2. Isaiah 62:1–5. This is a poem celebrating a love triangle involving the prophet Isaiah, the city of Jerusalem, and God. But there isa problem to be faced. It's the unpleasant space between what *is* and what eventually *might be* someday. On the one hand, there is the difficult his-tory of Jerusalem being rejected and ruined. And yet, we're promised a new name someday, the name "Hephzibah" meaning "My Delight." Be-cause God delights in us, our very beings and places of service can be-come like a wedding celebration. When Messiah arrives, crises will be resolved.

3. Corinthians 12:1–11. The task before the church in Corinth was to create a new kind of faith community, one centered in the Christian faith and celebrated in baptism. Paul's letter offers concrete advice, principles for discernment, models to be followed. He provides a picture of the Christian life as it should play out in the extended space between baptism and eschaton, between faith's beginnings and its consummation. How are we to live as Christ's church in the stressful time between when we first believe and when God eventually will take us home to be with him forever?

Members of this Corinthian congregation were dividing into factions based on preferred spiritual teachers. Each group was claiming superior status for itself. Paul urges that things be very much otherwise. The varieties of spiritual gifts are given by God's Spirit "for the common good" and not personal prominence. No spiritual gift should be used to disrupt the fellowship for one's own benefit. Human distinctions should never hold sway in the fellowship of Jesus. Between the first and last comings of Jesus, there must be an obvious humility and gracious oneness in all Christian communities.

D. Reflections of Leaders of the Wesleyan-Holiness Tradition

Words on the tombstone of John Wesley recall a man who had been a truly faithful and effective instrument of God's Spirit, one who properly lived out the demands of his baptism. As his brother Charles writes, baptized Christians are to join the angels and "lift up our voices and shout

Emmanuel's name." Until Christ returns, we are to be rejoicing instruments of his ministering Spirit. One way to encourage this is to educate the church's young in the direction of spiritual maturity and heart purity.

To the memory of the venerable John Wesley, A.M., late fellow of Lincoln College, Oxford. This great light arose (by the singular providence of God) to enlighten these nations, and to revive, enforce, and defend the pure apostolic doctrines and practices of the primitive church, which he continued to do both by his writings and his labors for more than half a century. And to his inexpressible joy, he beheld their influence extend-ing and their efficacy witnessed in the hearts and lives of many thou-sands, as well in the western world as in these kingdoms. But also, far above all human power of expectation, he lived to see provision made, by the singular grace of God, for their continuance and establishment to the joy of future generations. Reader, if thou art constrained to bless the instrument, give God the glory.[1]

> Glory be to God on high,
> And peace on earth descend;
> God comes down, He bows the sky,
> And shows Himself our Friend!
> God th' invisible appears,
> God the Blest, the Great I AM,
> Sojourns in this vale of tears,
> And Jesus is His Name.
> We, the sons of men, rejoice,
> The Prince of Peace proclaim,
> With the angels lift up our voice,
> And shout Immanuel's Name.
> Knees and hearts to Him we bow,
> Of our flesh, and of our bone,
> Jesus is our Brother now,
> And God is all our own![2]

John Wesley was a "radical" Christian. Christian radicality insists that at all costs the church must be a visible community that takes seriously the demands of discipleship. With his emphasis on the Holy Spirit, Wesley's faith was radically and biblically "charismatic" as well. Methodism was above all a movement of spiritual renewal. It was a mass movement of people coming to know the power of God and the power of genuine Christian community in their daily lives.[3]

The Wesleyan-Holiness movement, as embraced by its colleges and universities, is now struggling in the face of current American secularism. They will be revived only when institutions reclaim their heritage and return to John Wesley's balance of process and crisis. This means educating the whole person by the whole university, embracing holiness in student outcomes of the highest spiritual ends, spiritual maturity and purity of heart.[4]

---

1. On the tombstone of John Wesley, London, England, died 1791.
2. Charles Wesley, "Glory Be To God On High."
3. Howard A. Snyder, *The Radical Wesley*.
4. Jonathan A. Raymond, *Higher Higher Education*.

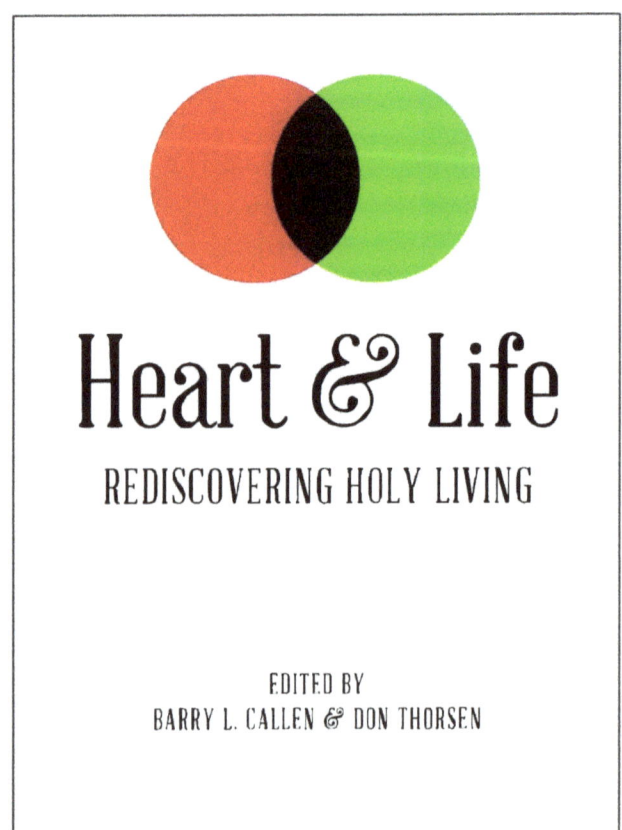

Week 11
DISCOVERING TRUE COMMUNITY

Much becomes clear in light of Jesus. Here's a prime example. God's people are many and diverse, and yet these many are to be wonderfully one in our eyes, as they are in God's. Being together *in Christ* is the source of the church's oneness, the possibility of a united although highly diverse community not otherwise known among fallen humans. In Christ, all things are held together (Col. 1:17b) and all people are valued equally.

The church is the unique held-together community of Christ's disciples, one body regardless of its various racial and national origins or the wide range of thinking and practices of its members on numerous secondary issues. The church must champion the vision of its essential oneness while it also is celebrating and being enriched by the diversity of its manyness. The disciples of Jesus are called to model before a badly divided world the beauty and peace of a truly united human community. Failure here is a great danger to the success of the church's mission in the world.

A. Prayer

Speak to me, Lord. Speak to me so that I might speak for you to the whole world. Give me the right words to testify to your reign of love, and then give me the courage to live and witness so that the world might know your name and hear your summons. Make increasingly clear to me that Christian faith is not an individualized business but a corporate enterprise. Mold me into true membership in your faith community, dear Jesus, seeing and valuing the whole of it. Make me a member who builds bridges of love and reconciliation within the faith fellowship and between it and the unbelieving world outside. May this divine-human community, the church, the body of your Son, be a shining example of what should and can be because of the redeeming and unifying grace of God. I want to be part of the answer and not more of the problem!

B. The Voice of Rabbi Jesus: Luke 4:14-21

> I am head of the church, my own body on earth today. I choose to lead the church not as a heartless dictator, modeling superiority over my lowly subjects. Early in my ministry I was led into the wilderness and there I refused the tempting pathways that destroy a servant ministry. As my disciples, you must do the same. Become known as those who spread grace and love and foster unity in the human family, not those who flash swords and lean on worldly power. Be reconciled and reconcilers. Help my people be known as the hope of the world and not seemingly just more of it.

What you, my disciples, are to proclaim in the future must not be dominated by your private thoughts and personal preferences. It must be a divinely derived testimony, like when Ezra long ago read to the people from my Father's revelation. You must speak under Spirit-induced compulsion. Your witness will be of little worth if it's not empowered by my Spirit and made understandable to the listeners through the Spirit's work. God's Spirit descended on me like a dove while I was praying after my baptism. Then God led me into the wilderness for testing. I refused anything other than being a servant minister of healing grace, especially to the downtrodden in this world. Choose to live and minister this way.

Without the Spirit of God, true ministry will be impossible. The *dunamis* (dynamic power) of my Spirit is the main thing my church has going for it. Never think that impressive buildings, budgets, staff, or volume of members necessarily represent or enable the power of my Spirit. That kind of misunderstanding is a menu for church disaster.

My Spirit is anxious to continue teaching you on my behalf. I'm providing you with select portions from the revealed Word of God and from a particular tradition of my church with wisdom you need. Read carefully and continue listening closely to my Spirit who will guide your minds and hearts to understand properly and apply effectively.

C. Light from the Revealed Word

1. Psalm 19. Here is a depiction of creation coming into being through the proclamation of God's voice. We are invited to recall the witness given to God's splendor by the textures and glory of creation. We are reminded of the significance and wonder of God's law. Finally, the psalmist calls us to a humble recognition of human frailty in the face of these majestic glories of God. A true faith community forms around such reminders and humility. Only in this ways can the intended oneness of God's people ever come to be.

The psalmist gazed into the skies and saw the glory of God. For the Old Testament person, "glory" was the obvious clothing of God. This clothing wasn't hiding God's true person but revealing it in his gracious actions. Disciples of Rabbi Jesus will discover their intended identity together as the church only as they respond and begin to reflect the Holy One's presence and guidance. We are called to be one people in Christ by the power of his Spirit. We are called to put on the clothing of God in order to reveal to others God's true essence. We must be holy as God is holy.

2. Nehemiah 8:1–10. During renovations of the Jerusalem city wall after the people had returned from the Exile, a scroll was found. It was the Scripture of Israel, lost and forgotten during the disastrous years away. The people assembled and listened intently all day long to the rediscovered Word of God being read aloud. As they listened, they came to realize the great gap between their actual lives and God's will for them as his chosen people.

Ezra stood before the people of Israel and read to them. The people soon knew that they had entered the presence of the living God. Their first reaction was to cry out in repentance for their sin. Beyond that initial reaction came the realization that the revelation of God was for their benefit, not their condemnation. As a community hoping to become united in faithfulness to God's Word, the people realized that they could achieve their God-given mission only if they were faithful to the Word. The true people of God centers its life around the Word of revelation and its call to reconciliation and mission.

3. 1 Corinthians 12:12–31. St. Paul points to the practical reality of Nehemiah's quest. Christians are inducted into a new humanity that requires and enables a new form of community. It should be a faith community marked by an appreciation for differences among its members, without a rigid hierarchy of social status. The good of the whole body is to prioritized. Pauluses the figure of the human body to explain this process of interdependence. All members of the church are to be equally enlivened by the same Spirit of Christ, and all are called to do Christ's work in the world, knowing that it's done best together as they merge their divine gifts.

Highlighted is the needed discernment of the giftings and functions of disciples of Jesus. Spiritual gifts are to be used *for the common good* rather than to elevate the status of any particular individual member (12:7). Because the faith community is the body of Christ, caring for the com- mon good is what faith in Jesus must look and act like. Presented to the Corinthians is a ranked list of some prominent spiritual gifts. The or- ganizational principle of the list is that the gifts that build up the whole are at the top. Speaking in "tongues"—which was being used by some Corinthian believers as individual claims to special status in the church— is included but put at the bottom.

D. Reflections of Leaders of the Wesleyan-Holiness Tradition

Only a holy church can be a united church representing well the Spirit of Christ. Thank God for a church triumphant, all pure in this world below! This at least is our calling and goal. When we really know that we have been confirmed as children of God together, then the fruit of the Spirit begins to flow—including an overflow of peace and unity in the body of Christ.

We must love God before we can be holy at all, this love being the root of all holiness. It has been confirmed, both in this and every age, by a cloud of living and dying witnesses. It is confirmed by your experience and mine. The Spirit bore witness to my spirit that I was a child of God, gave me evidence of it, and I immediately cried, "Abba, Father!" And I did this (and so did you) before I was conscious of any fruit of the Spirit. It was from this testimony that love, joy, peace, and the whole fruit of the Spirit flowed.[1]

> I want the Spirit of power within,
> Of love, and of a healthful mind,
> Of power to conquer inbred sin,
> Of love to Thee and all mankind,
> Of health that pain and death defies,
> Most vigorous when the body dies.
>
> O that the Comforter would come!
> Nor visit as a transient guest,
> But fix in me his constant home,
> And take possession of my breast,
> And fix in me his loved abode,
> The temple of the indwelling God![2]
>
> God's church is alone triumphant,
> In holiness all complete;
> And all the dark pow'rs of Satan
> She tramples beneath her feet.[3]

Christian identity and church membership are to be rooted in Christian experience, persons being transformed into the image of Christ by action of the Spirit. Affiliation with a church body apart from new life in Christ is false membership and poor theology. True belief is to be experienced and practiced, not merely verbalized.[4]

To be oriented to the presence and work of the Spirit is not necessarily to be mired in subjectivism or committed to anarchy in church life. Spirit orientation is the conscious determination of Christian believers to be free of artificial and forced structures of belief and church life and, conversely, to be committed to present spiritual reality, serious discipleship, and credible covenant community.[5]

The class meeting became the primary means of grace for thousands of Methodists. It served an evangelistic and discipling function. John Wesley realized that "the beginnings of faith in a person's heart could be incubated into faith more effectively in the warm Christian atmosphere of the society than in the chill of the world."[6]

---

1. John Wesley, *The Witness of the Spirit, Discourse II.*
2. Charles Wesley, "I Want the Spirit of Power Within."
3. Daniel S. Warner, "The Church Triumphant."
4. Barry L. Callen, *Forward, Ever Forward!*
5. Barry L. Callen, *Radical Christianity.*
6. Howard A. Snyder, *The Radical Wesley.*

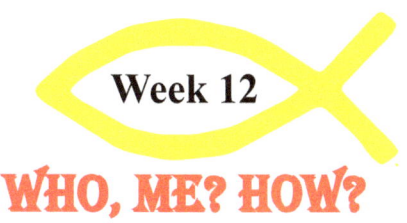

Week 12

WHO, ME? HOW?

In this Christian season of Epiphany, we marvel that Jesus Christ appeared for all the world to see. Like Jeremiah, we now recognize our calling to proclaim this good-news message to all. As Jesus said: "Go into all the world and proclaim the good news to the whole creation" (Mark 16:15). But who are we to do such a great thing? How could we ever get it done? Me, Lord? How?

One of the many things that must be clarified by Rabbi Jesus is our role as disciples n God's great mission, and particularly our resource for being able to accomplish such a major calling. How are we, limited as we are, to go about fulfilling our responsibility as serious followers of Jesus? There is the known problem. Wherever Jesus is faithfully preached and truthfully presented, there will be offense. Are we ready for that? How can we get ready?

A. Prayer

I need at least two things, Lord, and I need them badly. I need to hear your voice defining clearly my responsibility as your disciple. Then I need to know how to do what you ask. I also need the courage to share your good news with people who much prefer to hear other things more in line with their private comforts and self-justifications. Be my rock, my fortress, my informing and sustaining God. Dear God, please fill me with a love that will overcome and outlast all obstacles to the spread of your gospel. Although I am so small, I believe I can be adequate if I rely on your unlimited greatness. Only with you will I ever make it. Come to me, precious Spirit of Christ!

B. The Voice of Rabbi Jesus: Luke 4:21-30

> Yes, it's you who now are called to change the world. I'm relying on you, my disciples who form my church. Go everywhere and both tell and live the good news of my Father in me for all people. Don't expect to always be welcomed by your hearers. I am your Rabbi and Lord—and my own people called for my crucifixion. Even so, the great evangelizing task can be done. It must be done. You are the called ones responsible to spearhead its doing. Your essential resource will be the gifting and guidance of my Spirit who promises always to be with you.

Trouble came early for me. My neighbors were incensed that one of their own had the audacity to sit among them and suggest that they would not be the vessels for the unfolding of God's future. Here's what those Nazareth folks thought. How could "the chosen" become unchosen and their special privileges shifted to others? The insider, me in my own hometown, suddenly became the hated outsider. I wasn't what they wanted. My neighbors and former friends didn't want to hear that the living God had come to break through their arrogant and calcified religious ways. Be ready for the same opposition in your own ministries.

My Father will not be domesticated, homebound, confined by temples or cathedrals, or limited by your fears and limitations. When God sends, dare to go and the needed resources will be there. God will not be stopped by the selfish ways of religion gone wrong. His agenda will not be shifted to our own. My Father is far more than anyone's tribal deity. Unfortunately, the church of my disciples always will have those in it who are upset with a preacher not condemning their favorite enemies and comforting them in their cherished self-justifications.

My Spirit is anxious to continue teaching you on my behalf. I'm providing you with select portions from the revealed Word of God and from a particular tradition of my church with wisdom you need. Read carefully and continue listening closely to my Spirit who will guide your minds and hearts to understand properly and apply effectively.

C. Light from the Revealed Word

1. Psalm 71:1–6. Who, me? But how? The wicked are asserting themselves against the psalmist with a cruel and unjust power. It's the "righteous" who may be blown away. Even so, God is regarded as a refuge, a deliverer, a rescuer, a rock, a fortress—the One to be leaned on and praised regardless of negative circumstances. The expression "from my youth" (vs. 5) suggests a wealth of discipleship years and learning between the initial calling and the psalmist's present life. His many years of serving God had produced a matured intimacy characterized by a present belief that God is a dependable support. There's a hard-won wisdom in this psalm.

Jeremiah's response to the Lord's calling to a prophetic ministry is also wisdom for us today. As the psalmist puts it, "Upon you I have leaned from my birth; it was you who took me from my mother's womb." God plans, calls, enables, and can be trusted. Jeremiah protested to God, "Hold it. Look at me. I don't know anything. I'm only a boy!" (Jer. 1:6). God's reply was, "Don't say, 'I'm only a boy'." Are you called to bring a world-changing message to all the earth? Yes, you are. Then don't say that. If God calls, *God will provide*.

2. Jeremiah 1:4–10. Jeremiah resisted the call of God because he believed himself not up to the task. Jeremiah is the "everyman's" prophet. He shows us that fear, anxiety, resistance, inadequacy, even resentment are understandable reactions to the call to represent God in a very troubled world. Even so, these human feelings do not disqualify from serving God's intentions. Nothing disqualifies but our lack of faith and unwillingness to answer the call and receive God's provisions for its accomplishment.

God somehow mysteriously, graciously, chooses us of all people. The "greats" in the Bible were also ordinary persons whom God used in extraordinary ways. The same was true of first disciples of Jesus. They were an unlikely lot indeed. No matter. They were effective voices for God, and not because of anything within themselves that earned them that privilege. Their adequacy came because of their proper responses in faith to the call of Rabbi Jesus and the spiritual provisions of his Spirit.

3. 1 Corinthians 13:1–13. We who are the disciples of Jesus are like children who know only in part. Paul chides the Corinthians for imagining that they are spiritually mature and in full possession of the richness of the Spirit. He reminds them that he had spoken to them "as infants in Christ. I fed you with milk, not solid food, for you were not ready for solid food" (3:1-2).

Christians must live and serve in the troubled present. The coming kingdom of God has been inaugurated but not yet fulfilled. While we should be confident in the power of the Spirit, we also must be humble and discerning, aware that our prophecies are partial, our knowledge incomplete, and our vision dim. Whatever spiritual gifts we may have are gifts that are fleeting and will not outlast the most enduring gift.

What remains, the enduring gift, is love, God's gracious and unshakable grasp on our lives. It's the source of our security and the freedom that allows us to be patient and kind. Love is less another spiritual gift and more the way in which God intends us to practice all our gifts. There is something more important than being right or powerful or honored or safe in this world. It's relating to others with integrity and generosity. Loving with abandon is to be holy as God is holy.

D. Reflections of Leaders of the Wesleyan-Holiness Tradition

How do we proceed with our call from Christ? John Wesley announced his answer. Every way possible, including capitalizing on the power of community. His brother Charles added that from the depths of love we must find creative ways to care for others, showing how true believers live and witness. We must keep Satan asleep, attend to the means of grace, and be where God will find and guide us. One way to do this is to maintain a disciplined devotional life.

"Sir," said that unhappy man at my first interview with him, "I hear you preach to a great number of people every night and morning. Pray, what would you do with them? Whither would you lead them? What religion do you preach? What is it good for?" I replied, "I do preach to as many as desire to hear, every night and morning. You ask, what I would do with them: I would make them virtuous and happy, easy in themselves, and useful to others."

Whither would I lead them? "To heaven; to God the Judge, the lover of all, and to Jesus the Mediator of the new covenant." What religion do I preach? "The religion of love; the law of kindness brought to light by the gospel." What is this good for? "To make all who receive it enjoy God and themselves, to make them like God, lovers of all, contented in their lives, and crying out at their death, in calm assurance, 'O grave, where is thy victory! Thanks be unto God, who giveth me the victory, through my Lord Jesus Christ'."[1]

> Let us each for others care,
> Each his brother's burden bear,
> Thy church the pattern give,
> Show how true believers live.
>
> Free from anger, and from pride,
> Let us thus in God abide,
> All the depth of love express,
> All the height of holiness.[2]

Satan has got men fast asleep in sin and it is his great device to keep them so. He does not care what we do if he can do that. We may sing songs about the sweet by and by, preach sermons and say prayers until doomsday, and he will never concern himself about us if we don't wake anybody up. But if we awake the sleeping sinner, he will gnash on us with his teeth. This is our work—to wake people up.[3]

Wesley believed in the power of community, so much so that he made it the heart of the Methodist movement. Convinced that there could be no spiritual maturity without discipline, he developed societies, classes, and bands. These groups developed practices designed to assist people in spiritual discipline as means of sanctifying grace.[4]

How do I find God? You don't have to find him; you have to allow him to find you. That means, stop running away. Turn toward him in an attitude of expectancy. Faith is expectancy. Act as though God *is*, and is with *you*, and with you *now*. Practice the presence of God.[5]

Beware of assuming that the Christian life can be vital and light-bearing in neglect of the devotional life. It can be conventionally moral, highly respectable, even to a considerable degree altruistic without it, but it cannot be the Kingdom-seeking, cross-bearing, richly fruitful life that God requires. Without the devotional life, the light of faith tends ever to flicker as the winds of life blow upon it.[6]

---

1. John Wesley, *An Earnest Appeal to Men of Reason and Religion*.
2. Charles Wesley, "For a Family."
3. Catherine Booth, *Life and Death*.
4. Cheryl Bridges Johns, in *The Holiness Manifesto*.
5. E. Stanley Jones, *Abundant Living*.
6. Georgia Harkness, *Foundations of Christian Knowledge*.

WEEK 13

IT'S EASIER TO PLUCK BLACKBERRIES!

God calls and we are to respond. Isaiah the prophet answered the Lord's call this way. "I'll go. Send me!" The New Testament explains how Paul, despite his anti-Gentile background, became an apostle to the Gentiles. Jesus called Simon Peter to switch his fishing goal. "From now on you will be catching people" (Lk. 5:10).

God's in the calling business. There is to be no sitting around plucking blackberries when an amazing divine invitation beckons elsewhere. Plucking blackberries? The poet Elizabeth Barrett Browning wrote, "Earth's crammed with heaven, and every common bush afire with God; but only he who sees takes off his shoes. The rest sit round it and pluck blackberries."

Let's meet people who do hear God calling, who do take off their shoes, and pay the price to avoid missing the challenge and joy of following God's voice. Yes, it would be easier to keep sitting, to keep plucking blackberries. No matter. We must get up and go! Beckoning are both new dangers and enduring hope.

When we do go to evangelize in the name of Jesus, we must never forget this. Whatever our best efforts, it's always the Spirit of God who does the real work of human transformation. Even so, our human partnership in the process is critical.

A. Prayer

My God, I do hear your still small voice calling me in a difficult and undesired new direction. Staying with my normal routines and old friends would be so much easier than launching into your big unknown. Please don't let me make the wrong decision—and I know that avoiding any decision is a wrong decision. Have patience with me. I feel so unprepared for what you are wanting of me. Help me believe that you will provide whatever is necessary if only I will say, "Yes!"

B. The Voice of Rabbi Jesus: Luke 5:1–11

> Hear my voice, dear friends. I'm calling you to the most important enterprise of all, my Father's mission of redeeming love in this world. Push out with me and dare to fish for lost sinners. Be patient and know this. If you go and at first catch nothing, keep trying. I'll always be close by. I will be encouraging you to keep going, keep believing in the unexpected, having faith in the seeming impossible. When you get frustrated, don't focus on the failure. Just keep remembering who I am and try again. If I've sent you, there will be fish. In my kingdom, frustration is only the front door to the coming fulfillment.

Know this. My call to you disciples, whatever the future problems, will not be in vain. Your experience will be much like that of the prophet Isaiah. You will react with objections and questions and become very aware of your unworthiness. But don't stop there. Also hear my voice of reassurance. First be commissioned and then obey and persist, whatever the cost. The very gates of hell will eventually not withstand your coming with my good news.

The psalmist of old has it right. "The Lord will fulfill his promise for me" (Ps. 138:8). My promise to you is that I will be with you always. I know you better than you know yourself. You can do it. I will do it through you.

It won't always be easy to see my Father at work in the midst of your troubles. You'll be inclined to expect immediate results from your Christian labors. Know this. It's easier to pluck blackberries, but the level of ease isn't the real issue. No matter what, leave the plucking behind and press on. Stay the course. In God's time and way, all divine promises will be fulfilled.

My Spirit is anxious to continue teaching you on my behalf. I'm providing you with select portions from the revealed Word of God and from a particular tradition of my church with wisdom you need. Read carefully and continue listening closely to my Spirit who will guide your minds and hearts to understand properly and apply effectively.

C. Light from the Revealed Word

1. Psalm 138. We in the modern West live in an "age of anxiety," even before the 9/11 attacks on the United States. Now, after those horrible attacks and the political crises and pandemic that have followed, the anxiety has metastasized. We "walk daily in the midst of trouble." We need to encounter God and learn how to be divine witnesses in a world of terrorism and mass deaths. God shows the way by choosing to attend to the helpless and vulnerable—those on the margins of faith and life and in most distress. The high and mighty of our world won't do this "lowly" thing. They are too self-occupied to focus on the plight of those who are weak, insecure, insignificant, in jeopardy.

Home from an awful exile, the Jews were sustained by knowing that God's loving kindness had acted, hearing their cries and rescuing them. Now it was time for God's rescued people to begin acting in grateful response, not just sitting around being pleased by God's past actions. God calls, sends, and searches out all our actions, or lack of them (vs. 3). The saved dare not stay in church and be paralyzed by paradise! Those many now in distress are waiting for God to come to them through the loving actions of God's grateful people. A voice from above beckons that way. Our challenge is to respond appropriately.

2. Isaiah 6:1–8 (9–13). The prophet's response to God, and God's current invitation to us, is "Here am I; send me!" The hard facts of Isaiah's commission came only after he went, and sometimes they led to apparent failure. No wonder he came to regret his offer to serve God. Isaiah's "How long, O Lord" is no polite inquiry about the duration of his mission. He had learned that success would have to be measured by faithfulness and not the volume of fruit. In the end, the success of divine grace is assured not by the striving of God's witnesses but by divine power and timing. To stand in the presence of God is to be brought to your knees.

The sin being confessed here is more than the occasional violation of what parents once told us not to do as kids. It's the gaping chasm between who we are and who God is. We moderns have counselors, therapists, and television doctors to help us handle sin as minor misdeeds. However, what if our sin is with a capital "S." What if our uncleanness is not what we once did in high school or in the back seat of a car, but the relational gap between ourselves and God that's so wide and deep that no human can help us overcome?

God calls and we are to respond despite our unpreparedness and personal histories. We must become aware that the One who calls is able to forgive, close the God-human gap, and provide for all our needs as we agree to go on our divine missions.

3. 1 Corinthians 15:1–11. Apparently some members of the Corinthian congregation believed that there is no resurrection of the dead. Paul goes on at length to demonstrate that believing in the resurrection of Jesus is both necessary and plausible. The point is that the gospel Paul proclaims is a call to action, to a new way of living in the present age, one that is rooted in a sure hope for the age to come. When called by God, we are to respond with the assurance that ultimately, maybe beyond our own efforts and even lifetimes, God's intentions will be fulfilled. From the graveyard can and will burst new life.

We are called to share the gospel story, namely, "that Christ died for our sins in accordance with the Scriptures, and that he was buried, and that he was raised on the third day." We don't create this good news, we are recreated by it. We don't need to "succeed" in our gospel efforts, only be faithful in its sharing. Someday, from the very dust of death, we will be resurrected to life eternal! "We proclaim Christ crucified, a stumbling block to Jews and foolishness to Gentiles, but to those who are the called, Christ is the power and wisdom of God."

Who is a "saint" of God? It's one who capitalizes on the wonderful fact that in this life it's possible to enter into a relationship with God so close, so precious, that even death cannot break it. Such a relationship is called "holiness," a true resurrection life in the present, from the future, by the grace of God.

D. Reflections of Leaders of the Wesleyan-Holiness Tradition

We have been given a wonderful message of love and the invitation to spread it to the remotest corners of our hurting world. We must provide for the flock of wanderers who are searching for home. People need to know that they are loved. The evangelists of Rabbi Jesus must never forget that the primary Actor is always the Spirit of God.

Men and brethren, help! Was there ever a call like this since you first heard the gospel sound? Help to relieve your companions in the kingdom of Jesus who are pressed above measure. "Bear one another's burdens, and so fulfill the law of Christ" (Gal. 6:2). Help to send forth able, willing laborers into your Lord's harvest: so shall you be an assistant in saving souls from death, and hiding a multitude of sins. Help to spread the gospel of your salvation into the remotest corners till the knowledge of our Lord will cover the land as the waters cover the sea.[1]

> Jesus, thy wandering sheep behold!
> See, Lord, with tenderest pity see
> The sheep that cannot find the fold,
> Till sought and gathered in by Thee.
> Thou, only Thou, the kind and good
> And sheep-redeeming Shepherd art:
> Collect Thy flock, and give them food,
> And pastors after Thine own heart.[2]

The message of Jesus Christ is good news because it is a message of love. When we share the gospel, we are making that love manifest. We note and help meet the physical and social needs of persons. We offer food if it is needed, and friendship if it will be received. We love. We also share the living reality of God's love. It is good news for people to hear that they are loved and that God loves them so much that God became flesh, was born of a woman, and lived as a man to teach everyone who would like to know how to become a son or daughter of God.[3]

Remember that the primary mover in evangelism is the Holy Spirit. While it seems like it is all about *me* or *you* as an evangelist, in reality it is the Holy Spirit who prompts, leads, convicts, teaches, and transforms. The primary practice of an evangelist is not, surprisingly enough, to evangelize; rather, it is to pray for openness to the principal evangelist, the Holy Spirit.[4]

---

1. John Wesley, *The Larger Minutes of the Society*.
2. Charles Wesley, "Jesu, Thy Wandering Sheep Behold."
3. John Tyson, in the *Wesleyan Theological Journal*.
4. Priscilla Pope-Levison, *Models of Evangelism*.

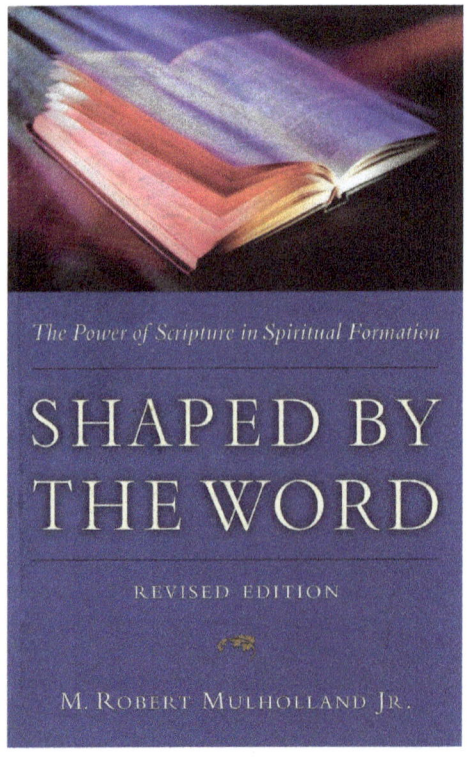

WEEK 14

TURNED ON ITS HEAD!

It's the opposite of what you might think. Reality often is our human expectation turned on its head. Happiness is often found in going the other way. Following Jesus is taking the road of life not usually traveled. We should come to church to be reminded of what's really real. So many people live in little worlds of their own making, or that someone dumped on them and they fell for. Don't be taken in by fake news! It's truth standing awkwardly on its head, and it's everywhere.

Because of Jesus, Christians have a quarrel with the world's definitions of reality. As disciples of Rabbi Jesus, we are to align our lives with the new reality that Jesus calls into being. What should be going on in worship services? Every time Christians gather, here is the question that should be on the table for consideration. "What's real?" The world as it appears before our eyes may be more distracting shadow than actual truth. The kingdom of God arrived with Jesus!

There now is available a new vision of reality. God in Christ has entered the world and changed the picture. The point of sharing the gospel of Christ is not first to tell people what to do. First, it's helping them see what they ought to be seeing. And let's attend to our own business. Let's allow people to see in the church a community that's obviously been transformed into a divine fellowship! If they can't see that new reality, they won't be able to believe our words.

A. Prayer

Lord, I know that I'm realizing only slowly that the best way to stand confidently tall is to kneel humbly low. Only down on my knees, with eyes closed, can I begin to see clearly. Fill me with this unusual wisdom. You, blessed God, are setting upright our upside-down world. It's a logic of transformed life that appears so silly to the selfish crowds of everyday. Fill me with that foolishness that is wisdom indeed, that is life at its best, that is an eye seeing what's real and truly possible. By your Spirit within, may I actually live a new life that will appear real to others, not just clutter the world with more religious double-talk.

B. The Voice of Rabbi Jesus: Luke 6:17–26

> Be warned about the coming challenges, the mixed messages, the confusing sights. Know that you'll be blessed even in the midst of apparent failure and false reports of your true motives. I'll help you see the bigger picture beyond the confusing shadows. I am the light of the world, and that includes your very human and private worlds. Keep your eyes on me and you'll be seeing reality as it is and one day will be. Stay alive in my Spirit so that what you say and do in my name will be credible in the eyes of others. For them to ever believe, you must be evidencing the fruit of a resurrected life.

I know my teachings sound idealistic and unworkable. They turn normal human experiences on their heads. The blessing of God follows this new logic. Those who leave everything to follow me will know the riches of the kingdom of God, regardless of how reviled and defamed they might be at times by those seeing things differently. My Father is turning the world upside down, actually right-side up.

Discipleship with me must go beyond a simple "follow me" to a level of daunting sacrifice. I'm pointing you toward a fearful tree, my coming Cross. Looking at that scene reveals my Father at work—even though it looks more like the Devil's work. You must see my Cross as the world being wonderfully turned right-side up.

An old philosopher named Plato composed the insightful *Allegory of the Cave*. Humans are pictured as prisoners chained to the floor of a cave, forced to sit facing toward the back wall. People are moving back and forth behind them but can be seen only by their shadows reflected on the wall. Friends, you must question the images you vaguely see. They can be deeply misleading.

Through me, my Father is showing you what the real world actually is and could be. For those willing see his revelation, there comes a glimpse of a whole new world, the real world, the world beyond the flickering worldly shadows of the alluring but the false. The point of all my teachings is to open your eyes to this new wonderful reality.

My Spirit is anxious to continue teaching you on my behalf. I'm providing you with select portions from the revealed Word of God and from a particular tradition of my church with wisdom you need. Read carefully and continue listening closely to my Spirit who will guide your minds and hearts to understand properly and apply effectively.

C. Light from the Revealed Word

1. Psalm 1. There are 150 psalms. The editor put this one first for a reason. It's why Matthew put the Beatitudes at the beginning of the teachings of Jesus. They properly preface all that follows. Happiness is life turned right-side up! There are two pathways and only one leads to life. It's not the one most people assume.

In contemporary society, happiness typically is measured by what one manages to take from the world's bounty. The happy person, according to Psalm 1, is the reverse. Happiness is not what one takes but what one contributes to the bounty, bearing fruit that sustains others and sprouts leaves that shade others from the withering sun of life's harshness. Those who "delight in the law of the LORD" (vs. 2) are like strong trees whose roots have gone deep into a nourishing reality unknown by others.

Reality is not a maze of selfish smoke and mirrors. Put simply, it's God in Christ for our salvation and the resulting lives of self-giving service that open reality's possibility to others.

2. Jeremiah 17:5–10. A stark contrast is shown between those whose hearts are turned away from God (v. 5) and those who "trust in the LORD" (v. 7). A devious heart, one set against God, can do well in this world, at least temporarily before becoming an eventual disaster (v. 6). Those whose trust is in God may struggle for the moment and yet will wind up being like trees that bear fruit in the worst of circumstances (v. 8).

To biblical people desperate for water in a desert environment, the tree was symbolic of life that had withstood drought and storms. We see such trees with their trunks, branches, and leaves, but the secret to their lives is not what we see. It's what we cannot see, the roots, those thirsty tentacles reaching deep into the earth and finding hidden moisture unknown above. Life happens in the darkness of subterranean places. We need special eyes to see down there.

Military power, technological innovation, social status, and economic achievement tempt us to judge them as the sources of security and personal meaning. However, reliance on these renders us insufficiently rooted for the trials that confront, sometimes now and certainly hereafter. We must trust in the Lord and not ourselves. That involves going deep down where real life can actually begin.

3. 1 Corinthians 15:12–20. The good news is that Christ can turn on its head the dangerous wrongness of life lived in defiance of God. It can free those who once believed in the perverse waywardness of the heart. The resurrected One enables resurrected life for serious disciples. A future vision can reshape our present living, so that what we now do in our bodily existence really matters for our futures (1 Cor. 6:12–20). The gift of the Spirit is the divine power and presence connecting now and later on, providing for the now from the resources of the later on.

The object of one's faith and trust matters greatly. Trust in the Lord leads to resources so that our lives can produce fruit even in times of drought. Faith in Christ is not worthless or empty because the object of this trust is none other than the God who raised Christ from the dead. This object, really the *Subject*, may appear to many as foolishness, but appearance and reality often are very different things.

Christ's resurrection is the first-fruit that provides the horizon of our destiny and the navigation coordinates for our present existence. The gift of the Spirit brings the future into the present as immediate reality and future promise. God's presence and power in the Spirit enable us to stay on course as the new humanity in Christ. That's the world right-side up!

D. Reflections of Leaders of the Wesleyan-Holiness Tradition

The perceptions of individuals are their realities. Today, widespread "conspiracy theories" and "fake news" have made reality dramatic opposites for differing viewers. God's revealed love has opened hopeful visions of possibility that non-believers aren't seeing. We who belong to Rabbi Jesus must see and seek a future that surpasses the present, and do so together as a transformed community of faith.

God is already renewing the face of the earth. We have strong reason to hope that the work he hath begun, he will carry on unto the day of the Lord Jesus, that he will never abandon this blessed work of his Spirit until he has fulfilled all his promises, until he hath put a period to sin, and misery, and infirmity, and death, and re-established universal holiness and happiness, and caused all the inhabitants of the earth to sing together, "Hallelujah, the Lord God omnipotent reigneth!"[1]

> O for a closer walk with God,
> A calm and heavenly frame;
> A light to shine upon the road
> That leads me to the Lamb![2]

The greatest strength of Wesleyan doctrine lies in its ability to mobilize the believer to seek a future that surpasses the present. It turns the Christian life into a project constantly open to new possibilities.[3]

From a Wesleyan perspective, the vision of the kingdom of God cannot be separated from Christian fellowship. There is a mutual means of grace by which the reign of God is embodied as a social reality. The divine embrace takes hold of each person while gathering them all into a kingdom community, so that their life together might bear faithful witness to the future of the new creation, all being encouraged to long for God's justifying and sanctifying grace.[4]

Evangelism is not the besetting problem of the church. The *church* is the besetting problem of the church. But the church is also a point of promise, a touchstone for the unchurched. The church can become a compass for a disoriented world *if* it embraces the qualities that exemplify *good* evangelism—hospitality, relationship, integrity, a message of the good news of the gospel. This sort of community embodies and *is* the good news.[5]

---

1. John Wesley, *The General Spread of the Gospel*.
2. Charles Wesley, "O, For a Closer Walk with God."
3. Theodore Runyon, in the *Wesleyan Theological Journal*.
4. Philip Meadows, *Wesleyan and Methodist Studies*, 2011.
5. Priscilla Pope-Levison, *Models of Evangelism*.

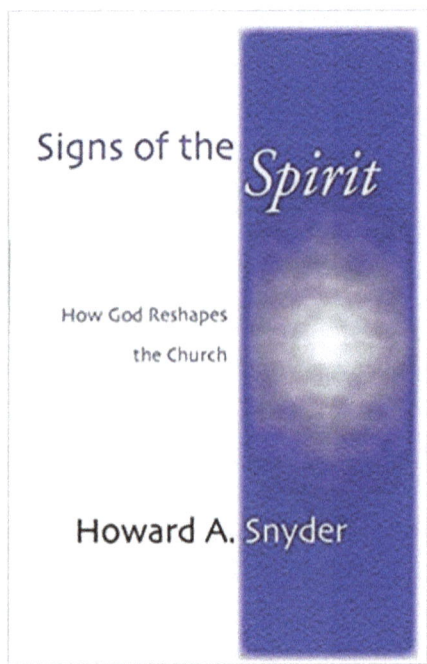

WEEK 15

NOW IN LIGHT OF THEN

Last week we were shown the importance of seeing what's really real. Now we learn that what's most deeply real can't be seen fully until the end of things. We must come to see ourselves and our human histories in the same God-working-behind-the-scenes way that Joseph of old finally did.

It's helpful to ask, "What led you to this church?" Here are today's typical answers. My mother went to a Methodist church, at least I think it was Methodist. I was looking for the Baptist church downtown and somebody gave me the wrong address, so I showed up here. I really enjoy good preaching and the preacher here is really good. I was dating this guy. He went to this church so I came with him. Music is important for me and I finally found a congregation that still had a choir. I could have joined lots of other churches, but there was this snowstorm and I couldn't drive too far that morning and showed up here.

Choice or chance? This seems to be the tension troubling most of our lives. Did God mean this for you or did it just happen? Do most things happen for no reason at all, or is there some grand plan just out of sight? Here's good news. The arrival of Jesus makes possible a productive life *in the meantime,* in the time between the uncertainty of *now* and the clarity of God's eventual *then.*

This much is very clear already. Jesus was no accident. God definitely meant him for us. As time goes on, we'll be more and more sure of this, and through him of many other things. Meanwhile, our *now* must come to be seen in light of God's *then.* The first fruits of tomorrow can be shaping our realities today. Eventually, God's planned *eschaton*, the finalization of all things, will make everything clear to us. But for now we proceed in faith.

A. Prayer

Help me, O Lord, to know that salvation is more than being forgiven of past sin. God has given me freedom from sin; now I want to give God the entirety of my life for his service—a big second phase of the salvation process. Empower me to act like a responsible citizen of your coming kingdom, Rabbi Jesus. It's hard to be in this world and march to a drummer playing so far away. Come closer, Lord. Your wonderful future will make clear all things, things so confusing to me now. The question I face is, How can I manage *now* in light of your yet-arriving *then*? Surely the presence of your Spirit is the answer. The Spirit enables the first fruits of the future that should characterize my transformed todays. Please, dear God, send me your Spirit!

B. The Voice of Rabbi Jesus: Luke 6:27–38

> Since all my true disciples are forgiven sinners, you must and can act out now your forgiveness. Do this by loving and forgiving even your enemies. You must act like tomorrow's people living today as loyal citizens of the coming kingdom. My spirit will show you how and make this hard thing possible. To be my "saints" is to be in sync with my Spirit's present work, even with many questions not yet answered. True saints are my disciples who are coming to see and act like heralds of the better tomorrow they are sure my Father soon will bring. Open yourselves to such faith, my friends. It's the only way ahead.

My ethical teachings are directed toward the present time, with an eye always on my Father's future. Generosity, forgiveness, and righteousness are the behaviors to cultivate and pursue diligently. The wrongdoers persist, enemies remain, and the unknowns can be troubling. The sad destiny of the arrogant non-believers is fixed. Love them anyway.

Love them in the present, motivated by the promise of what is to come for you—and hopefully somehow even for them.

Sacrifice your cherished sense of aggrievement toward your enemies, thereby rendering them not enemies at all, but fellow sinners forgiven by God. Let me distill my message down to its essence. Love others and love yourself because God loves you. Love the least of the people in your life every bit as much as you love yourself. That's my Spirit's way of living in you and through you.

Live *now* in light of my Father's *then*, even though you can't fully see it yet. Be true sons and daughters of the Most High by reflecting his holy nature through your merciful deeds. You are citizens of a new world. Look and act like it as you employ the gifts my Spirit gives each of you.

My Spirit is anxious to continue teaching you on my behalf. I'm providing you with select portions from the revealed Word of God and from a particular tradition of my church with wisdom you need. Read carefully and continue listening closely to my Spirit who will guide your minds and hearts to understand properly and apply effectively.

C. Light from the Revealed Word

1. Psalm 37:1–11, 39–40. Patience, patience, patience. That's the drumbeat of this psalm. "Do not fret" (vs. 1). "Soon" (vs. 2). "Be still and wait patiently" (vs. 7). "Refrain" (vs. 8). "Yet a little while" (vs. 10). Those who have the upper hand now will be brought low. The prosperity of the wicked will be reversed (vs. 38). The evildoers will wither away. Just wait, and act now knowing about their fate then if things don't change.

While urging patient confidence in the future that God is preparing, this psalm also recommends the behaviors appropriate for now in light of then: faithfulness, righteousness, and devotion. The present is not simply a time for passive waiting but one of actively pursue the things that further God's purposes and build meaningful lives. "Trust in the Lord, and do good" (v. 3). "Take delight in the Lord" (v. 4). "Commit your way to the Lord" (v. 5). Meanwhile, don't worry. Trust in God and in time all will be well. Just remember, God is at work and the future is secure. Knowing that should help you live properly in the present despite the many things not yet known.

2. Genesis 45:3–15. When the famine hit that Joseph had predicted, Jacob and sons back in Israel began suffering greatly. The brothers who had sold Joseph to Egypt were forced go there to buy food, and unknowingly to run into Joseph. Joseph was tested, being in the power position. He could be generous with whomever he wished. What about with his own family who had abused him? He finally reveals himself to his brothers and immediately asks about the health of his father.

The powerful phrase "but now" alerts us to Joseph's dramatic announcement of reconciliation. Yesterday was one way, but now God has meant it for quite another way today. Revenge is to be replaced with compassion. Joseph would let go of yesterday because he could see that God had been quietly at work bringing good out of evil. "God sent me before you to preserve life." Can we see the pattern of divine love woven into life's complexities? Such sight takes time, reflection, faith, and can make all the difference. Taking the long view leads to immediate generosity.

"God," said Martin Luther, "can shoot with the warped bow and ride the lame horse." It's not that everything that happens and everything we do occurs because God planned it that way. Not at all. It's that God shows an amazing resilience as we exercise our free wills. The point is that God's intent for the world isn't ruined by the inadequacy our efforts, at least not in the long haul. Paul said rightly that God works *in all things* for good for the ones who love God and are called according to his purpose (Rom. 8:28).

3. 1 Corinthians 15:35–38, 42–50. We may be inspired now by seeing what's finally to come, but how much of then can we see now? Details about our future bodies? We're curious, but Paul answers pressing questions of the Corinthians by admitting that he's talking about things he knows very little about. He's going by faith based on the resurrection of Jesus and the promise of our own new "bodies" one day. He's expressing the inexpressible, trying to put into words what goes beyond currently available human words. We do know this. In this world, everything is subject to decay and change. Not so with our bodies yet to come.

Disciples of Rabbi Jesus must avoid a toxic piece of faulty logic. If our physical bodies are only temporary shells to be discarded at death, why shouldn't we do with them in the meantime whatever we please? Paul will have none of that thinking or the evil practices it produces. Human life, pre-resurrection and post-resurrection, is *embodied* life. Christ died to redeem us as whole human beings. What we do with our bodies is of utmost significance for what we shall be one day.

The term "Christianity" doesn't appear in the Bible. Faith in Christ is far more than giving intellectual assent to doctrines or being formal members of any religious institution. Rather, it's a *way of life* often contrary to our own twisted inclinations. It's living our *now* in light of God's *then*. As Jesus people, our real identity need not include all that has attached itself to the word "Christian" over the centuries. It's being a true follower of Jesus in any time and place.[1]

D. Reflections of Leaders of the Wesleyan-Holiness Tradition

The biblical vision of *then* is wonderful indeed. But the glorious hymns to be sung above are also to be sung *now*, here below. Humans are created for relationships. The new creation in Christ is intended to provide the present conditions that enable human flourishing, a restored human-divine relationship, one that will extend even into eternity.

But the most glorious of all will be the change which then will take place on the poor, sinful, miserable children of men. There will arise an unmixed state of holiness and happiness far superior to that which Adam enjoyed in Paradise. In how beautiful a manner is this described by the Apostle: "God shall wipe away all tears from their eyes, and there shall be no more death, neither sorrow, nor crying, neither shall there be any more pain." Why? "The former things are done away!" And, to crown all, there will be a deep, an intimate, an uninterrupted union with God, and a constant communion with the Father and his Son Jesus Christ, through the Spirit![2]

> The church triumphant in Thy love,
> Their mighty joys we show;
> They sing the Lamb in hymns above,
> And we in hymns below.[3]

A Wesleyan view accentuates the social nature of humanity. Humanity's interpersonal relationships do not fade in a beatific vision of God, but grow and deepen more fully in final union with God. Humanity is made for relationship with other human beings, and within these relationships holiness and love intensify. The "new creation" provides grace to overcome what divides, empowering reconciliation between divided parties and supporting stable social conditions necessary for human flourishing. This perspective undergirds collaboration with other faiths to establish healthy, stable human relationships and social structures in today's world.[4]

---

1. For an essay titled "Please Don't Call Me 'Christian', " see Barry L. Callen, *A Pilgrim's Progress*, 3rd edition (2019).
2. John Wesley, *The General Spread of the Gospel*.
3. Charles Wesley, "O For a Closer Walk with God."
4. Christopher Bounds, *The Thirteenth Oxford Institute of Methodist Theological Studies*, 2013.

WEEK 16

CAN YOU HEAR IT?

The world is a chaos of sound. Advertisers aggressively compete for our attention. Many of us wear headphones to shield ourselves from all the noise, only to fill our ears with our chosen sound and still not be able to hear the quiet voice of God. Some of us are prone to hear voices when there are none. Sorting out the sounds is one of the great human challenges of today. Selective deafness is a modern malady. So often the Bible calls us to hear the voice of God. Will we? Are we able? Can you hear God's voice even now? You'll have to be especially quiet and really focus.

This is the Bible's grand announcement. *Divine music is in the air!* Can you hear it? Can you distinguish the divine voice from mere noise from the dizzying world? Be aware that once you've begun to hear the divine voice, you'll be responsible to be reshaped by it, allowing it to live through you. Hearing likely will require more "yutori," the Japanese for "life-space." We must allow adequate room for actually hearing.

A classic Christmas cantata of recent decades is titled "He Started the Whole World Singing."[1] It celebrates the amazing fact that "the words and the music were there all along." What can and should happen is that "what the song had to say was that love found a way to start the world singing a song." Can you hear that song? Have you joined in the singing? It's wonderful music indeed!

A. Prayer

Lord, often you went off by yourself to pray, seeking your Father's voice and direction. You escaped the crowd so that you could hear what most others could not. Most of my hectic life has tended to keep me somewhere in the deafness of the crowd. If the real problem is my need to prioritize the things in my life, then help me to somehow get that done. Focus me, Lord. Expand my listening space and capacity—teaching me to pray without always talking and choking out your voice with my own. Sort out for me the competing noises in my heart and head. Where is the sweet music of eternity? Tune my ears to the sounds of your Spirit. Take me off with you, Rabbi Jesus, to those quiet places with your Father.

B. The Voice of Rabbi Jesus: Luke 6:39-4

> Go with me often to those quiet places of listening and praying. If you can hear my Father's music, be aware that you then must sing and broadcast it widely. The voice of God seems small in the chaos of your times, but the heavenly music is really there and magnificent indeed. It will not demand your attention—that you must provide. Become regularly aware of how you focus your ears as my disciples. Listening is a sacred spiritual art form that you must cultivate intentionally. Pray always, and may many of your prayers be ones of listening for the heavenly music.

If you can hear the love music of my Father's beating heart, you also can do what my disciple Paul urges. No matter what your present circumstances, "be steadfast and immovable, always excelling in the work of the Lord" (1 Cor. 15:58). By hearing my Father's voice and then being changed by and acting on what you hear, you will be holy as my Father wishes. The experience of knowing me must result in a new way of living. Let me put it plainly with a hard question. Why do you call me "Lord, Lord" and don't do what I tell you?

Sin destroys the harmony between sound and ear, word and deed—and harmony characterizes my Father's music. You first must allow me to deal with the sin issue in your lives. A house built on sand is an unfortunate picture of my faith community being built the easy way, confession without life change, lip service without conviction, sermons not followed by unselfish service, ears that are deaf. You must avoid the temptation to seek cheap grace, no-cost discipleship.

Not one of you will sit at a keyboard for the first time and play Beethoven's Piano Concerto no. 4 in G major, or drive down the basketball court to slam a 360-degree dunk, or pass the state bar exam without significant study in preparation. What makes anyone think that becoming a mature and productive disciple of mine will not take time, work, practice, and dedication? You must hear my Father's music of grace, grow in your own musical skill, and practice until the song of Christ becomes your song, one you gladly play for others to enjoy until you hear that final trumpet sound!

My Spirit is anxious to continue teaching you on my behalf. I'm providing you with select portions from the revealed Word of God and from a particular tradition of my church with wisdom you need. Read carefully and continue listening closely to my Spirit who will guide your minds and hearts to understand properly and apply effectively.

C. Light from the Revealed Word

1. Psalm 92:1–15. Music represents a whole-body response to God's steadfast love. The musical references in this psalm resonate with Isaiah 55 where we learn that even the mountains and hills burst into song. "For you, O LORD, have made me glad by your work; at the works of your hands I sing for joy" (vs. 4). Remembrance of God's past provision for Israel should flow into faith in God's present and future care for his children. With the psalmist, we are to give thanks—with instrument and voice—for all that God has made, for the faithfulness of God, and for the promise of new life and growth in the house of the Lord.

The Sabbath was the day set aside for public worship and remembering the joyous rest God knows in eternity (Gen. 2:3). This rest wants to break through our darkened skies here and now. Can you hear the heavenly orchestra tuning in preparation for a concert designed just for you? The stupid and dull have their hearing aids turned off (vs. 6) or their batteries uncharged. God's people must be the turned-on ones who are hearing the melodies of life at its best.

2. Isaiah 55:10–13. This passage connects in a profound way with the church's situation today. Whereas the church once seemed to hold a central place in North American and European culture, the decline over the last several decades—in numbers, influence, reputation, and respect—has been steep. While Christians in America are not in literal exile, we have lost our privileged place. God's people once were in actual forced exile, the Temple in Jerusalem in ruins, and the future very uncertain. How welcome, then, to hear a prophetic voice of comfort declaring that Jerusalem's debt finally had been paid in full.

Whatever the earthly situation of God's people, the divine presence persists in the midst of history's turmoil and evil. Israel needed to hear God's voice clearly and at close range. That divine voice was calling for remembering. Whatever new things emerge, whatever old things pass away, one thing always is sure and true and eternal—*the lovely music of the Word of God.* Can you hear it?

There's no going back. We must leave behind what needs to be left, follow Jesus forward, and trust God for the future. When we look forward with Isaiah, what do we see and hear? A new creation coming into view, the mountains bursting into song, the trees clapping their hands, the earth blooming with lush new growth where thorns once pricked, and God's people going on in joy, being led forward in peace. Can you hear the rustling rhythms of this marvelous music? If you do, will you join in the song?

3. 1 Corinthians 15:51–58. Paul makes this emphatic statement of God's triumph over all things: "Thanks be to God, who gives us the victory through our Lord Jesus Christ" (15:57). Death has been swallowed up in victory. Paul links God's transformative work of resurrection to the sounding of a heavenly trumpet (15:52). Can you hear it? That trumpet will sound one day and all will hear, for better or worse.

John was exiled on the island of Patmos because of loyalty to Christ. He nonetheless managed to describe heaven as awash in song. It's victory notes already could be heard faintly. "Then I heard every creature in heaven and on earth and under the earth and in the sea, and all that is in them, singing, 'To the One seated on the throne and to the Lamb be blessing and honor and glory and might forever and ever!' And the four living creatures said, 'Amen!' And the elders fell down and worshiped" (Rev. 5:13-14). What a song, and we all are invited to the endless concert!

Paul's reporting on the resurrection is no exercise in escapism by rash future speculation. Rather, it undergirds a call for our effort and excellence in present Christian life. Death may be the final enemy, but it won't have the final word. Therefore, *live now*. Our current living is free to excel in the work of the Lord because we need not fear the grave. Life has purpose, the gifts of God are given to be used fully for that purpose, and our labors will not be in vain (v. 58).

D. Reflections of Leaders of the Wesleyan-Holiness Tradition

Our hearts are ever to be with the Lord. That's our listening posture for hearing the Divine. The hearing will enable a feasting on God's grace, with doctrines becoming more living experiences than theoretical statements.

A Wesleyan "prays without ceasing." And this is true prayer, and this alone. His heart is ever lifted up to God at all times and in all places. In this he is never hindered, much less interrupted, by any person or thing. In retirement or company, in leisure, business, or conversation, his heart is ever with the Lord. Whether he lie down or rise up, God is in all his thoughts; he walks with God continually, having the loving eye of his mind fixed upon him, and everywhere "seeing Him that is invisible."[2]

> He speaks and listening to his voice
> New life the dead receive.
> The mournful, broken hearts rejoice,
> The humble poor believe.
>
> Hear him, ye deaf; his praise, ye dumb,
> Your loosened tongues employ;
> Ye blind, behold your Saviour come,
> And leap, ye lame, for joy.[3]

Jesus, Jesus, Jesus!
Sweetest Name I know,
Fills my every longing,
Keeps me singing as I go.[4]

The hymns of John Wesley taught the people the fundamental truths on which Christianity was founded and helped them understand their new spiritual experience. He offered them Christ as directly in his hymns as did any of the evangelists in their sermons, and the very metres he chose helped them to remember the offer, and to ponder over and over again the fullness of its meaning. Doctrine was no longer contained in abstract and prosy definitions, unintelligible to the great majority; it lived forevermore in simple, inspired phrases so unforgettable that the singers became thinkers who presently made truth their own.[5]

---

1. Cantata by Bill and Gloria Gaither.
2. John Wesley, *The Character of a Methodist.*
3. Charles Wesley, "O For A Thousand Tongues To Sing."
4. Luther Bridgers, in *Jewel Songs,* 1911.
5. F. Leslie Church, in *More About the Early Methodist People.*

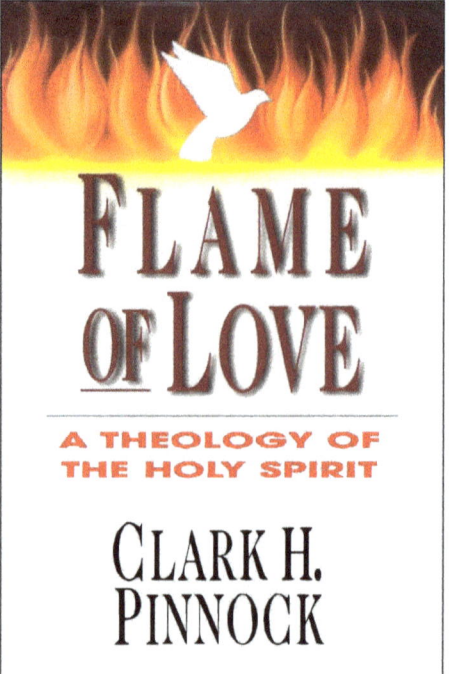

WEEK 17

HOW WIDE IS THE KINGDOM OF HEAVEN?

One final truth needs to addressed to complete the Christian's Epiphany (appearances) season. Where does God really live and who is invited to live with God in the divine precincts? We must recognize the depth and breadth and grandeur of God's light that has been revealed in Jesus Christ. That light brings real life to our lives and churches and seeks to brighten the whole world and its peoples—yes, *all of it and all of them.*

The chosen of God are not limited to a privileged few of a particular race or land or religious affiliation. They are the many who choose to respond in faith to the good news revealed in Jesus Christ. Those who never hear the name of Jesus nonetheless are also subjects of God's love and of the Spirit's redemptive ministry. We who are privileged to be fully aware of the work of God in Jesus must avoid arrogance and judgment about those less privileged through no fault of their own.

There are many religious systems alien to those that are biblically formed. Are all their adherents inevitably "lost" and without hope? We should withhold judgment, spread the good news of Jesus Christ as widely as we can, and leave ultimate decisions to the loving and redeeming heart of God.

A. Prayer

Broaden my heart, O God, so that its love can take in all those whom you love and seek to redeem. Forgive my arrogance that tempts me to think that only me and mine belong to your loving care. While I spread the good news of Christ as widely as I can, let me know that your Spirit goes before my efforts, and I presume also well beyond them. I understand from your Word that your "chosen" are those who choose to respond in faith believing, if not to my witness, then somehow to yours. Keep me sharing—and humble. Keep me loving the unlovable and make my heart big enough to believe that the Father of my Rabbi Jesus seeks to redeem the whole world and its peoples—*all of it and all of them.*

B. The Voice of Rabbi Jesus: Luke 7:1–10

> Not even in Israel have I found faith like this man's. So, here's a key lesson for you disciples. Don't artificially narrow the borders around your understanding of the territory of the kingdom of God. My Father is not anyone's tribal deity, and that includes the church that will carry my name into the world. Be bold in your proclamation and humble about the results, including about the status of those who never hear you or any other of my disciples. My Father finally will determine such matters, not you. I will judge you, not on your universal "success" but on your faithfulness. Others will be judged properly as the love of my Father determines the matter.

The healing of the centurion's servant breaks the stereotype that all non-Jews are enemies of Israel and outside the circle of God's love and redeeming grace. Toward the end of Luke's Gospel, another centurion renders the true verdict about me: "Certainly this man was innocent" (23:47). He exposed the complicity of my own people, the Jewish establishment, who called for my death. He also signaled the unusual spiritual insight potential of "outsiders."

The conversion of Cornelius, yet another centurion and a devout God-fearer, repeats the point that God's gift of salvation is offered universally. The collective testimony of the New Testament is but a foretaste of the grand scenario in eternity in which, John has announced, "a great multitude that no one could count, from every nation, from all tribes and peoples and languages" will gather to worship God and the Lamb upon the throne (Rev. 7:9-10). This is a big world, and my Father has a big heart. Seek such for yourselves.

My Spirit is anxious to continue teaching you on my behalf. I'm providing you with select portions from the revealed Word of God and from a particular tradition of my church with wisdom you need. Read carefully and continue listening closely to my Spirit who will guide your minds and hearts to understand properly and apply effectively.

C. Light from the Revealed Word

1. Psalm 96:1-9. Membership in the choir of heaven is open even to those who can't carry a tune and never saw the sheet music of Jesus in this world. Psalm 96 draws the worshiper's attention to the greatness of God's glory in comparison to the "gods" of Israel's neighbors. It's a song of expansive praise of the universal God. The God known by little Israel is the real King who reigns over all and loves all.

"All the earth" is urged to join in the song of thanksgiving, and all nations are to be included in the choir's membership. Any narrow defining of "the chosen" likely is not equal to God's boundaries of who's necessarily in and who's definitely out. All the peoples of earth are equally loved by God, have an opportunity to respond to God's saving initiatives, and are to be treated by God's faithful as respected "foreigners." After all, the Spirit of God is searching for all people with a love greater than our own, and God surely has witnesses other than ourselves.

2. 1 Kings 8:22-23, 41-43. In process was the dedication of the new Temple in Jerusalem built by King Solomon. For neighboring peoples, the high point of the dedication of their sanctuaries was the installation in the new shrine of a statue or image of the honored god or goddess. However, the God of Israel rejects such physical and limiting depictions.

Solomon's prayer focuses on the enthronement of God. The main theological affirmation is, "O Lord, God of Israel, there is no God like you in heaven above or on earth beneath." The Temple, site of God's presence, does not confine God or the knowledge and worship of God or the scope of God's concern and work. Neither the august Jerusalem building nor the whole nation of Israel ever corners the market on God's presence and loving attention. The reach of God goes beyond the human limitations of any nation or race or religious establishment.

What about those outside the Abrahamic religious traditions (Judaism, Christianity, and Islam)? While God may not be known fully and properly apart from the work of Christ and the ministry of his Spirit, dare we judge the "foreigner" prematurely? How are we to know what's going on with the Spirit's ministry in the hearts of others? What we do know is the loving and expansive heart of God.

3. Galatians 1:1–12. Troubling teachers had arrived in the congregation. Paul reacts by vigorously contrasting the divine origin of the gospel of Christ that he had received and preached with that of the "different" gospel that some of the Galatians were now adopting. Paul's gospel message was erasing human distinctions between Jew and Gentile. He was insisting that, at least in God's eyes, the "foreigner" is no longer to be defined as all those outside the commonly recognized people Israel.

Jew and Gentile were being equally welcomed by God's loving Spirit. This was proof positive of God's adoption into the restored divine family of everyone willing to receive God's gift of salvation through grace by faith alone. The gift of God's salvation has come, not as the exclusive privilege of a particular nation or even religious tradition, but on behalf of all people through Jesus Christ, the one Lord of all humanity. This was understandably difficult news for those schooled to think of themselves as the only chosen people of God.

D. Reflections of Leaders of the Wesleyan-Holiness Tradition

Who is invited to participate as subjects of the saving work of Christ? Salvation is for all who believe. Every soul is being welcomed by Jesus. God comes alongside all persons to reveal his nature and redeeming activity, providing the means to know him even when ears never hear the name of Jesus Christ. Divine love requires that disciples of Rabbi Jesus offer hospitality and hope to all.

Though we cannot think alike, may we not love alike? May we not be of one heart, though we are not of one opinion? Without all doubt, we may. Herein all the children of God may unite, notwithstanding these smaller differences.[1]

> Come, sinners, to the gospel feast,
> Let every soul be Jesus' guest;
> There need not one be left behind,
> For God has bidden all mankind.[2]

We are social creatures. Our personhood, values, worldviews, habits, attitudes, dispositions, moral judgments, and ethics are shaped in part by the influence of others. The company we keep is also the agency through which God comes alongside, reveals his nature, and provides the way and means to know him. While holiness is personal, it's not private or solitary. Holiness is a gift of God's love strengthened by the Spirit through the company we keep.[3]

God is never left without witness in the world (Acts 14:7; John 1:4). God is known in various ways in general human history, yet has come to be finally known in his Son. The Great Commission is to go to all nations and proclaim the gospel. It remains a pivotal Christian assertion that Christ is the truth even for those who do not recognize him as their truth. Where we are headed as faithful believers is to a house of "many mansions." Some of these mansions may remain opaque to our view. I leave all that to the loving wisdom of God.[4]

A characteristic of Christian spirituality is converting hostility into hospitality. Such hospitality is fundamental to Christian identity. It's "a framework that provides a bridge which connects our theology with daily life and concerns."[5] It also connects Christians with their Hebrew heritage generally and to Rabbi Jesus particularly. God is a generous and gracious host. Israel was a stranger, an alien, a people with no home, wholly undeserving when God chose them, called them, and granted them a home and future. Having been powerless sojourners in a foreign land (Deut. 10:19), they were called themselves to welcome strangers (Ex. 23:9). Christians should risk keeping the welcome mat out and well-used to the glory of God (Rom. 15:7).[6]

God's saints will exercise openness to the voice and wisdom of the Spirit. They will make room for their fellow believers, different or not, and they will be anxious for friendship with those still outside the faith community, hostile or not. To live in God's house is to breathe the Spirit's air and be involved in the Spirit's life and mission. [7]

---

1. John Wesley, *Catholic Spirit*.
2. Charles Wesley, "Come Sinners to the Gospel Feast."
3. Jonathan S. Raymond, *Social Holiness: The Company We Keep*.
4. Thomas C. Oden, quoted in Barry Callen, *Heart of the Matter*.
5. Christine D. Pohl, *Making Room: Recovering Hospitality as a Christian Tradition*.
6. Insightful essays addressing this hospitality to those of all faith traditions are found in the *Wesleyan Theological Journal* (by Randy Maddox, 1992, and Philip Meadows, 2000).
7. Barry L. Callen, *Catch Your Breath!*

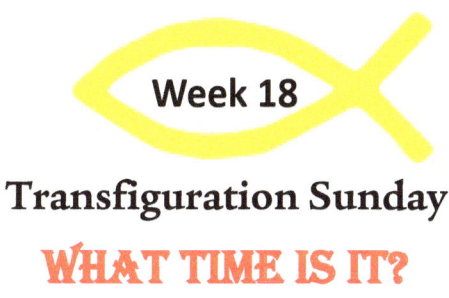

Week 18

Transfiguration Sunday
WHAT TIME IS IT?

Life at its best involves focusing on the really big questions of life and answering them properly. Here's one such question. What time is it? The Transfiguration of Jesus was halftime in his earthly life and ministry. The stories before this event introduced Jesus to the world and chronicled the rise of his popularity through healing miracles and compelling teaching. After the transfiguration, Jesus turns toward Jerusalem and the terror of the coming Cross. This time of central pause is about clarifying the two big questions. Who was Jesus really? What had he come to do?

The transfiguration is key to understanding the journey of all disciples of Jesus. It's an intermission between two distinct acts of our own faith journeys. The first act is getting to know Jesus and the second is preparing to follow him to the very end—and beyond. There are first-act and second-act disciples. Group one includes the believers who have limited themselves to getting their sinful pasts forgiven. Group two extends to those who are forgiven and actively going on to allow Jesus to shape them into holy and serving representatives of God, even in the most difficult of circumstances.

If the first act of faith group is accepting the privilege of calling ourselves Christian, the second is making the Christ-like sacrifices needed to demonstrate our new-creation identity by being actively about the mission of Rabbi Jesus. First we become personally acquainted with Jesus as Savior and then we choose to make him our Lord in all of ongoing life. The first, we might say, is being "saved" and the second "sanctified," that is, becoming real disciples in the image of and in action with the Master.

A. Prayer

The world sets its own calendars and fills them with its own special days. Yes, but I want you to set mine, Lord. What time is it—should it be—for me now? I sought forgiveness and you granted it. Praise God! Now I realize that you are asking more of me. I think it's my time to see what all you really came to be, do, and expect of me as your new-born child. Am I ready to fully yield my forgiven self to being formed in your loving image and joining you in completing your mission? I know it's time for my selfish heart to be cleansed so that your mission and will be-come mine as well. Come again, Lord, come to me and make me *wholly Thine*.

B. The Voice of Rabbi Jesus: Luke 9:28–36

> What a generation yours is! It has virtually no sense of who my Father is and rarely any ultimate focus to life. How different you disciples of mine must be. Come to the mountain with me and witness my transfiguration. See who I really am and who you might become. Then, if you will, go down into the world with me, giving yourselves away as I have given my life away for you. My Father is holy, and going with me redemptively into the world is what it means for you to be holy as well. It's time for you to decide if you're all in and prepared to go all the way with me. It's now my transfiguration time and your possible sanctification time.

Here's one of the major differences between Moses and me. The glow on Moses' face did not come from himself. It only reflected the glory of my Father. Moses hid his face behind a veil and the glow faded over time (2 Cor. 3:13; Exod. 34:33, 35). My glory is the heavenly glow inherent in my divine identity, now being revealed to those who believe (2 Cor. 3:18a).

I'm properly depicted as the "radiance of God's glory and the exact representation of my Father's being" (Heb. 1:3), "more worthy than Moses" (Heb. 3:3). Check the grand vision in the book of Revelation where the glory attributed to the Lamb (Rev. 5:12-13) is on par with the glory of God (Rev. 4:9-11). The holiness of my Father often is misunderstood. It's to be seen in the vastness of creation and now in the flesh of one man, myself, your Rabbi. The *incalculable* One is now also the *incarnate* One, the man enfleshed for your salvation.

My Spirit is anxious to continue teaching you on my behalf. I'm providing you with select portions from the revealed Word of God and from a particular tradition of my church with wisdom you need. Read carefully and continue listening closely to my Spirit who will guide your minds and hearts to understand properly and apply effectively.

C. Light from the Revealed Word

1. Psalm 99. Why should we come to church? To see good friends, learn a little about the Bible, get some personal needs met, to do some good together in the community? Yes, but first and foremost we are to come to worship and be transformed by the holy God! God looms majestic, towers in splendor. Holy is our God, wholly other, and in Christ's Spirit wholly present. Honor God, worship his absolute rule. Know who God really is and then come to know who we are expected to be as his humble disciples.

This psalm's keynote is God's *holiness*. What time is it? It's time to realize who God really is and carry to all humanity in our own persons and actions this amazing realization. We are to tremble in God's presence, knowing that we are "fallen" (Rom. 8:20-23), unholy. But there is hope because of the nature of God's holiness. God's kind of power loves justice and works for *shalom*, our highest well-being.

God is always judging evil and always ready to forgive and redeem the lost. That kind of holiness is what God wants to share with us and implant in us. Why? So that we can take its healing fruits into the world. What time is it? It's transfiguration time. It's sanctifying time. It's sharing time.

2. Exodus 34:29–35. Moses actually spoke with God and came down the mountain to share the conversation with the people. His face was shining brightly and he didn't know it—it wasn't his light or doing. It was looking ahead to the time when, in Christ, we "are being transformed into the same image from one degree of glory to another; for this comes from the Lord, the Spirit" (2 Cor. 3:18). We can be transfigured much like the Messiah as God enters our lives and we become increasingly like him.

These verses in Exodus are famous for their connection to Michelangelo's magnificent statue of Moses. The Hebrew word translated "shine" can also mean "horned." This explains why the celebrated Italian sculptor portrayed Moses with horns. God, however, is actually unhorned, truly beyond, other, holy, worthy of a worship inspired by love. God is not to be considered fearsome, unapproachable, grandly disconnected from tiny specks in the universe like us. In fact, God is engaged, caring, and by choice not far away from us at all. The ultimate One chooses in love not to keep us humans at a distance.

3. 2 Corinthians 3:12–4:2. God is characterized best as holiness, an awe-inspiring, reverence-inducing, love-motivated power graciously reigning over all places and peoples. We must tremble before God. Even the earth shakes because God's divine immensity and nature are truly overwhelming. And yet, God need not be feared because the Lord is concerned with justice, hears the cries of hurting people, and forgives their sins. God's heart was seen clearly one day by viewing an ugly and yet also magnificent scene of Jesus on the Cross. The horns of this world would pierce him. Even so, the love of his "unhorned" Father would rescue him from the grave.

Simply put, God the ongoing Creator isn't finished with us. The Christian life is always a life of faith in progress. Our inability to be effective witnesses to the new life in Christ usually is because of our shallowness of connection with God. God is a marvelous mystery who nonetheless is readily available for us to experience in the living Christ. Paul witnesses to this amazing possibility. "I have been crucified with Christ, and it is no longer I who live, but Christ who lives in me" (Gal. 2:20).

Will you embrace this radical reality and allow God to embrace and transform you? Here are the four big transfiguration questions and their important answers:

1. Who is Jesus? God's perfect reflection—looking at Jesus is seeing God!

2. Who is God? God is the One hanging on the Cross for us in the person of Jesus!

3. Who am I? I can be a carrier of the amazing God-in-Christ news for this world!

4. What now? Leave the glorious mountaintop of transfiguration and engage graciously the hurting world below.

D. Reflections of Leaders of the Wesleyan-Holiness Tradition

Forgiveness of sin should be followed by being stamped and sealed with God's Spirit so that the forgiven become holy, wholly God's, reflecting to the world God's very nature as "saints in the light." A saint is being God's alone by having allowed the transforming love of God to "reach the depths of our being." It's allowing holy love to reign in the heart.

We are sealed with the Holy Spirit of God by receiving His real stamp on our souls, being made partakers of the divine nature and "qualified for the inheritance of the saints in the light" (Col. 1:12). Indeed, this is the design of His dwelling in us.[1]

> Jesus, thy boundless love to me
> No thought can reach, no tongue declare;
> O knit my thankful heart to Thee,
> And reign without a rival there!
> Thine wholly, Thine alone, I am,
> Be thou alone my constant flame.[2]

We have already provisionally died with Christ through our participation in his crucifixion; now we must permit that death to reach to the very depths of our being as we cease from self and begin to live wholly to God. The death of the "old man" is thus a process initiated by conversion and realized in entire sanctification. In principle we die with Christ in justification; in full reality we die with him when we yield up ourselves to God as Jesus gave up his spirit to the Father on the cross.[3]

Who is a Christian? It's a grateful person "knowing Father and Son and walking along the pathway of cross and resurrection through the power of the Spirit. We must be personally crucified and buried with Christ and rise with Christ in new life in the Spirit."[4] In his sermon "The Wedding Garment," John Wesley made plain that "orthodoxy" is a small part of religion and must not be mistaken for the substance of the faith—which is holy love reigning in the heart.

---

1. John Wesley, *On Grieving the Holy Spirit.*
2. Charles Wesley, "Give Me the Enlarged Desire."
3. William Greathouse, in the *Wesleyan Theological Journal.*
4. Clark H. Pinnock, *Flame of Love.*

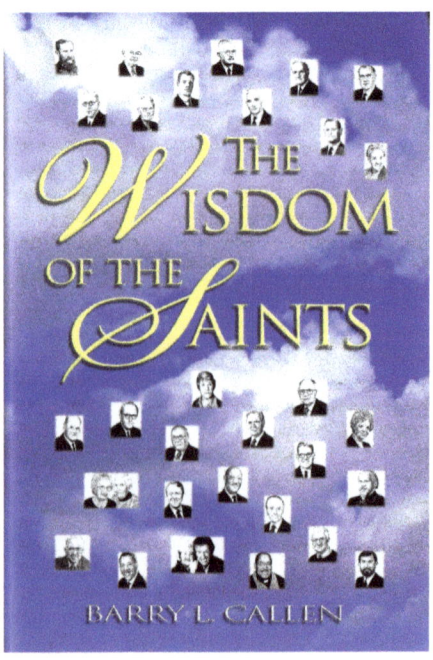

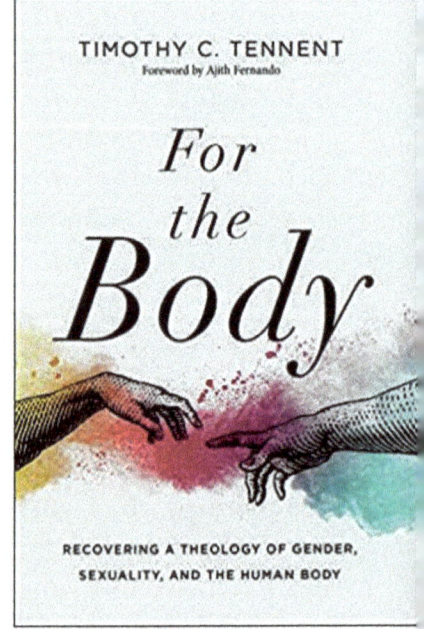

WEEK 19

First Sunday of Lent

LANDLESS PEOPLE, BACKWATER SAVIOR

We must lower our worldly expectations about a warrior Messiah and the presumed promise of a victorious and prosperous church. Jesus didn't call a host of angels to wipe out Rome, nor did he leave behind a fortune for his followers when his earthly end came. Jesus was a backwater Savior who sent out a landless group of disciples. Bad might happen to them, and often did. But, lowly as we are to be when following Rabbi Jesus, God promises to be with us always and provide what's necessary for our mission—for our needs and not necessarily for our desires.

We are disciples of the suffering Master, and we are called like him by carrying our own crosses, whatever they turn out to be. That's the negative. Here's the positive. We go into the world as divine agents. Therefore, we will be provided with whatever we need for our calling. We won't have whatever we want so that we can appear as the rich kids of some big-company executive. We will be given whatever it takes to be faithful and effective disciples of redeeming love.

A. Prayer

The culture around me judges success by what people achieve and possess. Help me, Lord, to understand how your time in the wilderness relates to my time of service in this world. Protect me from the temptations you endured and overcame. Strengthen me so that I can accept your wisdom and follow your example of self-giving love in the valleys of pain and despair. Help me want only what is necessary for me to be sustained and represent you well. Help me to rejoice in want or in plenty, in pain or in pleasure.

B. The Voice of Rabbi Jesus: Luke 4:1–13

> It takes more than bread for you to really stay alive. Temptation is only around the corner for you. Don't be lured by wealth or the glories of "success." Live simply, expectantly, lovingly. I will see that you have all you need. Faithfulness is your business; success is mine. When on the field of action, play for the approval of only one, my Father. The crowd cheers only when you manage to beat others as it wishes. You are not to be in the beating but the loving business.

Be careful, my friends. Some Jews and even a few of my disciples sometimes carry portions of Psalm 91 in little amulets to magically ward off danger. The Devil quoted Ps. 91:11-12 in tempting me to jump wildly for public amazement and personal gain. Remember that being good witnesses of mine shouldn't feature displays of supposed magical abilities or stunning affluence to impress anyone.

My Father can be trusted, even when you are caught in the worst of circumstances. The promise is that nothing can separate you from the love of God (Rom. 8:39). In fact, faithfulness to me as your Lord sometimes will send you into danger's path (2 Cor. 6:4-10). When in the wilderness, you will survive by God's grace and not our own self-sufficiency. The wilderness is the place of God's assured presence (Ex. 16:9-10) as well as my Father's undeserved but always adequate provision (Ex. 16:11-17).

J. R. R. Tolkien one day will conceive of a ring of power in his *The Lord of the Rings*. How desperately everyone will want the ring, including those with noble intentions, but the ring destroys anyone who keeps it, even Gandalf the wise wizard, and even Frodo the humblest of the Hobbits. Power is not to be pursued. The church's calling is to empty itself of reliance on worldly power, taking the form of a suffering servant like me.

My Spirit is anxious to continue teaching you on my behalf. I'm providing you with select portions from the revealed Word of God and from a particular tradition of my church with wisdom you need. Read carefully and continue listening closely to my Spirit who will guide your minds and hearts to understand properly and apply effectively.

C. Light from the Revealed Word

1. Psalm 91:1–2, 9–16. The psalmist appears to offer assurance that evil will be kept away; harm can't get through the door of God's faithful children. Does that mean that believers are really safe, guaranteed protection, even prosperity in their lifetimes in this world? Hardly. God certainly loves his people and is adequate to prepare them for any circumstance. However, Jesus' rejection of worldly applause and protection for himself is caution enough. The Suffering Servant, our Rabbi Jesus, makes clear that his disciples must avoid lives of self-serving in favor of the challenges of cross-bearing.

There's good news. It's that God will be our "dwelling place in all generations" (Ps. 90:1; 91:9). This assurance doesn't promise an easy or carefree existence. Rather, it offers the same assurance that empowered Jesus despite his Cross, and that will empower we who follow him as we bear our crosses (Lk. 9:23). God is our home. We dwell in the shelter of the Most High. Living sometimes may be in ragged tents, the typical homes of pilgrims. Nonetheless, given the divine presence, even these modest dwellings will be adequate.

2. Deuteronomy 26:1–11. This passage is highly sensitive to the self-interested dynamics that our present time baptizes as "natural," our right to health, wealth, and happiness. It proclaims that we are not isolated selves with individual rights. Rather, we are children of God in community together, brothers and sisters who have only what we have first received, and who in turn should be giving as we have been given. We must dispense with our constant "entitlement" language.

Our standing before God is by divine grace alone that is not of our deserving.

The Israelite identity was an immigrant one, a "wandering Aramean." They and disciples of Rabbi Jesus should be reminded that God's people were themselves once poor, marginalized, oppressed strangers in a foreign land. We now are called to share our bounty "with the Levites and the aliens who reside among you." There must be no ethnic or denominational sectarianism. All are to attend to the basic needs of all. What little we may have belongs to us by grace and to others in need as we gladly minister to them.

3. Romans 10:8–13. As Christ's followers, what must we be prepared to believe and proclaim? Paul identifies Jesus' lordship and resurrection as the centers of Christian faith. In keeping with his consistent emphasis on the centrality of the Cross of Jesus, we must both believe these things and show a willingness to sacrifice everything on their behalf. Paul emphasizes humility, even humiliation if necessary. We must be willing to give up our pride and good standing in the eyes of others when called into the service of Christ. The power to survive humiliation comes in the news of the resurrection. For us, even death has lost its sting.

To confess the resurrection of Jesus is to believe in the triumph of love and thus be able to embrace a life not motivated by power or controlled by fear. To confess Jesus as Lord is to affirm that God has chosen an impoverished Southwest Asian man from a backwater of the Roman Empire to be for us the perfect reflection of God.

We are invited to turn toward the Cross of Jesus as a surprising place of freedom and victory—freedom to love fearlessly and to live beyond the boundaries we and the world around us so often impose. To love like Jesus is to reach out graciously and risk when necessary. It's believing that such disciples, the world's landless from its backwaters, one day will be given the Kingdom of Heaven. The "Beatitudes" of Jesus reveal this clearly.

D. Reflections of Leaders of the Wesleyan-Holiness Tradition

While humble, backwater disciples like Rabbi Jesus, we are being filled with God's own dynamism and likeness, being renewed day by day. There are false paths of faith, "spiritualities" that are really self-serving. The right path, our true identity as Christians, is a Christ-like centering around love. While the Holy Spirit is the necessary power in the Christian life, so that followers of Rabbi Jesus are not puny people to be pitied, we must be careful what we attribute to the Spirit's working.

While you seek God in all things, you will find Him in all: the foun-tain of all holiness, continually filling you with His own likeness, with justice, mercy, and truth. While you look to Jesus and Him alone, you will be filled with the mind that was in Him. Your soul will be renewed day by day after the image of Him that created it.[1]

> Come then, and loose my stammering tongue,
> Teach me the new, the joyful song,
> And perfect in a babe Thy praise.
> I want a thousand lives to employ
> In publishing the sounds of joy,
> The gospel of Thy general grace.[2]

Love is a Christ-centering so real that there is left no place for morally superficial mysticisms. Love for John Wesley was the very heart and core of moral life. Love catches our whole selves up into a true integrity, leaving nothing out.[3]

There are many Christians who are forgiven but not controlled. They have never yielded their lives to Jesus as Lord, not going far enough to be caught up in the Divine purpose. Taking the Lordship of Christ seriously means that all of life is under his control. Along with his authority is a divine power to back it up—the Holy Spirit. We do not live alone or in our own strength.[4]

Thank God for the Holy Spirit! Thank God for the reality and experience of Pentecost. Thank God that Jesus did not leave us a powerless, puny, piddling, anemic church for the world! The Holy Spirit is making the Word of God come alive. He is breaking down barriers of hatred and selfishness that have divided Christendom for centuries. However, too much heat and controversy have accompanied the majestic work of the third person of the Godhead. Too much that is fleshly has been blamed on the Spirit. Too much that is weird and silly has been attributed to the Spirit. Far too much that is sectarian and traditional has been tied to the Holy Spirit. This is why I wrote *Glory to the Spirit* in 1990.[5]

---

1. John Wesley, *Discourses on Our Lord's Sermon on the Mount*.
2. Charles Wesley, "I Soon Shall Hear Thy Quickening Voice."
3. Mildred Wynkoop, in the *Wesleyan Theological Journal*.
4. R. Eugene Sterner, in Barry Callen, *The Wisdom of the Saints*.
5. Benjamin F. Reid, in Barry Callen, *The Wisdom of the Saints*.

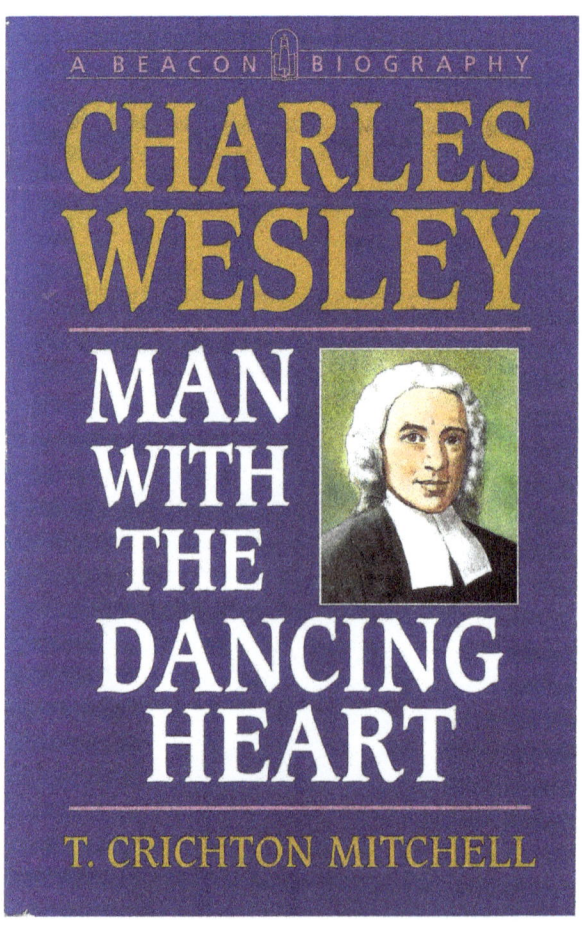

WEEK 20

POTHOLES IN SALVATION'S ROAD

Winter weather can rupture roads and ruin good cars with its potholes. Sometimes Christians seem to be living in a constant winter. There's trouble ahead for the church's tires. Even so, we can trust the promises of God. The problem is that their fulfillment involves ways and times not always to our choosing or expectation. This problem leads to the difficult challenge of figuring out how to manage the times of dangerous uncertainty during which we often must live.

Occasionally a pothole threatens to damage our faith's automobile, often rupturing a tire or even breaking an axel. Staying close to Rabbi Jesus likely will involve some rough roads. Lent is the Christian season of facing this difficult reality and planning for the needed repairs. How can we be fully insured so that the necessary repairs don't derail our faith lives? Patience and flexibility certainly are necessary. Admitting the problem is a first step in addressing it. Easter resurrection may be ahead, but there's difficult preparation work to be done before then.

The Wesleyan revival in England was in reaction to some serious problems that had developed in the life of the dominant Protestant church body in that country. Only a "heart-felt religion" freed of a restrictive church structure could fill this churchly pothole. Such problems seem to develop in all generations and countries.

A. Prayer

I admit, Lord, that sometimes I think having you by my side should smooth out all of life's roads. However, I've come to realize that such a thought is more dream than reality. It doesn't fit Rabbi Jesus at all. Ours is a fallen world and I admit to having a personal history of fallenness. So, as I travel some treacherous roadways in your service, help me navigate things wisely. Enable me to believe that needed repairs will be available when accidents do happen. I admit to really needing the help of your guiding and healing Spirit in this matter. I hear some believers claiming that belief in you, our Father, should bring health, wealth, and happiness. That surely wasn't the way it was for your Son, and likely not for me. Insure me, Lord, not with constant safety but with the surviving adequacy of your Spirit!

B. The Voice of Rabbi Jesus: Luke 13:31–35

> I said, "Tell that old fox I have no time for him right now." I was setting my priorities and affirming my primary identity. I and my Father are one and it was his busines I had to be about. It's the same for you, my disciples. Prioritizing always will open you to much possible unpleasantness. Sorry. It has to be that way. My path was not easy but it ended gloriously–and so will yours! When rough spots do come, rely on fellow believers and especially on the graciousness of my all-sufficient Spirit.

I had plans to steer a course toward Jerusalem. I knew that going there would set me on a collision course with the religious and Roman power establishments. I had been to Jerusalem as a child and as an adult pilgrim, so I harbored mixed emotions about the Holy City. I adored its heritage and wonders and always hoped for the fulfillment of its God-inspired dreams. Still, I was puzzled by the opulence and shocked by the corruption, and even cried over city's unwillingness to go my Father's way. I weighed Herod's threat, pondered the plot against my life, and knew that an ugly end was inevitable. No matter. I couldn't allow that to dominate my attention and dictate my actions. That's why I dared to tell Herod that I had no time for him. You will face similar challenges and must be willing to react with courage as I did.

My Father always longs for wholeness and peace for all of his children. My disciples, like everyone else, have the freedom to choose the best or worst in life. My Father and I don't operate with coercion. We prefer persuasion, gently calling the wayward to return to a life of holiness and righteousness. People can't be forced to love. If they refuse, however, judgment will come.

Here's a big pothole I want you to watch for and that you can avoid. You'll be tempted to say that things in this world are going to hell, so you might as well take your hands off, let them crumble, and passively wait on my return to make all things right. *Don't do this!* Such a "give up" attitude forgets that I've already come and my Spirit will always be with you to enable fresh possibilities of redemption and healing. My Father is weeping, working, and calling you to join in divine redemptive work. Don't let the Herods of the world distract you from trying.

My Spirit is anxious to continue teaching you on my behalf. I'm providing you with select portions from the revealed Word of God and from a particular tradition of my church with wisdom you need. Read carefully and continue listening closely to my Spirit who will guide your minds and hearts to understand properly and apply effectively.

C. Light from the Revealed Word

1. Psalm 27. Here's an expression of remarkable trust in God—especially seen in verse one. To paraphrase, "I'm tempted to champion your greatness, God, and I'm able to conclude that I've nothing to fear." But this psalm of assurance ends on quite another note. Why must I stay very close to God? Because there's danger just ahead! That was the experience of Rabbi Jesus. Rather than saying that he founded a church, it's more accurate to say that he found one in poor condition. God's chosen had failed to fulfill their calling. Jesus hadn't come to destroy but to renew the life of his Father's people. They had crashed into various potholes and needed some major repairs. Jesus was in the divine repair business.

God's followers must appreciate the dynamics of believing. Faith does not immediately or magically remove all threats and opposition. In fact, it almost invites them. The invitation to "wait for the LORD" comes with this need. "Be strong, and let your heart take courage" (vs. 14). Apparently, the psalmist was continuing to experience threat and opposition. Faith offers no immunity. It offers courage and strength to endure and proceed toward the abundant and productive life that God intends--despite the troubles faced.

2. Genesis 15:1–18. There sometimes is a great distance between what God has promised and what we believers are experiencing at the moment. The ancient promise to Abraham was, "in you all the peoples will be blessed." Still, the reality of the moment for Abraham was, no children! Abraham couldn't fathom the power and creativity of the God who had promised so much to him long ago. After all, much of it wasn't experienced reality, only future expectation.

Is the Lord able and willing to fulfill divine promises no matter how morally reprehensible the patriarch had been or how hopeless the current circumstances appeared? Yes, God will have the last word in our affairs. The pressing question is, "What do we do in the meantime?" The Lord had said that Abraham would be made into a great nation so that he and his family would become a universal blessing (Gen. 12:1-3). Unfortunately, there appeared no means at hand to make that possible.

Delays are common and the nature of fulfillments sometimes surprising. Abraham was fixated on the immediate potholes and could see no way forward. The temptation is to resort to a selfishness, insisting that the fulfillment of God's promises must come how and when we expect and prefer.

3. Philippians 3:17–4:1. True disciples don't back off when trouble looms. "Therefore, my brothers and sisters, stand firm in the Lord." It's abundantly clear that Paul loved the believers in Philippi. They were a source of significant support for him, especially at this difficult time when he is in prison. For each of us to survive, we need all of us to stand firm in the faith and stand together.

For Paul, the Cross of Jesus is central to the Christian story. It was a massive challenge for Jesus, something horrible and widely feared. For many modern Christians, however, the Cross has been reduced to a mere symbol seen mostly on a gold chain or in a stained glass window. Oddly enough, Paul "glories" in the Cross, and certainly not the decorative version. He celebrates what was a brutal reminder of sacrifice, blood, defeat, humiliation, and shame.

Being a follower of Jesus is both hard and counter-cultural. Pride in nation, race, and family cannot be elevated above our higher citizenship in the kingdom of God. To champion that divine citizenship necessarily involves coming to the foot of Christ's Cross and engaging in the painful sacrificing of all arrogance and selfishness. The Philippians lived in a Roman colony often humiliated by imperial power. To resist this power was dangerous indeed. Paul was in a Roman prison. He, the Philippian believers, and we need to know and courageously affirm our primary identity. We must be very consciousness of carrying a different passport, one issued by the kingdom of God.

D. Reflections of Leaders of the Wesleyan-Holiness Tradition

The Wesley brothers are clear that God is able, and thus there is hope in all circumstances. Note, however, that their focus is on forgiveness of sin and overcoming the waywardness of the human heart. Believers are not promised paths smoother than was their Lord's. We always must seek more understanding and allow the Lord to correct us every night. And we must never assume that proper conduct or correct theology is all that's needed.

We may dwell on the faithfulness of God and on the virtue of that blood that was shed for us to cleanse us from all sin. And God will then bear witness to His Word and bring our souls out of trouble. He will say, "Arise, shine, for your light has come, and the glory of the Lord is risen upon you." And, indeed, if you walk humbly and closely with God, that light will shine brighter and brighter unto the perfect day.[1]

> I thank the Lord who teacheth me
> To read his will aright;
> Yea, by his blessing do my reins Correct
> me every night.
>
> I set the Lord before my face,
> And trust in him alone;
> At my right hand the Lord doth stand,
> I shall not be o'erthrown.[2]

Trust and hang on God, even when he hides himself from you. Hunger and thirst daily after the righteousness of Christ. Be content with no degree of sanctification. Be always crying out: "Lord, let me know more of myself and of Thee."[3]

The Wesleyan revival in England was focused first of all on "heart-felt religion," not merely proper conduct, correct theology, or humanitarian service. This personal awareness of the assurance of God's favor was to become the cornerstone of the Methodist message and method. In his personal Aldersgate experience, John Wesley had felt his heart "strangely warmed."[4] That experience braced him for many difficulties soon to come.

---

1. John Wesley, *The Wilderness State*.
2. Charles Wesley, "Save Me, O God; For Thou Alone."
3. George Whitefield, *Works of George Whitefield*.
4. D. Michael Henderson, *John Wesley's Class Meeting*.

WEEK 21

STOP EATING BAD FOOD!

The luxuries of our neighbors may look really good to us, but they never will satisfy. There's something toxic about feeding greedily on the world's goods. When we're thirsty, we should drink clean water. When hungry, we should stop eating bad food when wholesome spiritual food is available.

We followers of Rabbi Jesus must position ourselves to receive the bounty of God. Daniel refused to eat the rich food of the empire (Dan. 1). We must "seek the Lord" wherever we are. Why? Because Jesus is the true Bread of Life. When he is available, and he now is, why go for the moldy crusts on the world's tables? Bigger barns only set the stage for bigger collapses. Greedily eyeing your neighbor's goods is step one to going blind.

Jesus joined the Hebrew prophets in warning about their faith tradition degenerating into an emphasis on *externals*. Of prime necessity, he insisted, is the rightness of the inner spirit. The struggle goes on against three opponents that constantly compromise faith's integrity. They are ceremonialism, creedalism, and legalism. Huge arguments over virtually nothing can be so distracting, like fussing over how much water to use or the right words to say at the baptism of a believer.

One can have at the same time theological correctness and a wayward heart. Love is greater than who wins an argument about the most proper apparel for a believer or which nuance of what church law will be mandated for all members in the church. We must not allow preferences over incidentals to destroy church unity and thereby cripple mission effectiveness. Doing so is serving really bad food to fellow believers.

A. Prayer

My good Father in heaven, please nourish me with living water and the real bread of life. May the true bread, my Rabbi Jesus, cause me to grow and strengthen so that I can bear good fruit to nourish a world hungering for hope. In myself, I know I am very gone wrong. With you, however, I know that all that can change. Be my personal menu, Lord. If we are what we eat, let me become more like you meal by meal. Keep me from feeding on the perennial bad food of the church's ceremonialism, creedalism, and legalism. Cold externals are hardly the spices of life.

B. The Voice of Rabbi Jesus: Luke 13:1–9

> As my disciples, you must have a real change of mind that results in fruit-bearing and life-nourishment sharing. Let me be clear. The "change of mind" I'm talking about is a really big deal. It's an entirely new life, a lifetime quest, the journey from a fallen lostness to a restored holiness before my holy Father. Come to me and be fed from the menu of life. Drink of the cup and eat of the bread I have given you.

The Greek word *metanoia* means to repent, "to change one's mind." This change is to be more than an intellectual change of what is thought. It signifies changing the focus of one's whole life, changing one's moral direction, a dynamic change in one's actual way of being and living. To repent like this is to live in a distinctly different way, my way. My disciple Luke points to the full ramifications of repentance when he says, "repent and turn to God and do deeds consistent with repentance" (Acts 26:20).

When you call people to repent, never focus only on the forgiveness of past sin. The call should include repenting toward the bearing of fruit worthy of repentance. New disciples of mine are to engage in the kind of repentance that results in a new way of living, in eyes newly open to see human need and hearts newly open to serve those needs. To bear fruit is the natural result of feeding on the richness of the Bread of Life.

My illustration about the tower suggests that sin brings its consequences. And then there's my illustration about the tree that doesn't bear fruit. Yes, it sounds a little harsh, but it's true that there's little worth in an apple tree that consistently fails to produce apples. My Father is a patient and compassionate gardener. Fruitlessness, however, eventually will bring negative results. Folks need nourishing food and drink, and my disciples are to be deliverers of the needed goods. To do that will require a real change of mind, the fullness of repentance, a holiness that is anxious to give itself away.

My Spirit is anxious to continue teaching you on my behalf. I'm providing you with select portions from the revealed Word of God and from a particular tradition of my church with wisdom you need. Read carefully and continue listening closely to my Spirit who will guide your minds and hearts to understand properly and apply effectively.

C. Light from the Revealed Word

1. Psalm 63:1–8. A connection between Psalm 63 and Isaiah 55 is evident in the first verse of each. The psalmist "thirsts" in a location where there is no water. Isaiah 55 issues an invitation to everyone who thirsts. "Come to the waters." What the psalmist needs and longs for is apparently readily available. "Seek the Lord while he may be found; call upon him while he is near" (Isa. 55:6).

What's the life-sustaining food longed for by the psalmist? It's the powerful, protecting, life-giving presence of a loving, compassionate, gracious God. We humans are made for such a nourishing reality. We thirst for God, the Fountain of life. We never will be ourselves without him. It's tragic when we settle for bad food and toxic water that may taste sweet but then fouls our insides. The Bible reacts with two questions and an invitation. Hungry? Thirsty? Come to the table, God's table. The Father has a place set just for you!

2. Isaiah 55:1–9. We are being beckoned to include ourselves among the recipients of God's bounty. What are the goals of the divine mission? They are to shower grace on a renewed history for God's people, bringing alive the worshipping community, providing a meaningful role for the people of God on the world stage, and restoring a link between the past and future of God's actions. People in exile are called to turn away from the lure of a secure material future in Babylon and seek after the lush spiritual reality offered in the steadfast love of God. Isaiah's suggested banquet of food and drink is a table overflowing with mercy and pardon for those who return to the Lord.

Isaiah provides insight into the subtle spiritual threat posed by the Israelites' life in exile. Many had become too easily integrated into Babylonian society. They had money to spend and were spending it on that which is not the bread of life. They were laboring for that which does not finally satisfy. They were caught up in a materialist economy foreign to the ways of God.

Sound familiar? Followers of the Lord are called to a salvation that turns away from alien spiritual cultures and sour banquets of alluring emptiness. Faith-filled people thirst and hunger for real nourishment, the good food and drink of the divine Spirit who calls us home to the table of God. It's supper time!

3. 1 Corinthians 10:1–13. It's vital to remember the central declaration of the gospel of Jesus Christ. While God is a righteous judge, above all he is a God of life-bringing grace and nourishing resource. While we were yet sinners, God loved us (Rom. 5:8; 1 Jn. 4:10). Jesus became notorious for eating with tax collectors, prostitutes, and other sinners. Paul himself was now a grace-filled follower of Jesus after having been a key enemy of Christ's followers. Diets change when real nourishment is recognized and received.

The promise is that God always provides needed food for his people. God was the Fountain of life that went with them wherever he led. The problem too often has been that those cared for by God turn to their own selfish interests and private meals seasoned by death. Paul warns that we must never try to get Christ to serve us instead of us serving him. No temptation is too great to withstand if our focus remains on the truly nourishing food and drink provided God.

D. Reflections of Leaders of the Wesleyan-Holiness Tradition

It won't happen all at once, but the marvelous feast of holiness can finally fill our life's tables. In due season we can begin yielding for others the good fruit of righteousness. What must be avoided is the bigotry of gorging on incidentals and choking others on a diet of what to do and what not to do. The Lord's Supper is real food. Eat often!

Experience and Scripture show that salvation is both instantaneous and gradual. It begins the moment we are justified by the holy, humble, gentle, patient love of God. It gradually increases from that moment as a mustard seed which at first is the least of all seeds but afterward puts forth large branches and becomes a great tree until, in another instant, the heart is cleansed from all sin and filled with pure love to God and man.[1]

> Make our earthly souls a field
> Which God delights to bless;
> Let us in due season yield
> The fruits of righteousness.
> Make us trees of paradise,
> Which more and more Thy praise may show,
> Deeper sink, and higher rise,
> And to perfection grow.[2]

On the great fundamentals we are all agreed. Pertaining to things not essential to salvation, we have liberty. To attempt to emphasize that which is not essential to salvation, and thus to divide forces, would be a crime. An unwillingness for others to enjoy the liberty that we enjoy in reference to doctrines not vital to salvation is bigotry and should be something from which the spirit of holiness withdraws itself.[3]

If holiness is reduced to a list of do this and don't do that, legalism is quick to follow. This was the problem with the Pharisees Jesus confronted. They looked only at the externals and forgot the significance of the heart and inner life. They also forgot that all righteousness comes from God. Paul is clear in his letter to the Philippians that he was perfect when it came to obeying the law. But that was not enough. He needed Christ to clean him from the inside out. One of the dangers of emphasizing the need for personal holiness is that we can forget its purpose and make it an end in itself.[4]

Being filled at the Lord's table is recalling and being filled with the redeeming Word of God in Christ made dramatically visible at the Cross. Wrote Charles Wesley, "And lo! My Lord is here become the Bread of life to me."[5]

---

1. John Wesley, *On Working Out Our Own Salvation*.
2. Charles Wesley, "Us Who Climb Thy Holy Hill."
3. Phineas Bresee, quoted in *A Prince in Israel*.
4. Diane Leclerc, *Discovering Christian Holiness*.
5. Elaborated by T. Crichton Mitchell in *Charles Wesley: Man with the Dancing Heart*.

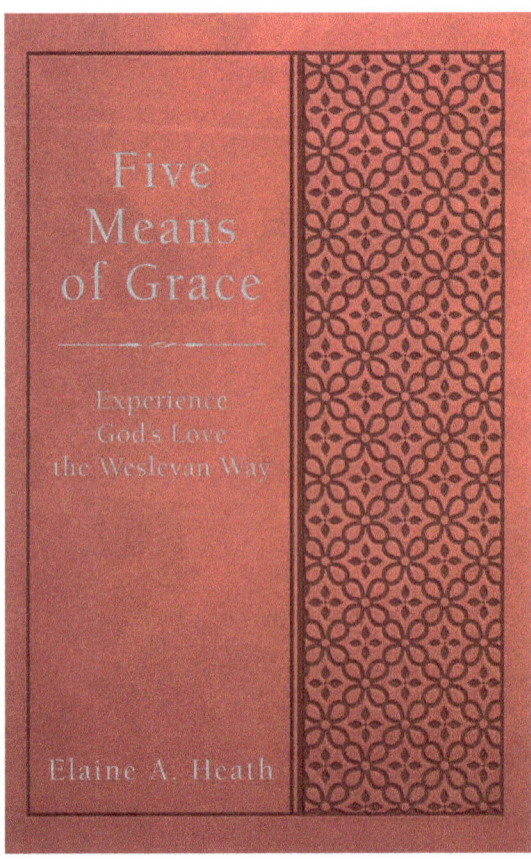

WEEK 22

GILGAL—LET'S ROLL!

Let's roll! Roll where? The Israelites finally had made it into their promised land. What now? Should they sit down and simply relish the benefits of the great promise fulfilled? Should they gloat over their good fortune to the envy of their displaced neighbors? No!

If once saved from past sin, are disciples of Rabbi Jesus at their full spiritual goal? No, being forgiven isn't enough. It's just the necessary beginning. What must come next is being in the church and in the world *the right way*. Christ has given a great gift that was promised. Now what? The salvation gift has been given so that we the forgiven can become great gift-givers ourselves.

The Hebrew "Gilgal" means "to roll." The freed Israelite slaves chose this name for the place where they initially found themselves in the promised land. They realized that much more was now expected and possible. The intent of being blessed surely includes the active blessing of others. So, now that we're here, let's roll!

A. Prayer

May the endless and amazing love of yours, my God, fill my heart today. Set me to celebrating the fulfillment of your salvation promise. Thank you for a heavenly experience through the blessing of a relationship restored and a spiritual promised land arrived. But may I also do the more that I know you expect. May I remember Gilgal. May my motto now be, "Let's Roll!" I and the church of Rabbi Jesus must move on, not arrogantly but humbly and confidently, sweetly spreading the good news of God in Christ for all. In a world where "no" is heard constantly by so many, may my witness bring a joyful "YES!" to life's potential goodness when lived faithfully in Jesus Christ.

B. The Voice of Rabbi Jesus: Luke 15:1–3, 11b–32

> There will be plenty of time to cry. The world hurts and will seek to hurt you, my friends. But right now it's party time! Your lost brother is found. A promised land is reached. Hope is fulfilled, so let's celebrate. This parable of mine is really about my loving Father who loves to welcome home the lost sinner. Never think you are more deserving than others just because you've been home longer than your brother or sister. And don't stop with celebrating. There are many more still lost souls needing found. Rejoice at the exciting event at hand and then determine to roll on!

The parable of the Prodigal Son, or better the truth about my Loving Father, join my parables of the Lost Sheep and Lost Coin. They drive home something very important, the profound joy filling the heart of my Father when those who are alienated from God ("lost") are reconciled ("found"). You, my disciples, are among the fortunate. Now you are to live actively your new lives in me. They necessarily include helping many others find this promised land of divine grace.

Can you imagine that young prodigal son coming to his senses after reading Psalm 32? Such celebration can be a catalyst for how the prodigal "came to himself" (Lk. 15:17). As my disciples, you are to be celebration catalysts in this troubled world. You've received your promised gift. Now roll the good news into the world with excitement and joy. You've been chosen and blessed so that through you many others can come to know the same joy. Celebrate is such ways that the embers of your joy will warm cold hearts nearby.

My Spirit is anxious to continue teaching you on my behalf. I'm providing you with select portions from the revealed Word of God and from a particular tradition of my church with wisdom you need. Read carefully and continue listening closely to my Spirit who will guide your minds and hearts to understand properly and apply effectively.

C. Light from the Revealed Word

1. Psalm 32. It's such a happy verse. "Be glad in the Lord and rejoice, O righteous, and shout for joy, all you upright in heart" (vs. 11). We sense an exhilarating opportunity here. There's a new way of living victorious lives in God's presence. The psalmist, once silent before God, has been forgiven and now actively shares that blessed state for our inspiration. We must receive it and do the same for others.

This theme of the thrill of new life by God's grace appears excitedly in each of today's biblical passages. Lent is a time of painful waiting and needed repenting. Just ahead will be the expected promise fulfilled. We begin now to repent so that we may move on to the rejoicing. God brings his people into promised lands and bids them move on by using their blessings to propel them into their mission of representing God's redeeming love to the whole world. Be glad. Roll on!

2. Joshua 5:9–12. This passage begins with this word from the Lord: "Today I have rolled away from you the disgrace of Egypt" (vs. 9). Egypt's reproach had tainted the Israelites who had been forced to dwell there in slavery. They were far from deserving God's generosity. The Lord's "rolling away" was a necessary cleansing, part of what makes the entrance into the promised land possible and so wonderful. The naming of the place as "Gilgal," Hebrew "to roll," is an exclamation point on God's liberating, cleansing, and commissioning actions.

Once in Gilgal, the people of Israel immediately shared in the celebration of Passover. The fathers, mothers, and grandparents who had fled Egypt decades before were now mostly dead. Remembering God's saving action must be passed from generation to generation. The urgency of keeping the traditional feast in Gilgal would inaugurate new life in the land with an act of worship. It was a rite of remembering all that God had done and one of offering gratitude for the fulfillment of God's past and future promises. Joining the psalmist, the people chose to remember, be glad, and rejoice.

3. 2 Corinthians 5:16–21. Lent is not usually seen by Christians as a season of celebration. Even so, the divine sacrifice of Christ on the Cross now has delivered new life. Thus, Paul calls us to celebrate in the same sense that we celebrate the Lord's Supper. We celebrate Jesus' faithfulness to divine righteousness even amid horror and injustice. We celebrate God's goodness even before receiving it fully and implementing it adequately. In Jesus' unjust execution, we can see the triumph of faith over worldly domination and the grace that ensures our own redemption, now and even more later.

Remember that Paul carried harsh memories of his own evildoing. As Saul, he had approved the stoning of Stephen who was full of grace, power, faith, and the Holy Spirit (Acts 6:5-8). He had "ravaged the church by entering house after house, dragging off both men and women" (Acts 8:3). But God's forgiving grace had intervened. Anyone now united with Rabbi Jesus receives new life and gets a fresh start. That's surely reason for celebration!

One other thing is clearly worth celebrating now that we have received our promised salvation. We are called to be faithful, *not successful*. We are called to grace-infused ministries of reconciliation with eyes turned toward God's new creation. Answering this call is our responsibility. Finally bringing the intended results is beyond us. It's ultimately the work of God. Even so, once in the promised land, it's time for us to roll with God's ongoing mission and accomplish all we can. Once gifted ourselves, it's time to share this joy with others.

D. Reflections of Leaders of the Wesleyan-Holiness Tradition

Yes, there comes peace and harmony when God's promise is fulfilled. But the necessary next step is "forth in Thy name, O Lord, I go." While the going is not forced, we are called to and empowered to accomplish God's work. God is not to be seen as a specialist in coercion. He chooses to work "strongly and sweetly." Integrity in Christian mission and worship must be God-centered. If it is, thorns can be turned into crowns!

There is no mixture of any contrary affections: all is peace and harmony. Being filled with love, there is no more interruption of it than of the beating of his heart; and continual love bringing continual joy in the Lord, he rejoices evermore.[1]

> Forth in Thy name, O Lord, I go,
> My daily labor to pursue,
> Thee, only Thee, resolved to know,
> In all I think, or speak, or do.²

John Wesley construed God's power or sovereignty fundamentally in terms of *empowerment* rather than control or *overpowerment*. This is not to weaken God's power but to determine its character. As John Wesley was fond of saying, God works "strongly and sweetly." That is, God's grace works powerfully but not irresistibly in matters of human life and salvation, thereby empowering our *response-ability* without overriding our *responsibility*.³

Wesley's abiding concern was to preserve the vital tension between two truths that he viewed as co-definitive of Christianity: without God's grace we *cannot* be saved; while without our grace-empowered but uncoerced participation, God's grace *will not* save.

In proper Christian worship, we are encouraged and enabled to encoun-ter God as revealed in Jesus Christ, who is present by way of the Holy Spirit and made known to us through faith, which is a gift of the Holy Spirit. Through the worship experience we do not simply know more *about* God but we come to *know* God ever more deeply. Authentic wor-ship not only remembers who God is but encounters the living reality of God through the Spirit. It avoids formalism, merely going through the motions, and "enthusiasm," substituting enjoying feelings for knowing God.⁴

With God's help, we can handle whatever we face. We face the mission of colonizing the earth with the life of heaven. Necessarily involved will be finding ways to change thorns into crowns. Our hope rests in the resurrection of Jesus. Jesus was afflicted with unjust thorns and forced to wear a mocking crown. Even so, he knew and shares with us a great peace that comes from such mocking being turned into eternal rejoic-ing. A crown can be made even out of thorns. Jesus' was. Pilate told his advisers to "to make the tomb of Jesus as secure as you can." But barricading the tomb of God was like shouting "Stop!" to the rising sun.

Therefore, since we are being called forward by God, the God of unlimited new life, let's roll![5]

God's plan for a holy people, which we refer to with terms such as "salvation" and "redemption," speaks not only to the transportation of humanity (from a destiny of eternal punishment to a place of eternal joy) but, more importantly, to the transformation of humanity (from their current condition to the kind of people God intends them to be). The salvation that God has made possible is not primarily interested in altering humanity's eventual *location*; it's focused more on altering its very being to the perfect love of holiness. And for the church to be the church, its holiness must be real, active, and visible.[6]

---

1. John Wesley, *On Patience*.
2. Charles Wesley, "Forth in Thy Name, O Lord, I Go."
3. Randy L. Maddox, *Responsible Grace*.
4. Henry H. Knight, III, in Callen-Thorsen, *Heart & Life*.
5. Barry L. Callen, *The Jagged Journey*.
6. Bernie A. Van De Walle, *Rethinking Holiness*.

WEEK 23

REMEMBER, THEN FORGET!

Remember God's great actions of yesterday—unless, of course, looking back blocks your openness to seeing God acting in fresh and amazing ways today! Yesterday has wisdom to share. That wisdom, however, can sour if we get stuck back there and lose connection with today's fresh possibilities. Going back in grateful memory should be a resource for going forward. There's an important sense in which we must remember and then forget.

The Old Testament rests on a basic assumption. The faith memories of God's people allow each new generation to re-live God's past deeds of redemption, opening them to God's continuing activity in their own lives and times. Remembering is essential, although there must be no choking on mere nostalgia. Remembering must fuel reliving.

Once a guest church leader was left alone in a pastor's study. He later reported gazing over the books on the shelves and deciding when the pastor's mind had died! Yesterday's wisdom is crucial; so is being actively about today's mission with fresh insight and energy. Old truths live on only as they find new applications. We must keep searching, thinking, looking forward, both rejoicing in yesterday and embracing the new life God offers now.

Remember, and then forget. Rejoice in yesterday, not for its own sake, but for what light it sheds on the present and coming future. Recall the *then* in order to live the *now*.

A. Prayer

Lord, teach me and thrill me with memories of your past actions. Also, save me from becoming lost in that past at the expense of being open to new things that may be on your mind today. Since your creating goes on, my God, save me from a common curse of church life, "We never did it that way before!" I know you, God, because of knowing your past actions, especially in Rabbi Jesus. Part of what I have come to know is that you are a God who is still re-creating. Still today, the lost are being found and the broken mended. Keep me open to the fresh possibilities of that nowness and newness. Connect me to the past only in ways that guide me into your todays and tomorrows. As I grow older, keep me young.

B. The Voice of Rabbi Jesus: John 12:1–8

> As my forgiven disciples, you now no longer are free to mull over the sins of your past. They are forever gone. Remember not yesterday's death but tomorrow's resurrection. Learn to focus on what my Father is doing now, and determine to look ahead and be part of that. Quit standing and sadly staring at my Cross. Absorb the great meaning there and then move on. Come and dance with joy around my empty grave. Ask me not, "How's it always been done." I much prefer the questions, "What are our next steps together, Lord," and "What do you want me to do now?"

Be open to a very new thing, my disciples. The world hung me on a cross to allow death to do its worst. Nonetheless, I live! Don't be paralyzed by what death once did to me or can do to you. I am resurrection life for you, the eternal life that overcomes the old and brings forth the new. That is the hope by which you must live and serve in my name.

My friend Lazarus had been dead for four days. I raised him and now he was hosting me at his house for dinner. Memory of the reality of death was still in the air. Also present was knowledge that death had not prevailed for him and hopefully would not for me. Mary sensed my coming death and glimpsed what might lie beyond. I praised her for her vision. However limited her view, at least she was reaching forward.

Instead of living under the oppression of times past, Mary wanted to be alive to the present moment of what my Father was about to do. She had the right attitude and was asking the right question. Her question was, and still should be for you, "What is God doing in this moment and how can I be part of it?"

My Spirit is anxious to continue teaching you on my behalf. I'm providing you with select portions from the revealed Word of God and from a particular tradition of my church with wisdom you need. Read carefully and continue listening closely to my Spirit who will guide your minds and hearts to understand properly and apply effectively.

C. Light from the Revealed Word

1. Psalm 126. The first verses of Psalm 126 look to the past, and the final ones look to the future. Both directions are important. God's people always need to live by both memory and hope. The ending verses pursue a new and transformed condition, not simply restoration, but renewal, even resurrection. The psalmist is not looking to the past in hope of a mere restoration to some old way of life—let's do it again as we always have. The hope is finding how to live into God's new way of being that's relevant for the changing circumstances of today and tomorrow. In our journey with God, with all the complexity of our personal histories, we are being readied by the season of Lent for the Easter celebration when God can be relied on to do a glorious new thing.

This psalm is a "song of ascent." Probably it was composed for use by pilgrims on their way up to Jerusalem. They knew the city's history with God, how over the generations it had served and also failed divine purposes. The Temple had been built and destroyed. God's promises had been fulfilled and left unfulfilled there. This complex set of circumstances acknowledges the changes in the fortune of God's people over time. Whether ancient Israelites or modern Christians, while we are journeying in God's steadfast love we always can experience *new life* no matter the darkness of the day.

2. Isaiah 43:16–21. There are important links between past, present, and future. Isaiah mentions "the former things, the things of old" (43:18). They are to be remembered and yet not dwelt on when "a new thing springs forth" (43:19). New contexts call for the story line to take new forms. God's new thing is continuous with yesterday and also freshly relevant for today. We are to remember in order to be informed and inspired, but never at the expense of becoming deaf and blind to what God is doing now, maybe something new, unprecedented, and truly wonderful.

This remembering and then forgetting the past is an introduction to a new event the prophet expects. It will be so world-changing that it actually will displace Israel's founding story. It will be a new thing, not a way in the sea (exodus from Egypt) but a way in wilderness (end of exile), not dry ground in the waters, but waters in the desert. This new will bring forward the old story of God-with-us in a new way. "Do not remember" becomes a call to let loose of things as they were and expect something new. While new, it nevertheless will be recognizable in terms of the past since it's the same God acting in both instances.

When should God's people not remember? When a nostalgic relation to some tradition ties believers to a past so tightly that they can't spot and thus fail to address present realities and opportunities. Forget yesterday if you think God is always intending to reproduce it today exactly as it was back then. This is a new day in which the Lord may be doing a new thing. We must rejoice and be creatively glad in it.

3. Philippians 3:4b–14. We who believe in the living God face a grammatical challenge. We must limit our use of *periods* and rely more on *commas*. God doesn't stop but keeps going, even if pausing on occasion because of our poor decisions. Embrace and rejoice in the new. There is a new way of understanding life through Jesus. We must break free of old assumptions and difficult memories. The Jews were very tradition rich and sadly too much tradition bound.

Paul walks the Philippians through his personal spiritual resume and then throws it in the trash. He was born, raised, formed, educated, even zealous in maintaining synagogue discipline, but none of that mattered anymore. This one thing I do, he announces. Forgetting what lies behind and straining forward to what lies ahead, "I press on toward the goal" (3:13-14). What had been ahead for Jesus was the Cross, now the symbol for how God turns human wisdom upside down. What was to be a door slammed shut was actually a door swinging open.

Christ shares in our death in order to break the power that death has over us. Through personal spiritual resurrections, we come to share in the risen life of Jesus. God has acted through Israel, and now through Christ Jesus, and continues to act outside the boundaries of many of our former understandings. God brings a new creation into being. Forget whatever is necessary in order to know this arriving newness.

D. Reflections of Leaders of the Wesleyan-Holines Tradition

God does reign over all and does not change in character or intentions. Nonetheless, sometimes "new songs do now his lips employ." We must be open to moving on, living out our baptism by being drawn on toward "the fuller reception of grace." We must remember our secularized world and then also forget it if it blinds us to today's great opening to things eternal.

Let God have the sole dominion over you, let Him reign without a rival, let Him possess all your heart and rule alone. Let God be your one desire, your joy, your love, so that all within you may continually cry out, "The Lord God omnipotent reigns!"[1]

> His name the sinner hears,
> And is from sin set free;
> 'Tis music in his ears,
> 'Tis life and victory.
> New songs do now his lips employ,
> And dances his glad heart for joy.[2]

Experiential sanctification is an ongoing process of daily rededication, reconsecration, mortification, and vivification of the whole person to God. It calls for believers to live out their baptism in time so as to allow new challenges and circumstances to draw them further on toward the fuller reception of grace and the deepening of purity of heart.³

A growing number of sociologists of religion are contending that secularism is now dead. The postmodern West is teeming with religion, with a growing openness toward and genuine interest in the supernatural. There is a mounting desire for sanctity. People are longing to encounter the sacred and searching high and low for the holy.⁴

---

1. John Wesley, *Discourses on Our Lord's Sermon on the Mount.*
2. Charles Wesley, "Let Heaven and Earth Agree."
3. Thomas Oden, *Classic Christianity: A Systematic Theology.*
4. Jason E. Vickers, *Minding the Good Ground.*

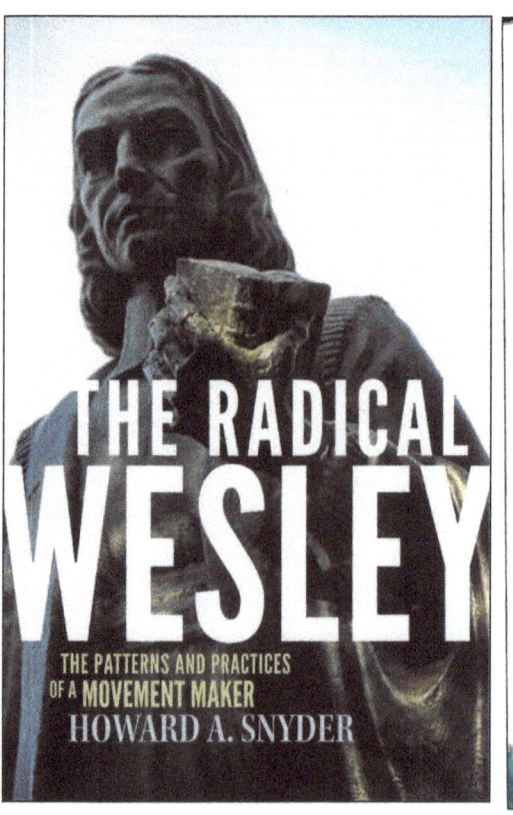

WEEK 24

Easter Day/Resurrection of the Lord

I'M STILL CREATING!

Originally, God created everything from nothing. Now, God continues to create from the scattered and spoiled pieces of the original creation. The opponents of Jesus conspired to have him crucified, a brutal and disgraced rendering of a living being back to the dust, an apparent reversion of Jesus to the nothingness of earthly oblivion.

Then came again the Creator's divine voice, saying, "Let there be." And there was! It again was order out of chaos, light in the darkness, new life, resurrection, Easter, amazement for all. This changed everything. Jesus being raised from the dead was a cosmic event that opened the future and now offers new life for us all. The very life of today's church is wrapped up in the ongoing dynamism of the tomb of Jesus being shockingly empty. The central message of the New Testament is this. Since Jesus lives, we too can live, now, wonderfully, and always.

Mary asked the key question, and all human history rests on the answer. Where had they taken the body? Who, the Romans? They may have had the power to kill and move the body if they wished, but not bring it back to life. No, God was the miraculous Actor here. The grave was empty and the future now wide open. Resurrection! God still creating. Nothing can cancel this new creation. God acts. Life wins!

A. Prayer

I live in a world, O God, that's full of doubt and despair and death. The casket is assumed to be the final end of us all. I need help and hope. Please train my dulled eyes to see that, no matter what, your love endures forever and even death doesn't have the last word. You always are creating hopeful newness, and this very day is one that you have gloriously made. In this day, then, whatever the negatives, help me to believe that the final victory always will be yours. May your very life, now pulsating in the Risen Christ, begin pulsating in me. Let me be able to sing with joy, "He lives. So can I. Hallelujah!"

B. The Voice of Rabbi Jesus: John 20:1–18

> Here was my question in that garden of sorrow. "Why do you weep as you approach my grave?" Mary cried because she was still without the big truth, the dra-matic answer. I told her that "they" hadn't taken my body anywhere. The world's powerful may have put me in the grave she was trying to visit, but all the rest of the happening was well beyond human ability to control. My father was the great Actor on resurrection day. He creates and re-creates. Count on this as you face what looks to you like final graves. I am the resurrection and the life, the once dying and now ever-living One.

Mary was confused. She assumed a "normal" explanation of my absent body. Faith in me as the Risen Christ always involves shock, struggle, and risk. Like Mary, you will live somewhere between grief and joy, despair and faith, questions and their apparent answers. Given what's happened, for Christians Sunday will always be the first day of every week. Bring to me your doubts, questions, everything you don't understand. Bring them to the tomb of your Lord and Master. I will cover them with my presence and life—because I am alive forevermore!

The women were on their way with spices and ointments to minister to my corpse. Things supposedly were as they always had been.

The powerful were crushing the innocent and had found a scapegoat to relieve their anxiety about a feared social upheaval. The followers of mine were running away at the moment of crisis. The one who loudly claimed to be the most loyal of all my disciples denied that he ever knew me. Even those closest to me could not imagine a real resurrection.

By contrast, you must remain open to what lies beyond the ordinary range of human understanding and expectation. Get ready to know the living Stranger in the garden of death who knows you by name and holds the keys to release you from death to a new future. When I return to my Father, my Spirit will arrive for you. Always think future and life.

My Spirit is anxious to continue teaching you on my behalf. I'm providing you with select portions from the revealed Word of God and from a particular tradition of my church with wisdom you need. Read carefully and continue listening closely to my Spirit who will guide your minds and hearts to understand properly and apply effectively.

C. Light from the Revealed Word

1. Psalm 118:1–2, 14–24. The call is to celebrate a great victory won by God. The celebration is grounded in God's love and faithfulness. "O give thanks to the Lord, for he is good." His goodness has no ending and is active in our human history, even taking broken stones and making them chief cornerstones. This certainly should be truly marvelous in our eyes. God the Creator never tires of creating. Death, where is your sting? Despair, where is your future?

Easter is re-creation day. The one who was dead is dead no more. Combining two of this psalm's verses tells the big story. This is the day when the Lord has acted (vs. 24). I shall not die but live (vs. 17). Now every day is the Lord's day, God's acting day, the day of new life. Let's be thrilled and act as though we really believe this amazing re-creation reality. God's love never quits. God's power knows no limits. God never will be conquered by death. God's strength and love will be my daily song.

2. Isaiah 65:17–25. This characterization of the new city of Jerusalem is quite amazing. It includes a welcome to the excluded "foreigners" (56:3-6), new worship as neighborliness (58:5-9), fresh commercial prosperity (60:6-11), and a new jubilee year (61:2). What had been mass destruction has moved to wonderful restoration (chaps. 40–66). The anticipation of God-given newness builds until we come to the climactic poetry of chapter 65.

God promises a wholly new future for Jerusalem, one that is not derived from a fixed pattern of the old. The future will be a new, free, unconditional gift. The triad of "new heaven, new earth, and new Jerusalem" means "everything new!" The only reasonable response is, "Be glad and rejoice forever in what I am creating" (Isa. 65:18a). Our God is in the business of restoration, resurrection, and eternal life.

Both the new city envisioned by Isaiah and the risen Christ of the New Testament declare boldly that God is not a prisoner or victim of any circumstance, including death. The Creator is still creating. Even the broken stones of a fallen creation can become cornerstones of a brand new tomorrow.

3. Acts 10:34–43. Peter's speech makes clear that the resurrection of Jesus changes everything he thought he knew about what God wanted from him. The divinity of Christ, so powerfully displayed in his resurrection, caused Peter to perceive that "God shows no partiality." The grace of God extends to "every nation" (vss. 34-35). All human fences run counter to the open boundaries of the kingdom of God.

Luke wants it understood that the resurrection of Jesus Christ is an event of cosmic significance. The very structures of the universe have been shaken. The socially constructed "givens" of what we always assumed to be true now must be rethought and reimagined in light of the exciting new events triggered by God's work in the Risen Christ.

The dynamic of the Easter mystery is the very life of the Christian church. It's the power of Christ himself now at work in us by the Spirit of Christ. All life is to change because of the presence and actions of the Risen Christ. Hope is alive regardless of circumstance. Joy!

D. Reflections of Leaders of the Wesleyan-Holiness Tradition

All things are now possible. All graves must stop their boasting in light of the Risen Christ. We each are to rise in heaven's re-creating light, see the cleansing stream of God's powerful love, and allow the ever-living One to be enthroned within. If Jesus lives, we too can live! Be open to a deeper and marvelous work of God's grace.

It is no small thing to lay out for God all which you have received from God. It requires all your wisdom, all your resolution, all your patience and constancy, far more than you ever had by nature but not more than you may have by grace. For God's grace is sufficient for you, and you know that all things are possible to the one who believes. By faith, then, bring every thought into captivity to the obedience of Christ.[1]

> Lives again our glorious King!
> Where, O death, is now thy sting?
> Once he died our souls to save;
> Where's thy victory, boasting grave?
>
> King of glory! Soul of bliss!
> Everlasting life is this,
> Thee to know, Thy power to prove,
> Thus to sing, and thus to love.[2]
>
> I rise to walk in Heav'n's own light,
> Above the world and sin,
> With heart made pure and garments white,
> And Christenthroned within.
>
> The cleansing stream I see, I see!
> I plunge, and, oh, it cleanseth me
> Oh, praise the Lord, it cleanseth me!
> It cleanseth me, yes, cleanseth me.[3]

Authentic Christian spirituality is personal life lived in union with Christ. It is a relationship with the incarnate and risen Lord through the power of the Holy Spirit, where his death is my death, *his resurrection my resurrection.* Spirituality in the New Testament sense is not a moral program, not a set of rules, not a level of ethical achievement, not a philosophy or strategy, but simply *life lived in Christ.*[4]

At the very heart of the gospel is the promise of a deeper working of God's grace in the heart of the Christian believer. It's a grace receivable by faith in the present moment, enabling us to be and to act in conformity of the great commandment, which is to love God supremely and to love every other person as we love our own souls.[5]

---

1. John Wesley, *The Good Steward.*
2. Charles Wesley, "Christ the Lord is Risen Today."
3. Phoebe Palmer, *The Cleansing Wave.*
4. Barry L. Callen, *Authentic Spirituality.*
5. William M. Greathouse, *Love Made Perfect.*

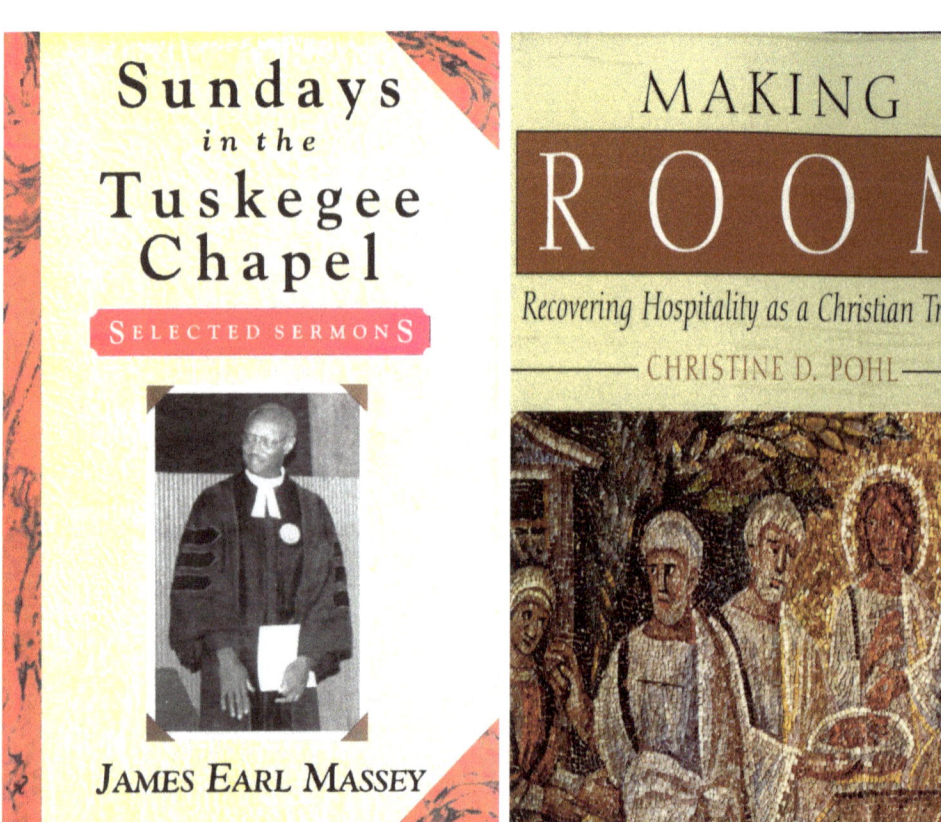

DARE TO RISK

Most of us specialize in personal defense mechanisms. We go all out to protect ourselves from danger and embarrassment. God asks a hard thing of us, an end to this selfish tendency. We are invited to risk stepping outside the artificial walls we use to protect ourselves. The issue becomes whether or not we are willing to follow our Lord into threatening territory well beyond our comfort zones. We know that Rabbi Jesus already has faced and overcome the contrary powers of this world, even death itself. Can we trust him with our fragile lives?

If we are faithful to our high call from God, there surely will be opposition. Even so, we are following the Ruler of the kings of the earth (Rev. 1). God sent the Son and now the Son sends us, danger notwithstanding. Easter is great news for us to share. As we go, some people will try to silence our voices because we will be threatening their comfort zones. No matter. We must carry on, daring to risk and relax in God's promised care.

A. Prayer

I admit, Lord, to being something of a timid and selfish person. I'm willing to be on stage, but not with a script that makes the audience uncomfortable. I'd prefer wearing a mask so the real me isn't seen. As I age, I do various things to try looking young. While it should thrill everyone, I know that your good news of resurrected life in Christ will be received reluctantly if at all by many of my friends. Their selfish and self-protective defense mechanisms will kick in and plan to kick back at me as necessary. Bolster my daring, Risen Jesus, so that I can stand tall and proud and be the prophetic voice you intend, regardless of what happens.

B. The Voice of Rabbi Jesus: John 20:19–31

> Just as the Father sent me, so I now am sending you. Since you're sent, dare to go regardless of the problems and unanswered questions. Don't be preoccupied with protecting yourselves by locking my truth behind defensive doors. I'm aware of your hesitations, your urges to self-protection. Know this. I bring you peace. I grant you safety—at least in the long-term. Look at my hands and side. I've survived the worst and so can you. The news is so good that you must not fail to share it openly. Receive my Spirit, stand erect, and go!

There they were, my first disciples, hiding themselves because of fear following my crucifixion. They didn't yet see the bigger picture. You must not follow their fearful example. I am offering you something that should inspire joy instead of retreat from the world. I have called you to be confident witnesses worldwide. I know that doing this will require much trust in me. I promise to breathe my Spirit into you. Receive that holy breath and allow my Spirit to make you bold and speak through you regardless of the circumstances and your own inabilities.

Recall that my Father, having "formed man from the dust of the ground," breathed life into his nostrils so that he became a living being (Gen. 2:7). Now you must become truly alive by the new breathing of my Spirit. Allow me to guide you into becoming an Easter community where the wounds of crucifixion do not paralyze. Your fears and failures must be overcome by the transforming joy of the new "in Christ" life. Resurrection faith means having the courage to look at my ugly wounds, and potentially your own, and still focus on the bigger picture of present mission and coming triumph.

My Spirit is anxious to continue teaching you on my behalf. I'm providing you with select portions from the revealed Word of God and from a particular tradition of my church with wisdom you need. Read carefully and continue listening closely to my Spirit who will guide your minds and hearts to understand properly and apply effectively.

C. Light from the Revealed Word

1. Psalm 150. Here's the last of the psalms. What turns out to be the bottom line of them all? Despite the dangers ahead, what are we left with after Easter? We should "praise the Lord!" We now know the high cost of our redemption and have glimpsed the Cross lodged in the heart of God. The causes for praise, despite all the world's negatives, are God's surpassing greatness, amazing love, and mighty deeds—particularly raising Jesus from the dead.

How should we go about this praising? We must step outside ourselves and move beyond self-preoccupations. We should blow, strum, bang, and stomp every instrument in sight, singing at the top of our voices. If we are breathing, we should be praising God so that all can hear the joy in our souls. When God calls to action, we should dare to move forward even in the face of danger.

2. Acts 5:27–32. It was inevitable. There would be a collision between broadcasting the good news about the Risen Christ and the status-quo political and religious establishments. Luke narrates a dramatic confrontation between the apostles, carriers of the Easter truth, and the high priest in Jerusalem, the point person for status-quo religion who had behind him the authority of Rome.

Are Christians called to civil disobedience when loyalty to God is made impossible otherwise? Dare we sometimes do what those first apostles of Jesus did? Soon they were being flogged (Acts 5:40) and commanded to shut up about Jesus in public. What happened? Considering it an honor to suffer for Jesus' sake, the disciples of Rabbi Jesus were barely beyond the door of the prison when they opened their mouths to start preaching again. "God," they confessed, "is our only authority."

Are we ready to take such a bold stand? Can we avoid reverting to violence even when victims of it?

3. Revelation 1:4–8. What are John's first words to the seven churches in Asia? "Grace to you and peace from him who is and who was and who is to come." The grace and peace offered is from the God who is timeless and rises high above all human rulers. Revelation 1:4–8 is a great doxology offered in honor of Jesus, "the firstborn of the dead and the ruler of the kings of the earth" (vs. 1:5). The language is unabashedly political. The praise of Rabbi Jesus subordinates "kings of the earth"—all of them—to the final rule of Christ. This political accent is reinforced by the use of "kingdom," "dominion," and "almighty" language.

God is everywhere "doing Easter"! A dominant theme of the Bible is the Easter truth that refuses any silencing by established authorities of this world. Moses contradicted the arrogant rule of Pharaoh. Daniel resorted to acts of defiance against the wicked rule of Nebuchadnezzar. The early Christian apostles got in trouble for proclaiming boldly the good news of the Risen Christ. Rather than fearing this world, they worked to transform it by stepping outside their defense mechanisms and risking reliance on God. To whom are we ultimately loyal? To whom are we ultimately accountable?

D. Reflections of Leaders of the Wesleyan-Holiness Tradition

We who rejoice in the resurrected Christ are sent to spread the good news, risky as that may be in some settings. We must dare to love and serve as Jesus did. Available to us is strengthening and serving power that enables a necessary cleansing and maturing as witnesses. The Living One must come fully alive in us! We then must risk standing in the middle and not escaping to the safer extremes.

Now, seeing you can do all things through Christ strengthening you, be merciful as your Father in heaven is merciful. Love your neighbor as yourself. Love friends and enemies as your own soul. And let your love be long-suffering and patient toward all. Let it be kind, soft, benign, inspiring you with the most amiable sweetness and the most fervent and tender affection. Let it rejoice in the truth, wherever it is found—the truth that is after godliness.[1]

> O that the world might know
> The all-atoning Lamb!
> Spirit of faith, descend, and show
> The virtue of his name,
> The grace which all may find,
> The saving power impart,
> And testify to all mankind,
> And speak in every heart.[2]

The biblical word *epiteleo* means perfecting, to mature, to bring to full stature, to complete. Purity is subtraction. Maturity is addition. Entire sanctification is not merely the negative goodness of a cleansing of the heart wrought at the moment of faith, but it is also the aggressive and progressive living, growing, and maturing, the applying of the principles of Christian ethics to every part of life.[3]

As Jesus was empowered, the church is empowered for its mission by the Spirit. Outward forms are not enough—the power must be at work in us (Eph. 3:20). The kingdom of God is not just a matter of talk but of power (1 Cor. 4:20). Outsiders ought to be able to sense the life-changing presence (1 Cor. 14:25). More than churches full of people, God wants (and the world needs) people full of the Spirit.[4]

There is a core connection among baptism, discipleship, and mission. On the one hand, baptism propels us into a Spirit-filled life of discipleship in which we overcome the power of sin, flesh, and the devil. On the other hand, we are set free for a Spirit-anointed life of mission to become co-workers with Jesus in the kingdom. This mission-shaped discipleship does not come naturally; it is not accomplished in a moment; it is going to be costly; and it must be intentionally developed.[5]

There is danger in remaining in the middle of the road and keeping proper balance between opposing poles. One is vulnerable to attack from both sides. Consistent Wesleyan theology is precisely fitted to occupy this mediating position, but it is a precarious position. Too often it has succumbed to the pressures and escaped to the safety of one or the other of the extremes.[6]

---

1. John Wesley, *Discourses on Our Lord's Sermon on the Mount*.
2. Charles Wesley, "Spirit of Faith Come Down."
3. Milton Agnew, in *The Holiness Pulpit*.
4. Clark H. Pinnock, *Flame of Love*.
5. Philip R. Meadows, *Remembering Our Baptism*.
6. H. Ray Dunning, *Grace, Faith, and Holiness*. See Barry L. Callen, *Caught Between Truths*.

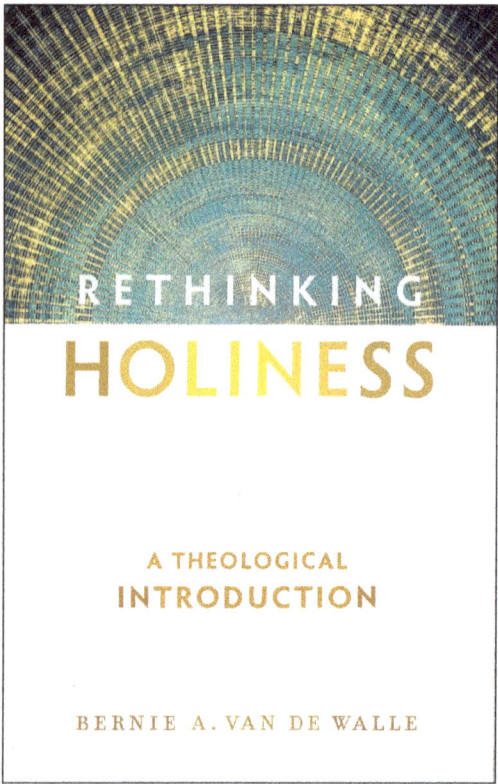
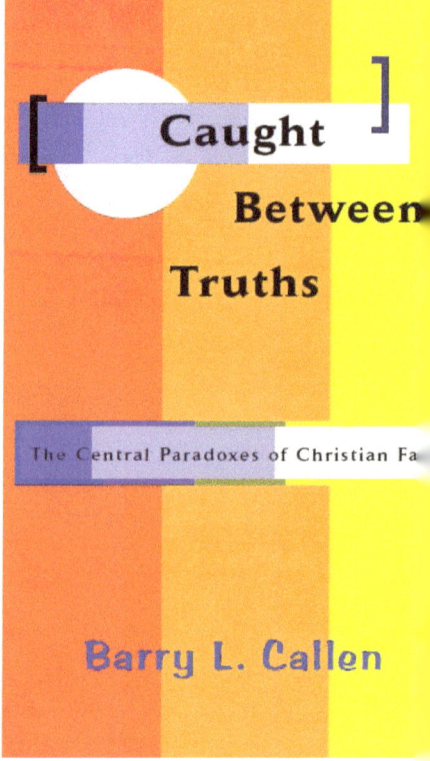

WEEK 26

HUMAN WALLS MUST GO!

Humans have been doing it for all recorded history. We build fences and walls to keep friends in and enemies out. Jesus breaks this mold. He was a bridge builder who jumped fences and punched holes in walls. He was an enemy of stereotyping and discrimination. Being a true follower of his won't win most popularity contests, but it will heal many ruptured relationships.

Jesus is Lord of all, Jews and non-Jews. We disciples of this Master are not to limit the love of God to our home crowd, to any crowd. Our mission is to all people, even when that's not comfortable and contradicts our negative stereotypes of certain others. Even the defensive wall we sometimes awkwardly erect between ourselves and those who suffer must come down if we want to receive true blessing.

The trajectory of the New Testament is hardly the standard human one. It's in upward, onward, and outward directions, beyond traditional walls, to our enemies, in fact to everyone. In fact, we are called to specialize in loving outsiders. Poet Robert Frost was right. "Something there is that doesn't love a wall." The something is a Someone, Rabbi Jesus. These words of an old song should define Christians. "Don't fence me in!" It's not so much that we want our freedom; it's more that we are anxious to reach lovingly to others without obstacles in the way.

A. Prayer

Lord, I'm so human. I cherish my prejudices, the high if subtle walls between myself and those many outsiders I've been taught to fear and dislike—and hope you do too. My family, country, club, denomination, and friends have pointed me to belief that my walls are appropriate, best, and necessary. Still, I now recognize that your Son, Jesus, spent his earthly days tearing down such artificial walls that so divide and damage the human family. He paid a high price for doing that, and so will I if I dare to do the same. How I need courage to be the person you want, O God. The only way to get such courage is to be filled with your Spirit. Come, liberating Spirit of God! Release me from my prejudices that clash with your universal love.

B. The Voice of Rabbi Jesus: John 21:1–19

> If you love me, as you enjoy saying you do, feed all of my sheep and don't put on a crowd-pleasing show as you do it. I live by loving, not by entertaining, dividing and destroying enemies, and impressing crowds. You are to do as I have done. Again, do you love me? Then feed my lambs, all of them. I came to love and save the whole world, not some preferred segment of it (Jn. 3:16). I dislike walls, as should you. Don't shield yourselves from those who suffer. Share freely with them and you will find me there.

I affirm the correctness of John portraying me as the Lamb who was slain and therefore is worthy to receive all honor and glory (Rev. 5:12–13). Disciples of false Christs build walls that limit their love and ministries. You must know me as the Good Shepherd who lovingly cares for my sheep—all of them, particularly the lost and desperate ones rejected by others.

You should be my humble and gracious disciples. Remember that the truly "meek" are not weak but strong in the power of love. This is a hard lesson to learn because it's so different from typical human thinking. You are to be my supposedly weak ones who go into the world in the unmatched power of my Spirit. Don't go about trying to impress the world with religious drama and spiritual magic. The devil tempted me to jump off the Jerusalem wall and drift harmlessly into the valley below to amaze to the crowd. I refused. It would have been a silly stunt, a dead-end drama. I wasn't a politician running for office. Yes, my resurrection was spectacular, but recall that it happened when no one was watching.

Don't play to the crowd, just follow my Spirit quietly and humbly and with courage. The crowds stay onboard only as long as you keep putting on your big show. Falter and they are gone. Instead, be gentle, loving, giving up yourselves, feeding my sheep, gladly doing the little things that really make a difference. It takes time to grow into mature disciples who know how to be humbly strong and relentlessly loving. I'll stay with you through this sanctifying process. Meanwhile, dare to keep bringing down walls of hate and prejudice.

My Spirit is anxious to continue teaching you on my behalf. I'm providing you with select portions from the revealed Word of God and from a particular tradition of my church with wisdom you need. Read carefully and continue listening closely to my Spirit who will guide your minds and hearts to understand properly and apply effectively.

C. Light from the Revealed Word

1. Psalm 30. Here is celebration of a dramatic overnight turn. What God does in the dark is turn us from sadness to joy, from distress to well-being. The result is that "joy comes in the morning" (30:5). Recall this psalm when it was on Paul's lips. He knew the tortured memories of having been an early persecutor of the Jesus people. His morning joy was his entry into a very new vocation and identity. It came by his abrupt embrace of the reality of the resurrection of Jesus. In this marvelous fresh day of faith, Paul could write, "May the God of hope fill you with all joy" (Rom. 15:13). His heart was full and bubbling over.

Paul's previous prejudices had walled him inside a web of mistrust and hate. It was so joyful to finally be freed in a Jesus morning so full of grace. His three days of blindness and the resulting transformation illustrate the arc of Psalm 30. Deliverance from the pit initiates a time of mourning that then is turned to dancing. The pit of prejudice erupts into praise to God because of salvation being available *for all* through Rabbi Jesus. Collapsed walls were allowing an invasion of joy.

Who's a "saint" in God's eyes? Verse 30:4 announces that it's someone who has become an extension of God's *hesed* (loving faithfulness).

Saints are, by God's grace, members of the covenant community who are experiencing God's loving care and gratefully becoming active in jumping fences and passing the freedom and joy on to others.

2. Acts 9:1–6, (7–20). The explicit command of Jesus was for Paul to witness about the Risen Christ to "Gentiles and kings" and "the people of Israel" (vs. 15). His perspective suddenly moved beyond religious tribalism. He was to reach out to all humanity, the universal sphere of Christ's domain, with redemptive love. For Paul, it now was not either/or, his own people or "the others." It had become a glorious both/and. None are to be excluded or judged secondary and unworthy of God's love and care.

The challenge to Paul and the congregations he would help form was how to hold in one Jesus community both Jewish followers who adhered to the Torah of Moses and Gentile followers who never heard of the Torah. How to manage this difficult tension dominates in particular Paul's epistles to the Romans and Galatians.

Reaching to "the other" is still an urgent matter for the church. We face a new multi-culturalism today that jeopardizes old entitlements and threatens traditional constituencies who say, "We've never done it that way before" and "Those people don't understand us and will upset everything we cherish." If so, so be it. True followers of Jesus aren't impressed with these stand-pat questions.

3. Revelation 5:6–14. The most powerful character in the drama, the only one capable of opening the scrolls, is said to be a Lamb with seven horns and seven eyes, looking as if it's been slaughtered (vs. 5:6). How odd that power was invested in the apparent weakness of a helpless lamb. The angels surrounding God's throne, and the living creatures and elders, are singing together like a wonderfully coordinated celestial choir: "Worthy is the Lamb that was slaughtered to receive power and wealth and wisdom and might and honor and glory and blessing!" (vs. 12).

This vision of John features an unlikely Lamb saving us. What power does a lamb have to save anyone, including itself? In many sacrificial rituals, a lamb is the chief victim. How can the victim save the perpetrator? This Lamb of God is seen in the midst of God's throne. An embarrassing sight? A Lamb dripping with blood now occupies the place of power, alone entitled to approach the throne, for it alone is said to be worthy.

This strange image of heaven is news that disrupts usual human understandings and breaks down our selfish and protective walls. Jesus' sacrifice reveals the true heart of God and becomes the basis of our own self-giving and bridge-building power (Col. 2:15; Heb. 2:14).

D. Reflections of Leaders of the Wesleyan-Holiness Tradition

When there are disagreements among Christians over this tradition or that preference, we are to "deny ourselves" and be "careful in our conversations." Our goal should be "the divine light within" rather than winning petty arguments. The common experience of love is the basis of our unity as believers. It's what propels us outward to others. True blessing comes when entering into the suffering of others.

Be exceedingly careful in your conversations that they may be worthy of the gospel of Christ. Don't let the liveliness of your spirit lead you into levity; cheerful seriousness is the point you are to aim at. And be willing to suffer with Him so that you may reign with Him. Deny yourself, take up your cross daily, and follow Him.[1]

> The gift unspeakable impart;
> Command the light of faith to shine,
> To shine in my dark, drooping heart,
> And fill me with the life divine.
> Now bid the new creation be!
> O God, let there be faith in me![2]

The experience of God's love to man, resulting in sanctification, becomes the foundation of the unity of all Christians. Christian fellowship is based on brotherly love among all Christians, a love that overrides distinctions of doctrine, ritual or ecclesiastical organizations. It excludes all sectarianism and partisanship.[3]

I learned the lesson in a feeding camp in Ethiopia. There is more to being blessed than having or giving material things. I came to love the desperate mass of people there, to care about their suffering. I had touched the hem of the garment of understanding. I had entered into the suffering of another. I had discovered that the presence of blessing does not mean the absence of need.[4]

---

1. John Wesley, *Letters to a Young Disciple*.
2. Charles Wesley, "Father of Jesus Christ the Just."
3. Harald Lindstrom, *Wesley and Sanctification*.
4. Jo Anne Lyon, *The Ultimate Blessing*.

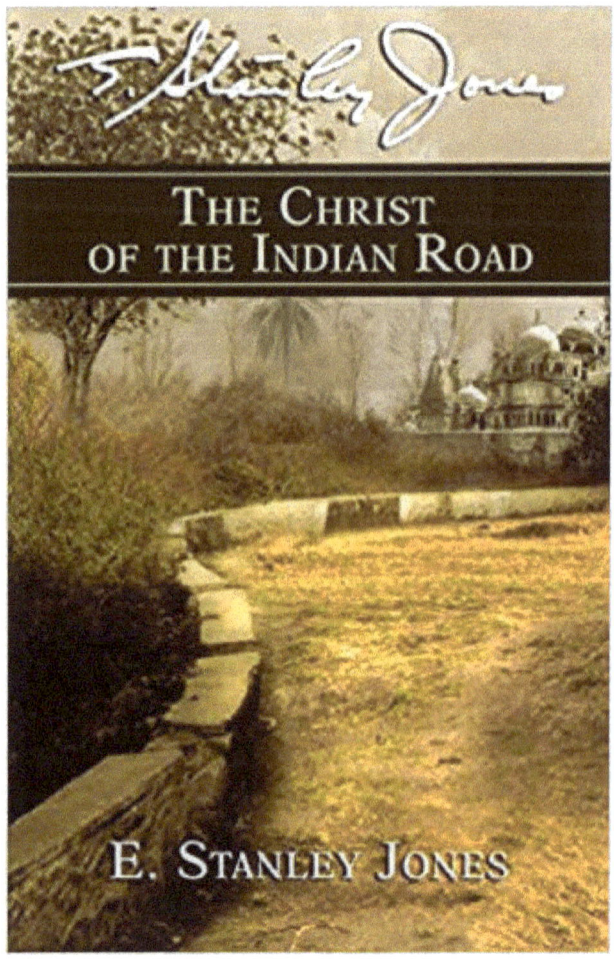

WEEK 27

WORDS MUST WALK

My talking about Jesus should also be my walking with Jesus. We disciples of the Master don't earn God's favor by what we do, of course. Still, what we say must be acted out in ways that show we've really received God's favor. Salvation is by faith alone, yes, but saving faith is never alone. It naturally goes into action or eventually goes sour.

The divine call to the church is to *be the church* by living as a holy, united, and redemptive force in the world. The church is not to withdraw and exist in some stagnant pool of detached self-righteousness. To the contrary, the church has a "political" mission that engages the world, not with an agenda of arrogance and coercion, but as a Jesus community that knows its true nature and power lie in servanthood and not domination of others.

John Wesley was right. God's expressions of power toward us, and thus of ours to others, focus on *empowerment* rather than control, manipulation, and overpowerment. Our words must walk in the world gently, peacefully, lovingly, and yet significantly. The Greek *eirene* (peace) appears in every New Testament book. It also should appear in the everyday actions of the disciples of Rabbi Jesus. We have received and must share the peace of Christ.

A. Prayer

I'm coming to learn, Lord, that if a picture is worth a thousand words, acting lovingly is a public display worth millions. I so want to be part of a church that's alive and living out its faith in concrete and very visible ways. Keep me from being caught up in the self-preoccupation and self-delusion of searching for "signs and wonders" about which I then can brag. Fill my life, O God, with loving actions that will be welcomed by others as apparent miracles of love from your gracious hand. Let me hunt for every lost one. When found, may I apply the healing ointments of your love. Send me into the dark valleys of others and, once there, may my words walk with loving actions that comfort them in their distress.

B. The Voice of Rabbi Jesus: John 10:22-30

> Everything I have done speaks louder than all my words. This is a key lesson for you. As I care for my sheep, they are to be caring for the sheep I have in many other folds. The real convincing is in the doing. You asked me to tell you straight out if I were the Messiah. My words didn't seem clear enough for you. I then allowed my acting to speak louder than my words could ever manage. Don't try to live by putting on impressive displays of divine showmanship. Be humble and loving, giving fully of yourself and yielding to others in love.

The Jews asked me during the Festival of Dedication whether I was the Messiah. I responded by continuing to identify myself and acting humbly as the "suffering servant" of God. This was not the image of a Messiah they wanted and anticipated, so they couldn't hear me well. They were looking for a military leader, perhaps closer to the figure of Judas Maccabeus, someone who would defend the people from foreign occupation. My disciples often are misunderstood, as I was. Be prepared for this and don't rely on violence as the answer.

No wonder I made my own people suspicious and then angry. Instead of fighting off the Romans, they thought I was wasting my valuable time healing a blind man (Jn. 9) and raising Lazarus from the dead (Jn. 11). You will face the same impatience. Choose your words wisely, whether or not they are welcomed. Keep them in line with who my Father is, what I was sent to do, and what I now have sent you to do. Act lovingly and many will come to believe your words.

You have to learn how to trust my eventual victory even while staring at that ugly Cross on which they hung me. The works that I have done in my Father's name testify to who I really am and what my Father intends and how he usually works. What I have done speaks louder than my many words. It will be the same for you. Don't just talk. Walk.

My Spirit is anxious to continue teaching you on my behalf. I'm providing you with select portions from the revealed Word of God and from a particular tradition of my church with wisdom you need. Read carefully and continue listening closely to my Spirit who will guide your minds and hearts to understand properly and apply effectively.

C. Light from the Revealed Word

1. Psalm 23. Sheep were common and shepherds essential in the biblical world. How natural that we humans are thought of as lost sheep and God as the guiding and protective divine Shepherd. We often are lost wanderers in this world. We long for a good shepherd who will come to us, show us the way to food, water, rest, safety, and home at the end of the day. Here's the biblical good news. The Word of God walks right into our lives and acts on our behalf, with this unspeakably wonderful result:

> Goodness and mercy all my life
> Shall surely follow me;
> And in God's house for evermore
> My dwelling place shall be.

With these assuring words ringing in our ears, we as God's people should be able to walk with confidence, even through valleys of dark and threatening shadows. There is a blessed home for us and One who knows the way. Rabbi Jesus said, "I *am* the way" (Jn. 14:6).

2. Acts 9:36-43. The Aramaic "Tabitha" identifies her as a Jew, and the Greek "Dorcas" indicates that she lived among Gentiles in Greek-speaking Joppa. Thus, Tabitha/Dorcas is an example of a recurring theme in the Luke–Acts writings. It's about the spread of the gospel of Christ from its origins in Judaism to its extension to Gentiles (everybody else), from one culture and religious heritage to many others. The salvation message of Jesus is to engage multiple cultures, languages, and peoples. Dorcas bears the distinction of being the only person in the New Testament specifically designated as a female disciple. She points us toward the whole world with good news.

A true disciple is a person, male or female, who follows Jesus out of the waters of baptism into lives directed by the Spirit of Rabbi Jesus. We must go to the world with a life of love that actively seeks engagement, bringing good news to those holding religious and political power, and doing so with words and acts of healing and reconciliation.

Dorcas had risen with Easter life to lead other disciples in attending to those most often neglected by society, but never forgotten by God. She was busy exercising a new version of power in which God uses what is lowly and despised in the world to bring to naught the things that are (1 Cor. 1:26–31). Dorcas was a seamstress who clothed others. She was a model disciple who walked redemptively, bringing a ring of reality to her loving words.

3. Revelation 7:9-17. The image of the great multitude seen in heaven reminds us that people of "all tribes and peoples and languages" (vss. 7:9, 14) will participate in God's ultimate victory. The white-robed and highly diverse multitude is bound together by their faithful witness while on this earth. We are invited and should be able to rise up and serve selflessly now because, in the end, God will wipe away every tear from our eyes (vs. 17).

This world, in all its fallenness, is a maze of fences and walls—and resulting hatred and wars. The world to come, by contrast, will involve an amazing crowd of diversity, wholeness, and togetherness made possible only by the sheer grace of the redeeming love of God. Those desiring to be part of that coming great multitude are to be working now on its behalf. May our mouths, feet, and hands celebrate the Christ together. May we do so in ways that cause walls to crumble, encouraging others to gladly join us.

D. Reflections of Leaders of the Wesleyan-Holiness Tradition

The actions of our lives must reflect faithfully the righteousness of our Lord. May God's will on earth be done, in part through our reconciling work. May God sanctify all our actions, increasing our hunger for Christ-likeness. We are called to be "perfect," reflecting the holiness of God. There's a word that needs defined with special care.

This is the name by which Jesus will be called: "The Lord our righteousness." Here's a truth which enters deep into the nature of Christianity and supports the whole frame of it. The Christian church stands or falls with it. It is certainly the pillar and ground of that faith from which alone comes salvation, the ground of that universal faith which is found in all the children of God. Unless a person keeps it whole and undefiled, he shall, without doubt, perish everlastingly.[1]

> Father, Son, and Holy Ghost,
> One in Three, and Three in One,
> As by the celestial host,
> Let Thy will on earth be done;
> Praise by all to Thee be given,
> Glorious Lord of earth and heaven!
>
> If so poor a worm as I
> May to Thy great glory live,
> All my actions sanctify,
> All my words and thoughts receive.
> Claim me for Thy service, claim
> All I have, and all I am.[2]

Once God's cleansing and energizing are accomplished, I will have an abiding hunger for Christ-likeness. This thirst will drive me onward toward the perfect example of Jesus Christ. I will experience ever-increasing joy, fellowship with other believers, love for the lost, a deep-settled peace in my heart, and a new energy for evangelism and involvement in the lives of others. God will continue to work in my life, conforming me to the image of His Son--in patience, gentleness, humility, satisfaction, meekness, mercy, and love. This is what God does in entire sanctification--purity from disobedience and power for service.[3]

John and Charles Wesley never disagreed on the importance of preaching holiness, but did disagree on whether or not the experience is an instantaneous crisis moment or a process that entails time and suffering. John worried that Charles set the standard of holiness too high, making it impossible for anyone to attain. Charles worried that it was too easy with his brother for some to profess holiness without showing evidence of the fruit of the Spirit. They each allowed for crisis and process, but with different emphases. John believed in a "perfecting perfection," a holiness experienced in a dynamic and not static sense. True holiness necessarily yields the fruit of the Spirit. The word "perfection" must escape the abstract and by God's grace walk lovingly in real life.[4]

---

1. John Wesley, *The Lord Our Righteousness*.
2. Charles Wesley, "Father, Son, and Holy Ghost."
3. Keith Drury, *Holiness for Ordinary People*.
4. Laurence W. Wood, *Pentecost and Sanctification in the Writings of John and Charles Wesley*.

WEEK 28

MULTIPLE SETTINGS, SINGLE MESSAGE

The law of love is more fundamental than the love of law. Don't rules exist to be followed? Yes, and no. God's purposes and expectations often extend beyond the horizon of longstanding and cherished human traditions, sometimes even beyond revered religious rules and supposed fixed laws of God. We expect our particular standards and processes to be honored by everyone, and we're inclined to judge harshly when they aren't, even if they don't fit new circumstances. It's especially hard to rethink the requirements of a revered holiness lifestyle, for instance, even though often it's obvious that various life restrictions are quite culture-bound and should not be thought of as universally binding.

The church must not hinder the movement of God by its obsession with what always has been and is locally thought best. It must open itself to celebrate what yet can be by the power of the Holy Spirit. Christian faith is conceived and lived out in varying ways in multiple settings. Cultural expressions, theological explorations, and worship practices are widely diverse across the expanse of the universal church. People faithfully following Rabbi Jesus don't always look and act exactly alike. Even so, there remains only one message. A huge church challenge in any time is finding and focusing on that unifying message in the midst of distracting diversities.

A. Prayer

God, you know that I love and intend to retain my particular home, language, church tradition, and familiar ways of understanding and practicing the faith. I know I'm very human. What's most familiar I tend to see as most precious and clearly right. But I know that such thinking is good and bad. It's bad when I devalue others in the church who also follow Christ but differ from me in some practical ways. I sometimes act against them while not even knowing them. Forgive me for my narrowness and unfairness to many of your loved people. Expand my heart to look and act more like yours. Soften my heart and broaden my view. Help me to focus more on the one message of saving love.

B. The Voice of Rabbi Jesus: John 13:31–35

> Love one another and people will recognize that you are my disciples. They might not like it, but they'll be amazed and at least know. Don't count them out just because they're different and may even oppose you. Love, forgive, and when necessary just move on. As you go, remember that your ways of thinking and doing things may not fit everyone as you wish they should. Relax in my love. Be flexible to the moving of my Spirit. Travel light and stay loose.

My special disciple John saw "a new heaven and a new earth" and heard my Father seated on the heavenly throne saying, "See, I am making all things new" (Rev. 21:5). The new commandment that I now give is to love and serve regardless of who it is and how different they may be, at least on the surface. You are to represent the freshness and flexibility and universal nature of God's new creation.

How are all things now being made new? By the presence and ministry of my Spirit. I am making it possible for you to love each other and even others with their many differences. All who are newly alive in me belong to you and you to them. Embrace them warmly and dare to think of their differences from you as enrichments and not threats to your fixed traditionalisms. This task is hard, I know, but my Spirit will enable it to be done if you will allow.

My Spirit is anxious to continue teaching you on my behalf. I'm providing you with select portions from the revealed Word of God and from a particular tradition of my church with wisdom you need. Read carefully and continue listening closely to my Spirit who will guide your minds and hearts to understand properly and apply effectively.

C. Light from the Revealed Word

1. Psalm 148. One can understand how a small tribe of people, seemingly under siege on all sides, might consider outsiders real enemies of God. Those thinking of themselves as "the chosen" can easily act harshly toward the "unchosen." Many stories in the Bible speak of what was understood to be divine mandates for the people of God, sometimes even calls to vanquish non-Jewish foes and claim their territory as God's gift to them. What is very clear in Scripture, however, is the announcement of the ever-expanding reach of God's steadfast love and mercy, stretching beyond the assumed "chosen."

At the end of this psalm is mention of Israel in particular: "He has raised up a horn for his people, praise for all his faithful, for the people of Israel who are close to him." While God's support of Israel anchors the end of the psalm, the vastness of God's concern and love makes up its bulk. God has his chosen, but they are chosen less for special privileges and more for a special mission, spreading the good news of the universal love of God who offers redemption equally to all.

There is one message—all is to offer praise to God. There are multiple settings for doing this, the moon and stars, depths of the seas, fields of cattle, forests of trees, and all the people of earth--nations, neighborhoods, cultures, friends and enemies. The challenge is never allowing the many settings to distract from focus on the single message. Here is only one God to be praised.

2. Acts 11:1–18. Peter is summoned to Jerusalem and not greeted with a parade to celebrate his faithful discipleship of Rabbi Jesus. Critics were waiting and claiming that his acts of healing and hope had evolved from a flawed and failed disciple who had denied Jesus three times (Lk. 22:61). Peter also was greeted with condemnation for something else, denying certain fundamentals of his Jewish tradition by his daring to eat with the uncircumcised Cornelius and his household. Surely, some fellow Jews were insisting, none can be a true Jesus follower without also being true to the many demands of the Jewish heritage.

This charge is nearly identical to the one leveled at Jesus when he shared table fellowship with those considered ritually unclean (Lk. 5:29-30). Peter's accusers viewed faith in Jesus as little more than a current subset of Jewish tradition. The bigger vision of Peter was challenging the newly forming church to expand its understanding of who belongs in the scope of the loving outreach of God. It was an understanding that was welcoming to the church not only Gentiles but women on equal footing.

Many Jewish people who now were followers of Jesus were having to rethink the importance of certain requirements for their traditional definition of holiness. Some life restrictions long held dear apparently had to be let go. God had given even the Gentiles "the repentance that leads to life" (vs. 18), and without the necessity of circumcision. It's humbling to have God show us that our love of the law, at least our version of the law, has become stronger than our commitment to the law of love.

3. Revelation 21:1–6. The Book of Revelation was written in the wake of Jerusalem's destruction by the Romans only a generation or so after the earthly life of Jesus. It dramatizes how apparently powerless believers can survive and even conquer Rome through their faithful witness, generous love, and enduring patience. The sea is portrayed as the abyss from which a dragon arises to torment the earth. Affirming the absence of the sea is seen here as a way of announcing a new creation without separations and exiles.

This sea-less city provides a unifying vision that compels disciples of Rabbi Jesus to understand freshly the one new people of God. They are a single redeemed people who come from many places and bring with them much diversity. The deep and divisive seas of race, nation, economics, culture, and language continue to torment us humans now, tempting us to live on isolated islands, in spiritual and intellectual ghettos of the faith. But the true church of Jesus is more than a select circle of like-looking and like-minded people. It's the one, complex, and yet united and rejoicing family of God.

D. Reflections of Leaders of the Wesleyan-Holiness Tradition

The ultimate law of God is the royal law of love. Because of this law, even the vilest offender can receive the gift of God's grace. The world will be impressed only by seeing our unity as disciples of Rabbi Jesus. The love of God is our unity, whatever our diversity. John Wesley and John Calvin shared the same gospel, but differed at least in emphases.

What law do we establish by faith? Not the ritual law; not the ceremonial law of Moses. By no means; but the great, unchangeable law of love, the holy love of God and of our neighbor.[1]

> Thy faithfulness, Lord, Each moment we find,
> So true to Thy word, So loving and kind!
> Thy mercy so tender, To all the lost race,
> The vilest offender may turn and find grace.
>
> The mercy I feel, to others I show,
> I set to my seal that Jesus is true:
> Ye all may find favor who come at his call,
> O come to my Savior, His grace is for all![2]

The common denominator is a clean heart filled with love for Christ and for each other. There is a profession of holiness that causes cleavage among good people. There is an experience of entire sanctification that promotes fellowship and unity among those of like precious faith. Only the latter can cause the world to believe.[3]

I appeal to those in the Wesleyan-Holiness and Pentecostal traditions to embrace the heart of both of our movements, namely the quest for love's knowledge. John Wesley understood love as the unifying force and life-giving energy of the Christian life. It's a knowing which is not a grasping but a letting go, a knowing that is not grounded in its own self-presence but in the presence of the source of all knowledge. Love's knowledge is relational.[4]

John Wesley and John Calvin both claimed to be biblical, but interpreted crucial parts of the Bible somewhat differently. Calvin conceived of the Christian faith more in terms of intellectual excellence, truth, and doctrine, whereas Wesley conceived of the faith more in terms of relational excellence, love, and empowerment. This does not mean either was unconcerned with the emphases of the other. It's just that Wesley was more relational in orientation than was Calvin, more focused on *orthokardia* (right hearts).[5]

---

1. John Wesley, *Justification by Faith*.
2. Charles Wesley, "Thy Faithfulness, Lord."
3. R. B. Acheson, in the *Herald of Holiness*.
4. Cheryl Bridges Johns, in the *Wesleyan Theological Journal*.
5. Don Thorsen, *Calvin vs Wesley*.

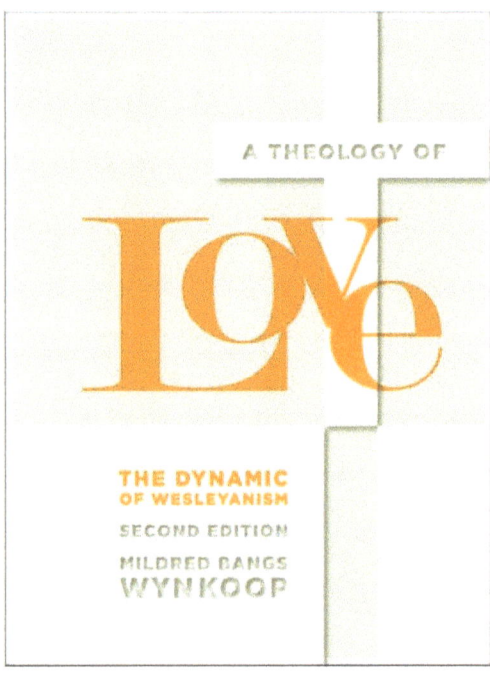

WEEK 29

ASCENSION OF THE LORD

GONE BUT NEVER ABSENT!

When a loved one dies, we tend to lose nearly all but our precious memories. We grieve the great loss and cling to the memories. However, when Jesus left this world things weren't limited to memories alone. He left and *is still here*!

The ascension of Jesus following his resurrection is less about his going *from* this world and more about our going *into it* well prepared because of his continuing presence. What we were promised at his departure was his ongoing presence and power in the midst of the church's urgent mission.

Jesus leaves, and remains, and we begin, but not alone. God sent his Son Jesus; now Jesus has left us his Spirit. We have become his body, his hands and feet traveling this world fulfilling our responsibility for doing the ongoing work of Rabbi Jesus. But we can't do it alone, and there's no need to even try. *We aren't alone!* Jesus directed that we wait on his Spirit to come and fill our very beings, set them spiritually afire, and thus accompany and enable us as we go.

A. Prayer

How hard it must have been, Lord, for those first disciples. Once you were resurrected and back with them briefly, you announced that you would be leaving again, and very soon. Terrible news it was! I confess, my God, that many days seem like you're distant from me, gone away again, leaving an awful emptiness behind. I need more than memories of you being with me once if I'm to engage your world-changing mission. Help me, Rabbi Jesus, to realize that, although you are gone physically, you actually are more present with me and your people than ever before. Fill me with your ever-present and all-satisfying and wonderfully-enabling Spirit. Otherwise, I know I'm facing failure.

B. The Voice of Rabbi Jesus

> Yes, as my disciples you are to go into all the world, but first it's Important that you stay put. Don't attempt your assigned mission until you are equipped with power from on high. You'll never make it on your own, and you need never be left alone on the frontlines of my kingdom work. Only go after you have been filled and infused and empowered by my Spirit. Hear this well. Without my Spirit, only frustration and failure will follow. Kingdom work requires kingdom gifts, and my Spirit is the essential Gift and gift giver in the kingdom of God.

My ascension marked the critical hinge-point in my Father's mission of restoring a broken world through my earthly life, teachings, resurrection, and now coming of my Spirit. My Spirit's arrival both consummates my earthly ministry and commences an expanded phase of my mission to all nations in all times. It's now to be happening through my Spirit-infused followers. The Spirit comes to birth the church and enable its true life and mission.

First, the divine mission was through my physical presence and sac-rificial work. Now it's to be through you, my faithful and Spirit-filled disciples. The Spirit enabled my very birth and now is anxious to birth in you the will and means to continue fulfilling my ongoing mission until I come again. I may be gone from you in a physical sense, but never will I be absent from you—never! It's so important that this be understood as you begin your own ministries in my name. My Spirit is anxious to continue teaching you on my behalf. I'm providing you with select portions from the revealed Word of God and from a particular tradition of my church with wisdom you need.

Read carefully and continue listening closely to my Spirit who will guide your minds and hearts to understand properly and apply effectively.

C. Light from the Revealed Word

1. Psalm 93. The amazing scene displayed here is a royal coronation, a kingly enthronement. It's hardly like the occasional pageant in England when a new king or queen is formally installed, with cameras allowing the world to watch. This is an ascension to the throne of God with only a few watching and no cameras available. As opposed to the world's kings and queens, this enthronement is to be forever stable, eternal, without limits on the peoples ruled or the power available to be exercised. God is enthroned as the universal, only, and eternal sovereign of all creation!

The celebration of the ascension of Jesus to the heavenly throne with his Father is not mostly about getting the physical body of Jesus out of this world. It's especially about God assuming rightful, term-less, and universal rule, with Rabbi Jesus at his right hand. All kings are under his feet (Eph. 1:22) and there will be the absolute and unending rule of mercy, compassion, and forgiveness.

This is a song worth hearing and singing in all generations as we humans gaze into the night skies. The Lord continues to reign and is robed in majesty. Nothing will ever cause him to be absent or asleep or overcome by some competitor. Even the floods will lift up their voices and the waves of the sea will thunder forth, but neither will ever overwhelm or silence the God most high.

2. Acts 1:1-11. The Book of Acts recounts actions of God in and through the early church. The ascension of Jesus is now over and the Spirit of Jesus has come. Once accepted and followed, God's Spirit is now functioning with a powerful presence that enables faithful followers of Jesus to turn the world right-side up. Jesus, gone, is very much present and even promising to come again. Meanwhile, his church, through his Spirit, has begun to impact the world on behalf of the arriving and still coming kingdom of God.

Faith too often is represented as bringing full clarity about God's activity—where God is located and exactly what God is up to in our confusing world. These opening verses of Acts remind us that a deeper faith requires trust in God's commitment to us precisely when we are confused about where God is located and uncertain about exactly what God is doing. What Jesus promises, and that for which we must wait, is the infilling of his Spirit. All questions won't be answered, but going out to represent God without at least the infilling and enabling of the Spirit is a strategy for church disaster.

Disciples often become discouraged and spend too much time waiting passively for the dramatic return of Jesus. Again, the ascension of Jesus is less about his departure and more a commission for us disciples to become accountable for the work that yet needs done by his remaining body, the church. The ascension is not so much an account of Jesus' departure as a confirmation of his power that now is present to accompany the church as it witnesses in his name, echoing the voice of his Spirit. Jesus will return—and *already has in his Spirit*. We are to wait patiently and work compassionately as we anticipate the ultimate coming again to conclude all history.

3. Ephesians 1:15-23. While Jesus may have departed, his Father has gifted the church now left behind. The eyes of the church are to be open to see certain things. One is quite paradoxical. God wins by losing. Paul was experiencing Christ's triumph even while preaching as a shamed prisoner (3:2-13). Carpenter Jesus had turned the wood of his ugly cross into a symbol of love and salvation that already was shaking the whole world. The loss of the death of Jesus was being swallowed by the victory vibrating in the life of his early church.

A second and related thing for the church to see is the divine definition of success. The world enjoys its momentary triumphs as triumphalisms. That is, when it wins, it gloats and happily takes all the marbles home. The church, on the contrary, is to embody God's higher way. We are to readily give up any spoils of victory because we understand that the victory is the triumph of God's Spirit, only in part accomplished through our modest efforts.

God calls the church to the counter-intuitive practices of love and service in order for it to experience God's victory in Christ through the Spirit. We will win most by giving ourselves away in love.

D. Reflections of Leaders of the Wesleyan-Holiness Tradition

Although we have seen Jesus rise beyond the skies to his native heaven, he remains with us in his Spirit to provide all we need to be the body of Christ on mission in a still-lost world. The resurrection was the inauguration of the kingdom of God and the ascension the King's enthronement.

And thus to believe in God implies to trust in Him as our strength, without whom we can do nothing, who every moment endues us with power from on high, without which it is impossible to please Him. God is our help, our only help in time of trouble, who compasses us about with songs of deliverance as our shield, our defender, and the lifter up of our head above all our enemies that are round about us.[1]

> Hail the day that sees him rise,
> Ravished from our wishful eyes!
> Christ, awhile to mortals given,
> Reascends his native heaven.
>
> Grant, though parted from our sight,
> High above yon azure height,
> Grant our hearts may thither rise,
> Following Thee beyond the skies.[2]

There is an enduement of power that comes with this filling of the Holy Spirit which Jesus wishes us to have, and which we all ought to covet for the sake of the progress of the kingdom. Power for service is the need of the hour. A lamentable weakness is the one painful universal characteristic of the church of God in our day. There is but one remedy, "Ye shall have power after that the Holy Ghost is come upon you." This

Spirit-baptism will not make all believers evangelists, but it would make all witnesses influential for Christ in the field where God has called each to live and work.[3]

The resurrection of Jesus was the validation that God's history-long plan to redeem the world through Israel had reached its climax. The new creation had begun, the age to come had dawned. The ascension of Jesus was the enthronement of the King following his conquest of evil and the inauguration of God's kingdom.[4]

---

1. John Wesley, *Our Lord's Sermon on the Mount.*
2. Charles Wesley, "Hail the Day that Sees Him Rise."
3. A. M. Hills, *Holiness and Power.*
4. H. Ray Dunning, *Biblical Heights for Today's Valleys.*

LOOK BOTH WAYS BEFORE CROSSING!

The final Sunday of the Easter season comes just before Pentecost. It's a great pivot time in the life of the church. We are called both to look back to the resurrection of Christ and forward to the gift of the Spirit to the church. We who belong to Rabbi Jesus are being commissioned to move from the high drama of yesterday and to the bold entering into today's world with truly good news. Before we do enter, however, we had better look both ways.

The double view involves remembering, looking back, always rejoicing in the resurrection of Jesus, and looking forward, receiving the ongoing presence of the Spirit of the resurrected one. Jesus became dramatically alive again in the first century. Through his eternal Spirit, he now remains alive in the twenty-first. Look back and never forget. Look forward and never fear because the Spirit of Jesus is here!

A. Prayer

I cross many dangerous roadways each week. Help me, O God, to be appropriately cautious, and not only for my personal safety. I realize that I must look both ways in my spiritual life and ministry as a disciple of Rabbi Jesus. I always must be looking back to the source, Yourself in the person of Jesus, and forward to the divine mission in the presence and power of your Spirit. To lose track of either the foundation of yesterday or the resources and responsibilities of today is to invite disaster. Help me to pay dual attention at all times. I'm not very good at this multiple task. Seeing in only one direction, I know, is to be dangerously blind. How I want and need to be a double-direction disciple.

B. The Voice of Rabbi Jesus: John 17:20-26

> There's a crucial mandate facing my church. You are to attend to your own oneness in my love, and only then address the broken world in a way it can believe. As I am one with my Father, may you be one with each other because of the wonderful ministry of my gifting and unifying and sending Spirit. You disciples are very different from each other. Nonetheless, don't allow that to fragment your fellowship. Your differences must become a resource for mission and not an obstacle to the life of my church. That transformation can only happen through the blending miracle of my richly relational Spirit.

Everything critical in the life of my church is born and should hold together in ways reflective of the relationship between myself and my Father. As we are one, may my church become one. You will be one with each other only as you are all living truly *in me*. Your common relationships with me are what make you a spiritual family together.

Face it, my friends. My disciples will never all see alike on everything or be organized into a single earthly institution. What you must do is *be* alike as serious children of God. I'll say it again. Your necessary unity resides in your common relationships with me. There always will be considerable variety among you. That variety must not be allowed to divide you from each other in ways that will appear scandalous in the eyes of those to whom you seek to witness on my behalf. Look both ways, first to assuring the unity my Spirit seeks to enable among you, and then to the broken and divided world that hungers for such loving unity, something it cannot achieve on its own.

My Spirit is anxious to continue teaching you on my behalf. I'm providing you with select portions from the revealed Word of God and from a particular tradition of my church with wisdom you need. Read carefully and continue listening closely to my Spirit who will guide your minds and hearts to understand properly and apply effectively.

C. Light from the Revealed Word

1. Psalm 97. This is one of the enthronement psalms that proclaims God as King. The first section features the grand appearance of God. All peoples and even the heavens respond in jubilant affirmation. The final section extends to readers of all generations the invitation to join the joyful occasion. The response to God's appearance must involve a celebration of God's majesty. It must include an ongoing determination to strive for righteousness and justice in the earth.

Verse seven recognizes the existence of some persons who don't acknowledge God's sovereignty. They report that such persons will "be put to shame." The call is for people of faith to embody and enact God's intent for righteousness and justice. We are to look back to the enthronement, be amazed and convinced and empowered, and then proceed forward to being God's dedicated and unified agents in this world.

2. Acts 16:16:34. The Book of Acts almost turns into an action movie, minus the fiction of course. There are prison breaks, shipwrecks, dramatic escapes, and a snake leaping from a fire. We are brought to the colonial city of Philippi and given a rollicking account of healing, persecution, and liberation. Paul and Silas exorcize a pagan sibyl, thus lessening the livelihood of an enslaved woman's owners. The liberating power of Christ had disrupted their dirty little enterprise and the agents of Rabbi Jesus would pay a high price.

The gospel of the Risen Christ sometimes is a disruptive force, and not in ways that some merchants of the world can easily embrace or will long tolerate. The disruptive effect may be more subtle than guns and bombs, although it's no less powerful in the long run. The gospel of Jesus exposes injustice. It makes clear the folly of imperial systems. It does not tear down evil empires with violence but announces that such empires already are teetering at the edge of self-destruction.

Disciples of Jesus should look two ways. First they should look to their own need of salvation and then to the defective social systems around them that enslave people with unjust policies and practices. Fear is the main tool of powers and principalities—the fear of suffering and death for all who dare oppose. This is why a resurrection proclamation is so threatening to human empires. When the fear of humiliation and even death no longer hold sway and dictate our actions, disciples of Rabbi Jesus are free to confront and challenge.

3. Revelation 22:12-21. It's the Easter season, the time of the Christian year when the church lives in the shadow of God's recent victory over death. We continue to celebrate this victory properly only when we look back on that day of triumph and then refuse to stop there. We also must dare to look ahead to the day when God will complete this victory by making all things new at the return of Christ.

But such forward looking must not be a passive and unproductive waiting. We are called to be active agents of God's justice and righteousness *in the meantime*. The final verses of the Book of Revelation close the Bible with a dramatic note of hopeful anticipation. Rabbi Jesus announces that he will be returning as promised. Disciples naturally react with a joyous "Come soon!" Meanwhile, it's assumed that our world mission will continue. Announced is the assurance that the sustaining grace of God will be with all the saints throughout all the days to the end of the age. Hallelujah!

D. Reflections of Leaders of the Wesleyan-Holiness Tradition

The difficult challenge is to be double-direction disciples. The whole gospel of Christ requires both affirming all that Rabbi Jesus has accomplished and serving the present age in his name. One day we will have a "strict account to give." God's tomorrow, therefore, calls us to God's business today. Th double direction for disciples involves looking back to the sacrifice of Jesus and forward to the gift of the present ministry and power of the Spirit of Jesus.

Christian faith is then not only an assent to the whole gospel of Christ, but also a full reliance on the blood of Christ, a trust in the merits of His life, death, and resurrection. It's a reliance upon Him as our atonement and our life, as given for us and now living in us. And, in consequence of this, it's a cleaving to Him as our wisdom and righteousness and sanctification and redemption, or, in one word, our salvation.[1]

> A charge to keep I have,
> A God to glorify,
> A never-dying soul to save, And
> fit it for the sky.
>
> To serve the present age,
> My calling to fulfill:
> O may it all my powers engage To
> do my Master's will![2]

To be overly preoccupied with the future at the expense of the present is to replace discipleship with dreaming. God, the source of all hope, also is the source of the commission for believers to go into all the world as redemptive forerunners of the future that already is breaking into the present, first through the life, death, and resurrection of Jesus, and now through the ministry of the Spirit of Christ and the faithfulness of the people of Christ, the church. To be with God *tomorrow* requires being about God's business *today*![3]

Christ overcomes the judgment that keeps flesh from the sanctifying work of the Spirit. He overcomes this fire in order to open a path to the Spirit for all flesh. Christ's exaltation as Lord is his ultimate victory, and his first act of lordship is the pouring forth of the Spirit upon all flesh (Acts 2:32-36). He overcomes the reign of sin and death so as to impart life. The Messiah who bears the Spirit becomes the Lord who imparts the Spirit. Christ's atonement has its victory in this wholeness of flesh and Spirit, which leads to the renewed community that witnesses to

Christ in the world through the power of the Spirit, who gives all glory to the heavenly Father.[4]

---

1. John Wesley, *Justification by Faith.*
2. Charles Wesley, "A Charge to Keep I Have."
3. Barry L. Callen, *Faithful in the Meantime.*
4. Frank Macchia, *Religions* (journal, 2017).

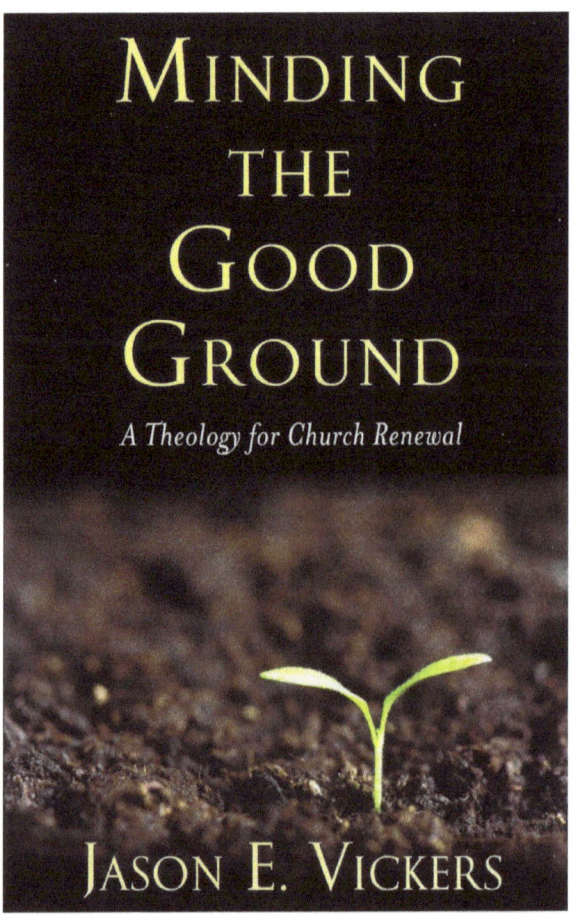

WEEK 31

Pentecost

BUILDING GOD'S TOWER

The Bible reports that once there was Babel, a tower of human pride and ambition (Gen. 11). Now under construction is a tower of God's Spirit, the church of God's reconciliation and love. It's to be a towering and unifying community that rises above all narrow tribes, nations, and denominations, blending believers together in one redeemed family worldwide. It's being built by the loving Spirit of God who unites rather than discriminates, isolates, and divides. God is building a community that gladly embraces all people who are embraced by God and accept his redeeming grace.

Out of many is emerging an amazing oneness. It's an inclusive rather than exclusive community. We call it the church. It defies human tribalistic tendencies and can be erected only by the initiative and unifying grace of God. Following the Risen Jesus faithfully involves disciples gladly belonging to this new community of his Spirit. Discipleship is based on active membership in this new body of people. They are being called to help change the world by replacing the old Babel tower. Members of the family of Rabbi Jesus are to be willing builders of the tower of love, this family of God. Pentecost celebrates the dynamic, the Spirit, who makes it all possible.

A. Prayer

I know that my daily attitudes and actions are constructing who I really am becoming. I so want to be in line with what you, my God, are all about and intend for me. I know that you are forming, gifting, uniting, and sending out a new people, the disciples of Rabbi Jesus. Together we are to be his new body, his gracious tower gleaming with fresh human possibilities. We are to be representing him by thinking and acting like him, and doing it together. Holy Father, I want to be holy as a reflection of you, a new creation of your Spirit, a true disciple of Jesus, a real member of your forming church. Please come to me and make it so! There's no way I can do this on my own.

B. The Voice of Rabbi Jesus: John 14:8–27

> The Father who resides in me and I in him is prepared to craft each of your words of witness into a divine act of revelation and blessing. The result of your faithfulness, and that of your fellow believers for ages to come, will be my church in action, a new tower of joy to bless the world. Can you see this big picture? Are you willing to be an instrument of such miraculous divine construction? My Father is building a bastion of love and you are called to be both blocks and builders. This construction is being founded on solid rock and thus will never be overcome by evil.

My Spirit's presence will make possible through you the same works that I accomplished. Indeed, through my Spirit you will do even "greater works than these" (v. 12). My earthly ministry was geographically and temporally limited, but you and the many soon to be with you are the growing community of believers who will continue to have the gifting and guidance of my gracious Spirit worldwide and in all times. That means that my Father's "wind," "breath," his very life will be blowing on and flowing through you. That life-creating and church-building breath is everywhere present and uncontrollable, sensed rather than seen, basic to your very lives as my disciples.

Don't stick your necks into this troubled world until you are prepared to be instruments of my Spirit. Be sure you are in my church before you attempt to represent it. Once in, my Spirit will teach you all necessary truth, advocate for you, and distinguish you from the world. The Spirit will build you into a very different kind of person in a very special community, making you holy ones, carriers of restoring and unifying love.

My Spirit is anxious to continue teaching you on my behalf. I'm providing you with select portions from the revealed Word of God and from a particular tradition of my church with wisdom you need. Read carefully and continue listening closely to my Spirit who will guide your minds and hearts to understand properly and apply effectively.

C. Light from the Revealed Word

1. Psalm 104:24-35. This is a creation psalm. We confess as we sing that the Spirit of God continually creates, bringing order out of chaos, enabling unity without destroying the richness of diversity. The Spirit is responsible for the origin and maintenance of all creation. We humans seek peace, order, and happiness through self-help plans, attempts to manipulate the people and settings around us. We humans grab resources and build selfishly, with frustration and failure inevitably the result.

The only real truth and hope lie in the wonder and mystery of the divine Presence who alone can order, guide, and enrich all that we ever hope will be or construct. God builds on, now constructing a community of love called the church, the body of Christ. God's the great builder, stretching out the heavens like a tent, laying the beams of his chamber on the waters, setting the earth on its foundations, and replacing the Babel tower of humans with one filled with the life and love of his Spirit.

2. Genesis 11:1–9. The building of the old tower was an act of foolish pride by an arrogant and seriously in-grown community of fallen humans. Their possession of one language and unified identity was motivated by a selfish ambition that finally brought God's intervention.

When walled together selfishly, insiders are privileged and outsiders demonized. Unfortunately, humans tend to have a tribal mentality that lives by discrimination. The assumption is that we are special, "they" are not, little more than a threat to be eliminated. God finally judges such arrogance by scattering the towered people into a chaotic multiplicity—diverse locations, languages, cultures, races, etc. They no longer communicate well with each other or successfully build anything together.

For Christians, Pentecost is a celebration of the *great reversal*. The new construction does not repeat the negative consequences of the old tower story. The new church resists retreating back into some monolingual, mono-cultural, one-superior-race community ideal. Rather, ethnic, linguistic, gender, and cultural differences are preserved, even treasured without community disruption. God delights in multiplicity, the richness of his creation.

What happens at Pentecost is that the Holy Spirit serves as the blending and binding agent. Each person is enabled to hear the good news of Christ and understand it in his or her own native tongue and cultural setting, and without devaluing the tongues and settings of others. We are enabled to become one family, the church, in the midst of all our differences. This surely is possible only by God's doing!

3. Acts 2:1–21; Romans 8:14–17. Jesus proclaimed in Nazareth that God's Spirit was upon him, launching a new creation. Pentecost is another outpouring of the same Spirit, this time not on Jesus alone but on his followers, the newly constituted church. It's an amazing new reality. Although the crowd in Jerusalem on that dramatic Pentecost day was from many nations, each person somehow heard and understood the gospel proclamation. God's intent is universal redemption, a tower of redeeming love, potentially the home for all humanity.

Paul explains that life "in the Spirit" and "led by the Spirit" is a fresh state of human existence in sharp contrast to living "according to the flesh" and "under the law." One role of the Spirit of Rabbi Jesus is building up the church, the body of Christ, the temple of God. The old Genesis tower was an edifice of pride and power. The new Spirit tower, the church, is to be a worldwide family of the redeemed offering true community for all people willing to join. In the church, all are to be led by the Spirit and gladly recognized and valued as loved children of God.

D. Reflections of Leaders of the Wesleyan-Holiness Tradition

God's creating again, forming the fallen into a community of the holy ones, calling ministers with holy motives. The goal is for us former sinners to be fully restored in God and reunited with each other, now graciously lost together in wonder, love, and praise. It all begins with experiencing the fire that falls in upper rooms where the humble are gathered and waiting on the Spirit's arrival. A special challenge is presented to church leaders.

Many of us are more immediately consecrated to God, called to minister in holy things. Are we ministers, then, examples to the rest "in word, in conduct, in love, in spirit, in faith, in purity"? (1 Tim. 4:12). Is there written on our foreheads and on our hearts, "Holiness to the Lord"? From what motives did we enter on this office? Was it indeed with a single eye "to serve God, trusting that we were inwardly moved by the Holy Spirit to take on us this ministry for the promoting of His glory and the edifying of His people"?[1]

> Finish then Thy new creation,
> Pure and spotless let us be;
> Let us see Thy great salvation,
> Perfectly restored in Thee.
>
> Changed from glory into glory,
> Till in heaven we take our place,
> Till we cast our crowns before Thee,
> Lost in wonder, love, and praise![2]

The "fellowship of the Holy Spirit" means that the relationship broken by sin is restored in the human heart by the ministry of the Holy Spirit, that every step in the revolution and restoration is in the interest of moral integrity, that it is Christ who is formed within under the Spirit's ministry, that in Christ personal purity is experienced, corporate unity of spirit is cemented, and the fellowship of His sufferings becomes a basis for the enjoyment of the fellowship in his glory. The doctrine of the Holy Spirit is not abstract but draws into relevance every thread of Christian theology.[3]

To be Pentecost people in the world requires first having been in an upper room where the fire fell and hearts were set ablaze. In the fire of the Spirit, mere religion dissolves, authentic spirituality emerges, and the true life of God shines forth. The good news is that Jesus Christ, having died on the cross and risen from the dead, dies no more. He now sits at the right hand of the Father and has become for us the life-giving Spirit (1 Cor. 15:45). Away with mere religion. Bring on the new life available in the Spirit of Jesus![4]

---

1. John Wesley, *Scriptural Christianity*.
2. Charles Wesley, "Lost in Wonder, Love and Praise!"
3. William Arthur, *The Tongues of Fire*.
4. Barry L. Callen, *Authentic Spirituality*.

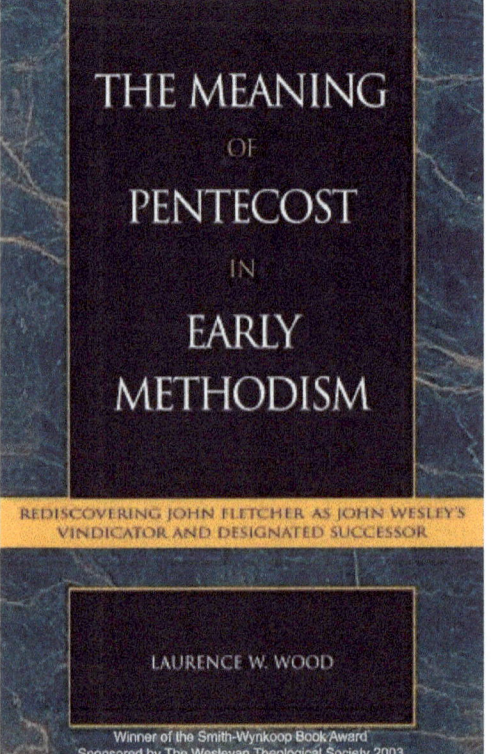

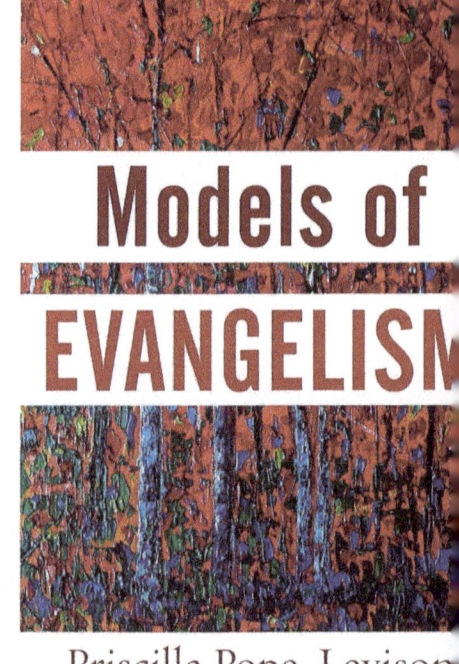

WEEK 32

Trinity Sunday

THE WISEST OF WOMEN

This is the only Sunday of the church year focused on a specific Christian doctrine. It's the Trinity of God. The well-known hymn "Holy, Holy, Holy" sings this truth with conviction and joy, "God in three persons, blessed Trinity." However, can God be three persons and still be one God? Why is the Trinity celebrated as so important in Christian faith when it appears contradictory?

This much is clear. In this case, our hearts can sing what our minds struggle to fully grasp. The Bible points to a woman who will teach us. She's said to be the wisest of all women, none other than the Spirit of Rabbi Jesus who is God remaining with us always as the great Teacher and Enabler. The Spirit, one "member" of the Trinity, is an extension of the Son who in turn is the full expression of the Father. The Spirit makes clear the Son even as the Son has made clear the Father.

Revealed to us by the Father is his true divine nature, amazing love, a marvelous truth known to us dependably only through the Son and now the ongoing ministry of the Spirit. Such is so basic theologically that it's judged worthy of being singled out for specific attention.

A. Prayer

Come, Holy Spirit. Be among me now and guide me into all that is true. Proclaim your good word so that I might glorify you fully and properly—Father, Son, and Holy Spirit. I admit that such a grand Trinity vision of God is too much for my limited mind. I'm sure that what you want for my understanding is possible only with your assistance. So please, help me know the true God in the Triune fullness. Then enable this understanding to inform all else I need to know so I can represent you properly in this world. And keep reminding me of this, something I've already learned. Intellectual understanding, while important, is never to replace experiencing your transforming grace and love. Becoming rightly related to you is critical to my rightly understanding you.

B. The Voice of Rabbi Jesus: John 16:12–15

> I have paved the way for you disciples to return forgiven to my Father. Now my Spirit will show you the way to a fuller understanding of my teachings and the best ways to go into this world as our redeemed representatives. The holy God wants to lead you as holy people into an unholy world to carry on my ministry of redemption. I, my Father, and now my Spirit are joining as one to prepare and send you. We are one from all eternity. Mirror us by being one with each other. And always know this. Apart from becoming holy yourselves, you never can really know my holy Father.

My beloved John bears witness to a deep union between the Father and myself (Jn. 14:10-11). Yet John was aware that the Son's return to the Father created a crisis for you disciples—the Son was now absent! That's what Pentecost is all about. If the Son's function is to reveal and glorify the Father, it now is the Spirit's role to reveal and glorify the Son, showing what belongs to the Son and what things are still to come. The Spirit interprets to you, my disciples, how I am "the way, and the truth, and the life" (Jn. 14:6), the only way that leads to my Father. My Spirit brings into your immediate experience the life transformation that my work has made possible.

The Gospel of John invites you to grasp the very being of my Father and live into my Father's future as my disciples. How? By being receivers of my Spirit. All will not be clear about the mystery of the Holy Trinity, a majesty exceeding human minds. No matter. The Spirit will encourage you to have fresh encounters with the revelation of the Father in the Son. You must be receptive to Spirit-guided growth in personal understanding and maturity. My church must not be locked into the limitations of the past but come to understand who I am and what I mean for its own time—and that's the work of my Spirit.

My Spirit is anxious to continue teaching you on my behalf. I'm providing you with select portions from the revealed Word of God and from a particular tradition of my church with wisdom you need. Read carefully and continue listening closely to my Spirit who will guide your minds and hearts to understand properly and apply effectively.

C. Light from the Revealed Word

1. Psalm 8. Psalm 8 is best read in response to Proverbs 8. There God is proclaimed by the wisest of women, personified Wisdom, the Creator and Sustainer of the universe. This psalm praises God for being the origin of all the creatures in the world, particularly human beings. It poses an obvious question. How can God, whose glory is set "above the heavens," whose fingers establish the moon and stars (vs. 3) in their places, be mindful of mere humanity on this one little planet (vs. 4)? Nothing but an amazing love could possibly be the answer. Jesus revealed that love and now his Spirit brings it alive for us in the present.

That answer of love is more wonderful than I can even imagine, unless God actually is filled with, in fact should be defined by amazing and reaching and restoring love. Such a breathtaking claim is the heart of the entire biblical revelation. The Spirit of God reaches across the creation and, through the Son, seeks lovingly to bring home to God the Father all who will.

2. Proverbs 8:1–31. Where do we go to find God? Or better, where in the world does God find us? How about in the wisest of women? Wisdom in the ultimate is personified as this wise woman who is said to be better than jewels and leads to life (8:35–36). Sister Wisdom tells us that God is reasonable and has created a rational world. When we humans order our lives accordingly, good things happen. We'll be walking in the right direction even if we haven't answers to all the hard questions of life in this troubled world. If we choose to go against the laws of God, the very order of things, we will do more than break God's laws; we will break ourselves on them. The laws will always stand.

The divine Spirit intends to teach us this. Jesus the Son is the "firstborn of all creation" and "before all things" (Col. 1:15–20). Who is God? Only a Trinity answer will do. The Father, yes, the Son, yes, and also the Spirit who conveys and activates this ultimate wisdom of triune reality. She, now present with us as divine wisdom, seeks to explain who God the Father is, reminds us of who Jesus the Son was and did in the flesh, helps us interpret the Bible correctly, and enables us finally to be all that the Triune God intends.

3. Romans 5:1–5. Today is Trinity Sunday, the first Sunday after Pentecost. It celebrates the current presence and work of God's Spirit. Paul gives assurance to the church in Rome that God's promises are fulfilled through Jesus' ministry, death, and resurrection, and now through the Holy Spirit of God. Christians live in peace with God because of Jesus Christ. Christians also know the love of God because the Holy Spirit is pouring into our hearts that love of God seen in Christ. There's the Trinity in action. It's more than a formal doctrine. It's to be a *lived experience* of all disciples of Rabbi Jesus.

Paul is explaining the way the Roman church should understand itself in relation to God and to the oppressive world it knew every day. Rather than hiding in the face of oppression, the church is to stand and even boast. It's to boast, not about itself, which would be silly and tragic, but only about the glory of the God on whom the church stands—the loving glory that raised Jesus Christ from the dead and, through the power of the Holy Spirit, now is being poured into the church (Rom. 5:5). The Spirit enables the church to be a community of memory and hope, one that knows truth's foundations and also is learning its current applications to all of life.

D. Reflections of Leaders of the Wesleyan-Holiness Tradition

The one God is finally known best in three. The Father's great mercy we see in Jesus. May we echo the eternal praise of the One who has given himself for us and now, through the Spirit, provides the needed power to do his holy will. Doctrine must be more than intellectualized religious ideas. In faith, we must take a "yes stance" that gladly affirms more than we can ever fully comprehend.

Above all, stand fast in obedient faith, faith in the God of pardoning mercy, in the God and Father of our Lord Jesus Christ who has loved you and given Himself for you. Ascribe to Him all the good you find in yourself: all your peace, and joy, and love and all your power to do and suffer His will, through the Spirit of the living God.[1]

> Holy, holy, holy Lord,
> God the Father, and the Word.
> God the Comforter, receive
> Blessings more than we can give!
> Mixed with those beyond the sky,
> Chanters to the Lord most high,
> We our hearts and voices raise,
> Echoing Thy eternal praise.[2]

Without the baptism with the Spirit renewing us in righteousness and true holiness, the doctrine of Christian perfection may be reduced to a "speculative, notional, airy shadow which lives in the head, not in the heart," as John Wesley once complained about William Law's mysticism. Only the Pentecostal power of the Holy Spirit of Christ can enable us to love God with all our hearts and our neighbor as ourselves, and to evangelize the world so that righteousness will cover the earth as waters cover the sea.[3]

The holiness of God's people rests in our decision to take the "yes stance" in our lives of faith. We say *yes* to the fullness of God in our lives, *yes* to the best possible use of God's ministry gifts we have received, *yes* to the fellowship and enrichment of other believers, *yes* to lives that nurture the well-being of God's creation, and *yes* to the hope that one day the full will of God will be accomplished here and here after.[4]

When we have finished our theologizing, we still shall not understand all mysteries. We are but human pilgrims following the pathways of knowledge, and to the end of the earthly way we shall still "know in part." And yet our faith in Jesus Christ our Lord can give us the *assurance* of things hoped for, the *conviction* of things not seen. And is that not, after all, the object of the quest?[5]

---

1. John Wesley, *Advice To a People Called Methodist.*
2. Charles Wesley, "The Trinity."
3. Laurence Wood, in *The Asbury Journal.*
4. Barry L. Callen, *The Prayer of Holiness-Hungry People.*
5. Georgia Harkness, *Foundations of Christian Knowledge.*

WEEK 33

Christian Life #1
SUNDAYS SHOULD BE SPECIAL

Just as the season of Epiphany transitions to Lent, spring is right around the corner. In the springtime, a wonderful transition occurs. What was once frozen, brown, and seemingly lifeless comes alive again. As the sun and rain come down and nourish seeds, so too God's Word reaches people of faith and remains until the time of their fruit-bearing.

We enter the spring season of the Christian year looking for the new growth, the fresh fruit. We thank God the Father for planting the seed in Christ and staying with us in the Spirit until we can mature toward the intended holiness and righteousness intended for the good of ourselves and the world.

Transformation is the doorway to eventual flourishing. Christ saves and we then are to serve. Such does not come automatically. The rhythm of the life patterns of the faithful is important to understand. Work and rest are equally necessary. Periods of fresh focus are required to stay on the proper action track. Regular worship brings needed perspective to daily challenges.

"Sabbath" is the biblical concept intended to bring into our lives of faith the required rhythm, rest, and periodic refocusing that release springtime and enable spiritual seeds to grow. Disciples of Rabbi Jesus mature spiritually and serve well only when regularly nurtured with necessary discipline and accountability. Sundays are the times of "practicing for heaven."

A. Prayer

Lord, I live my life in a hurry. I often hope for the best but don't hold still long enough to do the necessary planning. I'm committed to your service and only wish that I would spend more regular times that focus on growing in my faith, being with your Word, Spirit, and people. I'm finding that where I am and with whom I spend my time tends to shape me in wrong ways. Dear Lord, make me a Sabbath observer, not out of raw duty but out of sheer necessity. Your people have known the wisdom of this for many centuries. Enable me to know it for myself right now and actually do something about it. Teach me to really pray!

B. The Voice of Rabbi Jesus: Luke 6:39–49

> You will need to focus carefully as you face a difficult future in my service. It won't be easy to act lovingly and avoid crumbling under criticism. You'll need prayerful perspective and each other to survive. Worship my Father together and regularly. Frequently take the bread and cup I offer, ingesting insight and strength from my sacrifice for you. These are the symbols of me that will keep you from forgetting and losing your way. Make time for quietness so that you will be able to hear the gentle voice of my Father explaining the way ahead.

How should your enemies be treated? Punitive measures forced on the German nation by the victors after WWI partly fueled the dynamics that led to WWII. By contrast, the Allies' generous rebuilding programs on behalf of devastated societies in Germany and Japan after WWII aided in the rise of two of the stronger democracies and economies in the world today. Can you see the lesson there?

What am I saying to you dear disciples? Look ahead. Think carefully about the likely results of your actions. Act in love and not merely according to some set of traditional restrictions. Don't split hairs over how to observe the Sabbath. My enemies tried to trap me over such trivial things more than once. Be alive and flexible in my Spirit.

Know this. You need the rhythm of work, rest, and worship. Legalism is a danger. So is negligence. Of course, all days are holy periods when you are to be about my Father's business. However, a regular setting aside of one of them for discipline and accountability will keep you from being busy and not in close touch with my Father whom you are trying to represent.

My Spirit is anxious to continue teaching you on my behalf. I'm providing you with select portions from the revealed Word of God and from a particular tradition of my church with wisdom you need. Read carefully and continue listening closely to my Spirit who will guide your minds and hearts to understand properly and apply effectively.

C. Light from the Revealed Word

1. Psalm 92:1–15. This is a Sabbath song that often had to be sung in alien surroundings. It was the time of the great Exile. While the deportees were an ethnic minority group permitted to continue some of their religious practices, many Jews were being assimilated into the dominant Babylonian culture and losing their distinctive identity. Continued observance of the Sabbath was a way of constantly renewing that identity. It was a conscious remembering of what God had done for them and a deliberate hoping that God finally would enable them to return home.

The true spirit of Sabbath challenges God's children of all times to reflect carefully on their observance of what now is known as the "Lord's Day." It's not to be simply a weekly time of abstaining from work. It's the day of renewing the identity of believers by remembering God's promises and more fully preparing for the responsibilities of God's work. Failing to observe such periodic times of remembering, resting, and focusing invites the alien surroundings to take over and steal the distinctive identity of God's people.

2. Isaiah 55:10–13. We modern humans have become very aware of nature's unpredictability. Hundred-year droughts and floods now seem to come every couple of years. Tsunamis crash into subcontinents with little warning. New viruses show up and quickly bring destruction on human populations and national economies worldwide. The exiles to whom the prophecies of Isaiah were directed also knew that nature could surprise as well as soothe. Dust storms could blow up on the desert. Whirlwinds could break out in the forests. Droughts could go on for years. Fig trees could wither, and grapes dry and die on the vine.

The key metaphor here is the amazing effect of springtime's arrival. A time-lapse film can dramatize the first rivulets of water on dry land becoming a rushing river. The prophet celebrates this renewal process. Seeds long dormant split and send out roots. Insects and microorganisms long hidden burst forth from the ground. Plants attract birds that attract animals that attract more animals—and soon a place that was empty is teeming with life because of the rain that has watered the earth.

The "rain" of God's Word has gone out, announces Isaiah. Chapter 40 is full of calls to speak. "A voice says, 'Cry out!' And I said, 'What shall I cry'?" The answer: "Get you up to a high mountain, O Zion, herald of good tidings." Isaiah 55 moves on to the effects of this dramatic speech once uttered. The words of God's promise set in motion changes that reconfigured the entire cosmos. There is good news and much new-life potential. God's people must be attentive to this announcement and position themselves for assisting with its fulfillment. To skip regular Sabbaths could lead to weakness and distraction that allow a missing of the whole thing!

3. 1 Corinthians 15:51–58. There's hope because of the transformative power of the resurrection of Jesus and its promise for human flourishing, even beyond death. In the resurrection, the old life is gone; a new life of joy and peace begins. "Death has been swallowed up in victory." We hear echoes of Psalm 92. "The righteous flourish like the palm tree, and grow like a cedar in Lebanon" (vs. 12). "Lo, I tell you a mystery," announces Paul. Somewhere far from the shores of the conceivable lies the realm of resurrection. That which God created out of nothing was not created in vain. God will re-create by resurrecting from the dead.

This hope is amazing. "When the trumpet of the Lord shall sound, and time will be no more, and the morning breaks eternal, bright and fair," as the old hymn says, "I'll be there!" Paul, however, doesn't expect his readers to wait passively for God's transformation at the future resurrection. Instead, he encourages active participation in their own present transformation. "If anyone is in Christ, there is a new creation: everything old has passed away; see, everything has become new!" (vs. 5:17). Therefore, "Be steadfast, immovable, always excelling in the work of the Lord" (vs. 58).

Flourishing is now the order of the day, but it takes planning, focus, time, intentional action, and conscious togetherness as the church. Minus regular renewal Sabbaths, the possible flourishing likely won't happen at all.

D. Reflections of Leaders of the Wesleyan-Holiness Tradition

The grand spiritual goal is being set free for accomplishment as increasingly we are filled with the love of God. We must do our part to release within ourselves the "Spring of life." God's promise requires our participation of full surrender. Becoming "holy" is no automatic process. The growth road must be filled with many Sabbaths. We must be reminded regularly of the riches of the holiness tradition of Christian faith and determine to "practice for heaven."

I want that faith which none can have without knowing that he has it, for whoever has it is freed from sin; the whole body of sin is destroyed in him. He is freed from fear, having peace with God through Christ and rejoicing in hope of the glory of God. And he is freed from doubt, having "the love of God poured out in his heart through the Holy Spirit" which is given to him, which Spirit bears witness with his spirit that he is a child of God.[1]

> Holy Ghost, no more delay!
> Come, and in Thy temple stay!

> Now Thine inward witness bear,
> Strong, and permanent, and clear;
> Spring of life, Thyself impart,
> Rise eternal in my heart![2]

God wants to condition us for holy living. He wants to make us ready for life and labor in His will. God wants to work His purpose in us so that he can work out his purpose for us. Our responsibility is to give God our consent and steady cooperation. It is our privilege to have His help. It should be our longing to have His holiness. The promised life awaits only our full surrender.[3]

Too many Christians spend their time speculating about when Jesus will come again. They miss something of fundamental importance that enables holy lives in the meantime. At Pentecost, *Jesus already has come again!* The Spirit of Christ has come *to us* to be *in us* (experienced holi-ness) in order to move *through us* as ministering love to a broken world (expressed holiness).[4]

Too much congregational worship in the Wesleyan-Holiness tradition now takes its cues from consumer-oriented church marketing strategies. This risks the negative effects that such an approach can have on the memories, formation, and practices of the faith. One result is loss of the tradition's identity. A return to the historic liturgies of the church would create clearer church identity by bringing the whole of the Christian life into focus and regularly setting before the people their tradition's identity. The Wesleyan-Holiness tradition is worthy of retaining, being rich with images, symbols, and experiences of people who have longed to be made holy by God.[5]

---

1. John Wesley, *Journal*, 1738.
2. Charles Wesley, "Since the Son Hath Made Me Free."
3. James Earl Massey, *What Sanctification Means*.
4. Barry L. Callen, *Catch Your Breath! Exhaling Death and Inhaling Life*.
5. Steven Hoskins, in the *Wesleyan Theological Journal*, 1997.

WEEK 34

Christian Life #2

PLEASE, NOT ANOTHER HOLY WAR!

There's something we disciples of Rabbi Jesus must do, and do carefully. We must swear full allegiance to the one true God, and to none other, period. We must practice loyalty to God's kingdom in ways that avoid, whenever possible, starting another holy war! History tells us this will not be easy, just always important.

There are times when we who believe must stand for truth in the face of blatant untruth. When this becomes necessary there is a crucial choice to be made about how to be faithful. God alone is to be praised and followed. God also is the only one to make final judgments about others, those unbelievers and idolators who now oppose him and his people.

We are to praise God and share God's love with everyone, regardless of their idolatries and unacceptable demands on us. Meanwhile, we must be careful not to become idolators ourselves right in our churches. How easy it is to elevate personal thoughts and practices to the level of Christian truth. When we do, we usually insist that it must be believed by other disciples just as we believe.

The unquestionable truth is that we are to be in saving relationship with God through our faith in Jesus Christ, and in loving relationship with each other. Too often we make fateful judgments about others based on our beliefs. On occasion we even are willing to go to war to force dominance of our view. That's dangerous idolatry right in the house of God!

A. Prayer

What I believe about a range of things is very important to me, Lord. Of course I tend to judge others harshly if they disagree with me. Naturally I hate idolators, as I should (I think). They are the people who affirm something in place of you, the only true God. My harsh attitude toward them makes me aware of what I need. It's the humility and love necessary to leave judgment of idolators to you. It's also the grace to avoid becoming a "Christian idolator." Help me to keep the incidentals of my faith incidental, and to know what is incidental and what should be beyond question. This is hard and I need help. Dear Prince of Peace, help me stand for truth without starting another war!

B. The Voice of Rabbi Jesus: Luke 7:1-10

> This is a violent world in which to serve my kingdom of love and peace. Remember that I shouted at Peter to put down his sword. That was no way to win the Romans. My Father is all-powerful, and yet he is anything but a specialist in coercion. I expect you to honor and love all people, whatever their wrongness. You once were very much in the wrong yourselves and I came lovingly to you nonetheless. While I was handed a violent death for my efforts, in the long run I will triumph anyway. Be patient when suffering comes. Whenever you can, spread peace as loving reconcilers in this fractured world. Act like pieces of the solution and not obviously more of the problem.

The large theological question this Luke 7 story asks and answers is this. Can Gentiles have a place in the kingdom of my Father? The answer is clearly yes. The centurion has access to the kingdom because of his faith and nothing else. I healed the slave from a distance so that the faith of the centurion, who was outside the house of Israel, might be confirmed. I turned on its head the prevailing understanding of who was welcome at the table of God's grace.

Go and do likewise, my disciples, uncomfortable as that will be at times. The love of my Father is being extended to all people. No one is an outsider to the reach of my Father's love. Someone always will be thought of as a "Gentile," an unacceptable outsider. You must learn the lesson of love that refuses to think in this exclusive and even dangerous way. Spread love across the land, not war supposedly fought on my behalf.

My Spirit is anxious to continue teaching you on my behalf. I'm providing you with select portions from the revealed Word of God and from a particular tradition of my church with wisdom you need. Read carefully and continue listening closely to my Spirit who will guide your minds and hearts to understand properly and apply effectively.

C. Light from the Revealed Word

1. Psalm 96:1–10. There are thoughtful and spiritually sensitive people who don't orient their lives through worship of any presumed sovereign deity. They seek serenity and compassion through realization of who they are by gaining some spiritual connection with "all things." Their rituals and meditations are oriented to nothing but the attempted achievement of an elevated spiritual state, with no reference to God. They may resonate with this psalm's sense of human sharing with the rest of creation, but the note of God-praise isn't seen by them as necessary.

Granted, as the psalm assumes, all such "gods of the people are idols." How, then, should Christians relate to such "good" people who are sincerely committed to idols? Contact with people of differing faith perspectives is inevitable today. Inter-faith dialogue is a critical skill for international stability, let alone Christian evangelism. How can disciples of Rabbi Jesus profess belief in the one true God in a way that deals respectfully with those who believe otherwise? How does one say with conviction among the nations that "The LORD is King!" without starting the next holy war?

Since God "will judge the world with equity" (vs. 10), our encounters with "idolators" should be characterized more by sharing the joy we have found in the living Lord and less by our harsh judgments of their wrongness. We should love them toward the love of God, not stir their hate and fuel their likely retaliation.

2. 1 Kings 18:20-39. The conflict between Elijah and the many prophets of Baal echoes the comment in Psalm 96 that "all the gods of the people are idols." This vivid story is a scathing indictment of idolatry. Israel's God alone actually is God alive and working wonders. However we name our idols, they cannot save. Whenever we are faithful, right will win out.

It's imperative today that people of different faiths at least respect each other rather than embarrass or attack. So what do we do with this Elijah story and its theme of "let's prove that our God is better than your non-god"? Our violence-plagued world doesn't need people doing harm to each other because they feel their superior belief has been offended and retribution must follow. This critical issue now very much involves the relationships among Jews, Christians, Muslims, Hindus, atheists, immigrants, national borders, and so on.

Who do we welcome? What rules do we enforce, and how? Who deserves respect? To what extent must *they* become like *us* to be accepted? Does God need to be proved by us to others? It would seem that Jesus expects full allegiance to the truth he has revealed, and also a love even for our enemies, something central to that truth. How would the prophets of Baal been handled in his ministry?

3. Galatians 1:1–12. Paul was shocked and even aggressive. "I am astonished that you are so quickly deserting the One who called you in the grace of Christ and are turning to a different gospel—not that there is another gospel, but there are some who are confusing you and want to pervert the gospel of Christ" (vss. 6-7). Paul urges the Galatian Christians to ignore the false spiritual experts who were trying to claim their attention. (vss. 8-9). How should these false prophets be treated when rejected? Their false teaching certainly is to be exposed and not followed.

After the 9/11 terrorist attacks, Americans became more acutely aware of a world filled with religiously fueled fanatics. Hopefully, they also began to understand the need to make room for the honestly-held faith perspectives of others, while certainly not condoning or joining the violent intentions of a few, be they Muslim, Christian, or whatever.

There is urgent need for valuing tolerance of various worldviews in ways that result in increased sensitivity, humility, and respect for those different from ourselves. Insisting otherwise only incites holy wars that everyone will lose. Violence surely is not the way to advance faith in Jesus Christ.

D. Reflections of Leaders of the Wesleyan-Holiness Tradition

We must seek to live peaceably with all, finding in Christ the way of peace. Excessive institutionalism in church life fostered many negatives that the original Wesleyan revival resisted. What is the authentic "enthusiasm" of Christian faith that reflects Christ well and is not a personal and or corporate "fanaticism"? Forget holy wars. Humility is necessary. Final judgment belongs to God.

And suppose we cannot make these wars to cease in all the world; suppose we cannot reconcile all the children of God to each other; however, let each do what he can; if it is only two mites, let him contribute toward it. Happy are those who are able, in any degree, to promote peace and goodwill among men, especially among good men, among those who are enlisted under the banner of the Prince of Peace, and are therefore particularly engaged, as much as lies in them, to live peaceably with all men.[1]

> Find in Christ the way of peace,
> Peace unspeakable, unknown;
> By his pain he gives you ease,
> Life by his expiring groan;
> Rise, exalted by his fall,
> Find in Christ your all in all.[2]

The most dreaded malady of the religious establishment at the time of the Wesleys was "enthusiasm"—personal fanaticism which was thought to excite the unstable masses toward anarchy and rebellion.[3]

The enemies of the church today are not flesh and blood, but the spiritual powers of evil (Eph. 6:12). Therefore, we can cry out with the psalmist to put an end to these principalities of wickedness and to break their hold in the lives of people in this world. Some prayers (the "imprecatory" psalms), however, both cry out for judgment and call for the transfer of our anger over to God (Deut. 32:35, Rom. 12:19).[4]

The church will encounter other communities of faith that seek peace and justice. In the church's witness to the gospel of justification toward such communities, there can be no illusions of self-righteousness. Our witness is not to Christianity but to God. If the path to justification in resurrection and new creation is the Cross, the church cannot make any claims for itself in its witness. Our witness is exclusively to God's redemptive justice or saving righteousness in Christ through the Spirit.[5]

---

1. John Wesley, *The Lord Our Righteousness.*
2. Charles Wesley, "Weary Souls that Wander Wide."
3. D. Michael Henderson, *John Wesley's Class Meetings.*
4. Timothy and Julie Tennent, *A Meditative Journey through the Psalms.* 5
5. Frank Macchia, in *Theology Today* (2001).

WEEK 35

Christian Life #3

DOES GOD CONTROL EVERYTHING?

You would think that a poor widow would be the last to have extra food for Elijah. Wouldn't another widow be the last person Jesus should have related to in public, not to mention his also openly touching a man socially declared an untouchable? God's king sends his best soldier into mortal danger. Make sense? Paul, a hater of the Jesus people, certainly was a poor candidate to be commissioned as a prominent mouthpiece for God on behalf of those very people. The list of oddities in the Bible is long. Was God really in charge of all this?

We hate to question God's wisdom, of course, but sometimes we do have to wonder. Does God really know what's going on? Were these really divine decisions? We know it sounds almost heretical. Still, it needs to be said. Awful things do happen that we would think a fully capable and loving God would not have allowed. Choices made by humans and then attributed to God sometimes make little sense in light of Rabbi Jesus. If God does know everything that's going on, is God in full control when things happen that obviously violate his will? Why is there evil and why do good people suffer?

A. Prayer

I apologize, Lord, for daring to question you, but your great prophets of old asked hard questions and you received them graciously. Surely you haven't done everything people have claimed you have. Knowing Jesus, I realize that you can be the great unexpected One who acts in unexpected ways. Your ways are not always ours. Keep me open to your newness. Keep me humble when I think I could have made better choices than you seem to have made. I know you'll forgive me for being so honest. Even so, I wish I had more answers than I do. Help me to believe even when living under a cloud of unknowing.

B. The Voice of Rabbi Jesus: Luke 7:11–17

> My Father never wanted the stink of sin in his creation. When it came, his love planned a way to address it. That's why I came. I'm providing the way home for the lost. My original disciples certainly failed at first to see that my Cross could have been my Father at work. It did look like the world doing its worst again. Stay awake and open, my friends. My Father worked right through that Cross and now will work through you in wonderful and often unex-pected ways. Your anticipations won't always line up with his actions. So, be careful what you claim that God is doing. My Father is sovereign, but his great love allows some things to happen that are very opposed to his will. Such evil may win the moment but never has a long-term future.

My miracle at Nain is an example of the promise you'll find in Luke 6:21. "Blessed are you who weep now, for you will laugh." I was willing to risk rebuke for exercising my Father's special mercy for the least in human society. I often crossed socially acceptable lines in my acts of compassion. What made my Father smile appeared to human crowds as shocking and unrighteous behavior. A faithful church often will be misunderstood.

For a male Jew, the body of the dead was considered unclean. I was forbidden to touch it, but I did and spoke the word of life. My response to an unprotected widow was equally suspect. Eating with sinners made scandalous headlines denouncing me. No matter. My Father works his will as he chooses. Remain ready to be his instruments, and sometimes to live in faith without answers..

My Spirit is anxious to continue teaching you on my behalf. I'm providing you with select portions from the revealed Word of God and from a particular tradition of my church with wisdom you need. Read carefully and continue listening closely to my Spirit who will guide your minds and hearts to understand properly and apply effectively.

C. Light from the Revealed Word

1. Psalm 30 and 146. Here's a glimpse at the kind of faith that should sustain the soul in the face of a confusing present and ominous future. It reminds us of the claim often made in Scripture about the power of God as opposed to the power of the greatest mortals. Which of these can feed the starving, heal and redeem, even raise from the dead?

God's greatness is to be exalted, although something important must not be missed. God's actions in the world aren't to be viewed as the cause of injustice. God doesn't dictate all that happens. He has granted a freedom of choice that allows true love to blossom, and for now also enables the possibility of evil. God remains steady and loving and at all times is fully aware. Our sinful misuse of our freedom violates the divine will and creates circumstances that never should have been. This world cries out for a renewed holiness, humans restored in the image of their gracious Maker. Fulfilling that cry is what God is all about!

While not responsible for the evil consequences of many of our human actions, God does control the larger flow of things and will prevail eventually. There are powers now working against the purposes of God. As they work, God adapts, invents alternate routes, and sometimes chooses unlikely people to serve the divine purposes. In the short-term, much grieves God. In the long-term, the psalmist has it right. "The Lord will reign forever, thy God, O Zion, to all generations. Praise the Lord!" (vs. 10).

2. 1 Kings 17:8–24. Ahab did more to provoke the anger of the Lord than had all the kings of Israel before him. The prophet Elijah delivered to Ahab his failing grades from God, and then had to run for cover, fearing for his life. God's will prevails in this world, although it's often the case that human wills rule for a time.

God sometimes is working Plan B when the ideal Plan A has been derailed by wayward humans. Is a prophet of God having to hide a sign of the limits of God's power? Does hiding mean that God can't protect and care for his own without their having to run for cover? No, it means that God has granted the Ahabs of this world the freedom to go the wrong way, while God exercises loving patience and flexibility in finding a way to recover the situation for the eventual good.

God's plans, particularly the Plan Bs, often are surprising. They leave us scratching our heads, wondering if we heard God right and if God really knows what he's doing. In a time of drought, God tells Elijah to go to a suffering place and meet a widow who will care for him with the very little she has. We can't blame Elijah for muttering to himself, "I'd rather trust the ravens than depend on this impoverished widow. Does my God know what he's doing?" God's ways are not always ours, nor are they the ways God would have preferred if we humans hadn't forced negative circumstances. God's abundance is inexhaustible and can come in quite unpredictable ways. Even so, it will come!

3. Galatians 1:11–24. This is the story of Paul's call to be an apostle of Christ. He understands that his call embodies the same divine commission that motivated the prophets of old, despite their apparent lack of qualifications. Amos didn't have a prophet's license and Paul hadn't been with Jesus in the flesh like the original apostles. How does an unlikely man or woman qualify to be God's person in a time of crisis?

Our ability to recognize and embrace God's use of novel inventions is critical these days. Confused by the pace and scope of change, Christian congregations need to hear the word of hope being spoken here. It's a joyful thing to worship a very awake and creatively adaptive God who is ever pointing to new opportunities for human flourishing, despite contrary circumstances. Are we not like the impoverished widow and unlicensed prophets who prevailed and served despite the problems, and only because of the bounty of God's gracious and adaptive care?

D. Reflections of Leaders of the Wesleyan-Holiness Tradition

As relational love, God rejoices with us and sometimes has to grieve because of us. Whatever happens contrary to God's will, God will provide a way. We can glorify God regardless of what's happening at the moment. The Omnipotent always overcomes the defiant, at least eventually. The holy believer must resolve to walk daily with the Holy Spirit, seeking wisdom and acting as an instrument of divine love and reconciliation.

Christians know the mighty working of God's Spirit in their hearts, and the wisdom of his providence directing all their paths, and causing all things to work together for their good (Rom. 8:28). Yes, they know in every circumstance of life what the Lord requires of them and how to keep a conscience without offense, both toward God and toward their fellow man.[1]

>Omnipotent Redeemer,
>Our ransomed souls adore Thee,
>Whate'er is done
>Thy work we own,
>And give Thee all the glory;
>With thankfulness we acknowledge
>Our time of visitation;
>Thine hand confess, and gladly bless
>The God of our salvation.[2]

Love is the fundamental character of God. This means that God is intimately connected with the world, caring for it and committed to its good. It also means that God is necessarily sensitive to the world and vulnerable to its developments. God suffers in our suffering and rejoices in our joys.[3]

Character is constructed through a multitude of momentary acts and commitments. Christian perfection thus begins with choosing to walk with the Spirit. The choice, however, is not a once-for-all event. It must be renewed and reaffirmed. Christian perfection is a life that is given over to God in such a way that, over time, transformation occurs and freedom from sin is achieved. Christian perfection requires continuous resolve to remain walking with the Spirit.[4]

Giving freedom is part of God's steadfast love. God cannot fail to provide the freedom a perpetrator of evil expresses. John Wesley says, "Were human liberty taken away, men would be as incapable of virtue as stones. God cannot thus contradict himself or undo what he has done." We should not blame God when creatures misuse freedom. Creatures are blameworthy.[5]

---

1. John Wesley, *Christian Perfection.*
2. Charles Wesley, "Omnipotent Redeemer."
3. Delwin Brown, *What Does a Progressive Christian Believe?*
4. Sam Powell, *Holiness: Why It Matters Today.*
5. Thomas Jay Oord, *The Uncontrolling Love of God.*

WEEK 36

Christian Life #4

THE POWER OF EMINENT DOMAIN

Sometimes a society has the legal option of overriding the land ownership right of a private citizen for the sake of the public good. A property blocking completion of a new highway can be purchased at fair market value against the will of the owner. It's the power of eminent domain, an understandable one that can serve the public good or easily be abused. The Bible reports that Naboth was unfairly victimized by personal greed and not for public good.

Are we willing to buy or sell for private gain at the unfair expense of another? Do we in the church isolate certain groups of individuals for negative treatment—like women, people of a particular race or national origin, the poor, the recent immigrant? Who really has the power of eminent domain in the ultimate affairs of human lives? While the church is the people of God, that fact grants it no right to invoke God's power for its own selfish interests.

Perfect love restored entails both the renewal of the individual and the whole community of faith, causing both to partner with God in transforming the fallen world. Disciples of Rabbi Jesus, together as the church, are to *proclaim* and *perform* God's shalom in an unjust world.

A. Prayer

God, I'm so embarrassed. I've seen too many hurtful power plays in my nation and even in your church. It's so easy to subtly stereotype people and then injure them in favor of our preferred group interests. Please, God, forgive me for doing such a thing against anyone. Also, help me forgive when such has been done to me. You've sent me to convince others that your good news is for them. Keep me from being unfair to anyone as I seek to do the convincing. Don't let your good news become bad news for someone at my hand—or at that of my church's.

B. The Voice of Rabbi Jesus: Luke 7:36–8:3

> While my Father has universal eminent domain, it always is his preference to exercise his unlimited power gently and graciously. Justice belongs to all and salvation is available to all. You are to open doors, my disciples, not close them on people, especially on the most vulnerable. Build bridges and tear down walls without violating the property of others. Be the gracious host who rejoices in anyone who is kind to me and hoping for a new beginning in life. Never strip from anyone their human freedom and dignity. While being strong, always be gentle and fair.

As you serve in my name around the world, never forget the awful stories of Naboth and Uriah. And there's another woman from my own ministry who also was abused. She had an evil reputation and came into a home where I was a guest. She was so kind to me and upset my Pharisee host greatly. He belittled her and me, saying that if I was who I claimed to be, I would have known who she really was and would have had nothing to do with her.

The real sin in this incident was the ugly bias that divides the world into sinners and saints and assumes that my Father honors the divide and people can't cross it gracefully. Once separated into fixed categories, humans isolate and conquer the sinners as they choose. The fact is that all people are sinners and, by the power of forgiving love, all can be restored and become saints of my Holy Father. Turn no one away. Treat everyone with kindness. My Father can work in surprising ways and will redeem anyone who comes asking humbly in faith.

My Spirit is anxious to continue teaching you on my behalf. I'm providing you with select portions from the revealed Word of God and from a particular tradition of my church with wisdom you need. Read carefully and continue listening closely to my Spirit who will guide your minds and hearts to understand properly and apply effectively.

C. Light from the Revealed Word

1. Psalm 5:1–8 and Psalm 32. It was a time when the righteous seemed so outmatched by the wicked. Nobody was listening or caring. Know this when you are in such a circumstance. The righteous at least have an invaluable resource in God's listening ear. God hears the crying voice early in the morning, listening not only to the words but the hurt and urgency behind them. And the really good news? God is much more than one who hears. He also is capable of acting in any circumstance. After all, it was God whose mere word "made the heavens by the breath of his mouth!" (vs. 32:6).

"Listen to the sound of my cry, my King and my God, for to you I pray." This petition comes from one who worshipped God as the absolute King who has eminent domain over all things. In contrast, the psalmist's enemies, the "bloodthirsty and deceitful," serve the gods of their own appetites. They are willing to sacrifice the innocent along the way. In the midst of such awful times, it's well to recall the pathos in a song like "Nobody Knows the Trouble I've Seen." God knows and cares and can overrule!

2. 1 Kings 21; 2 Samuel 11. Elijah's message to King Ahab concerned the abuse of power, specifically murder and unjust land annexation. The victim of this imperial-sanctioned violence was Naboth who happened to own a vineyard bordering the palace of King Ahab. Naboth said he wouldn't sell. Jezebel, Ahab's wife, takes over, engineers Naboth's killing, and allows an easy take-over of the desired land. King David wanted access to the beautiful wife of Uriah. Her husband's death was arranged and the deal was done. Talk about royal abuse! "Little" people are easily abused.

Powerful people have a long history of seizing lands from indigenous communities, family farmers, and poor communities. They use selfish logic, like manifest destiny, colonization, protection of a superior race, all variations of inappropriate eminent domain. Such powerful people pay little attention to the effects of their actions on the violated individuals and sometimes even on their whole communities.

Scripture compels us to ask about the ways in which people are willing to lose our moral center in order to possess what they think they deserve or just want. In what ways are we as people of Rabbi Jesus called to speak prophetic truth to property-violating and even death-dealing persons and systems of selfish power? Are even leaders of God's people sometimes guilty?

3. Galatians 2:15–21. There are very wrong power plays even in church! By withdrawing from the Gentiles at Antioch, Peter insinuated that Jews were superior to Gentiles in God's eyes. That superiority supposedly justified discrimination. Instead of testifying to a divine grace that doesn't honor selfish social boundaries, Peter's action attempted to establish an ethnic fence around divine grace. By sharp contrast, Paul's life-changing encounter with Jesus "put to death" ancient stereotypical perspectives about Gentiles. In their place arose a new life of faith open to the surprisingly inclusive and most gracious ways of God.

The Jews have no advantage of birth over "non-Jewish sinners." Paul testifies to no longer being a Law-man in favor of now being God's man of love with respect for all people. No group is to be advantaged or disadvantaged by virtue of gender, racial heritage, or national identity. In matters of salvation, God alone has eminent domain and intends the universal availability of his restoring grace.

D. Reflections of Leaders of the Wesleyan-Holiness Tradition

How easy it is to fall short of the "religion of love." We must love and not use our neighbors. We who belong to Rabbi Jesus are to be light to the world and not more darkness! We are to proceed in confident faith, not concerned about being perceived as the "rubbish" of the world. Why worry? We belong to the God to whom all things belong! As necessary, we can and should sing even in the night.

Endeavour to help each other in whatever we are agreed leads to the kingdom. So far as we can, let us always rejoice to strengthen each other's hands in God. Above all, let us each take heed to himself (since each must give an account of himself to God) that he fall not short of the religion of love; that he be not condemned in what he himself approves.[1]

> The two commands are one:
> Ah, give me Lord, to prove
> Who loves his God alone.
> He must his neighbor love,
> And what Thine oracles enjoin,
> Is all summed up in love divine.[2]

Analysts of contemporary culture describe a fallen world. It is the world in which we live in the 21st century, one marked by forces that dehumanize mankind because those forces are antithetical to the elements that characterize the image of God which embodies the nature of true and authentic humanity. How important it then is for those who claim to be holiness people, sanctified by consecration through the power of the Holy Spirit, to "reflect the divine image," to be shining examples of what the Creator God intended the creation to be, in a word, to be the "light of the world."[3]

Jesus made clear that his disciples were to wait before they were to work for him in the world. The work would put them on the world's margins; thus, the only effective way to accomplish the task was to be instruments shaped and directed by Christ's Spirit. Jesus could live on the edge because he was firmly centered in the love of God for a lost and resistant creation. Disciples can do all things that God intends when divinely strengthened (Phil. 4:11-13). To live in Christ is to live by God's loving grace, through the ever-present Spirit of God, as an extension of the emerging post-resurrection life of Jesus.[4]

The Christian Negro spirituals are songs from the night. They are shafts of light and often documents of social protest. They are outcries of longing for needed change. They have a persistent perspective regarding God. There is a profound conviction that no problems or masters have the last word where faith reigns. This is the music of searchers who had found something eternal and Someone immortal.[5]

---

1. John Wesley, *Letter to a Roman Catholic*.
2. Charles Wesley, "The Two Commands Are One."
3. H. Ray Dunning, *Reflecting the Divine Image*.
4. Barry L. Callen, *Radical Christianity*.
5. James Earl Massey, *Sundays in the Tuskegee Chapel*.

WEEK 37

Christian Life #5

GOD AS RELATIONAL LOVE

God, while singular and supreme, nonetheless is the loving God who desires restored relationships. Love naturally reaches out. God announced himself to be unacceptably separated from Israel's worship. It wasn't truly relating to God, but mostly was only soothing and servicing the desired personal ends of the worshippers. God distanced himself from this. The Jewish exiles almost gave up because of the seeming absence of the active warmth of the Divine-human relationship.

Elijah paid a heavy price for his faithfulness and finally was assured in his depression that he was not alone. God lovingly comes to his own. Jesus came to his own people but, sadly, they did not receive him with a mutual love. Then he went to the outcasts and Gentiles, people who lived with rejection, and many found in relationship with Jesus a real friendship with God.

God is best defined as *relational love in action*. A fallen creation has broken the intended relationship. The result? Rather than being vindictive, God has gone into action, anxious to reach out and redeem by a pure gift of love.[1] O that the lost will recognize and accept this amazing gesture of pure love! A holy and "apostolic" church may appear insignificant on the scene of major religious institutions, but that's where the "optimism of grace" keeps pointing.

A. Prayer

I would understand, Lord, if you left us sinners to our deserved destiny. That's what we selfish humans would do to each other. But your Son has shown us something else, something very different and wonderful. Love reaches, searches, lifts life to its intended heights. How I need loving relationships to be fulfilled as a human being. Especially do I need to know your gracious and loving presence, O God. May your Spirit lead me always to Rabbi Jesus. As promised, may the Spirit of Jesus pour divine love into my soul and inspire me to share that love with the least and the lost of this world. Please, Lord, and thank you!

B. The Voice of Rabbi Jesus: Luke 8:26–39

> My Father is the great lover who seeks to shower love on the creation and pour transforming love into and through all of you. Can you avoid harsh judgment that keeps you from loving the most desperate and undeserving? Not on your own you can't. You must form churches that are schools of love. They must offer gracious spaces where the wounded and isolated can come to be heard, cared for, and restored. My Father reaches out for healing relationships with all people because of the great love that he is and shares. That's exactly what I call you to be and do—be great lovers in a love-starved world.

I met a man who had been driven out of his village, wore no clothes, was homeless and living in the tombs of the dead. I released him from his demonic misery. This dramatic action foreshadowed the time I would send my disciples to be witnesses to all people, "in Jerusalem, in all Judea and Samaria, and to the ends of the earth" (Acts 1:8). Like me, you are to go to society's outsiders and probably suffer for your gracious efforts, as I did. Dare to consider it a privilege.

The restoring grace of my loving Father reaches beyond every barrier that human sin and society have built. God is relational love in action, always reaching and restoring. Learn to reach out lovingly as part of my Father's ongoing work of redemption.

My Spirit is anxious to continue teaching you on my behalf. I'm providing you with select portions from the revealed Word of God and from a particular tradition of my church with wisdom you need. Read carefully and continue listening closely to my Spirit who will guide your minds and hearts to understand properly and apply effectively.

C. Light from the Revealed Word

1. Psalm 42. The last lesson of Rabbi Jesus made clear that God has eminent domain in all things—as none other has. There is only one God and he has all possibilities and no competitors. "My soul thirsts for God, for the living God." I am lost without God. I am created to be in relationship with God. That's our human problem, holes in our hearts that only God can fill. Here's the amazing fact that speaks so wonderfully to our lostness and great thirst and empty hearts. God loves, comes, and seeks full relationship restoration with us!

God is filled with relational love and greatly desires to be close to and spiritually intimate with each of us. God is anxious to provide exactly what we need. Why, then, are we so down in the dumps and crying the blues? The psalmist reports great news. "God promises to love us all day long and sing glorious songs to us all through the night" (vs. 42:8).

One meaning of the Christian doctrine of the divine Trinity is that God is by very nature a rich relational being. As such, God is complete within himself. Even so, God is so full of relational love that he reaches out for us. He now has sent his Son to enable us relationally starved ones to join in the divine richness of relational fulfillment. My soul surely thirsts for being found by that lovingly relational God!

2. 1 Kings 19; Isaiah 65. In response to Jezebel's death threat, Elijah flees for his life, leaving the northern kingdom of Israel and crossing over to Beer-sheba in the southern kingdom of Judah. Here he parts from his servant and proceeds to migrate alone through the desert. Soon malnourished, exhausted, and isolated, he recedes into a suicidal depression. "I was ready to be sought out by those who did not ask, to be found by those who did not seek me." What a dangerous and relationship-deprived sadness was his.

Just as depression set in, so did the healing presence and care of God. Suddenly an angel touched Elijah and said, "Get up and eat. *You are not alone.* I care for you. Now get back to it." Starting with Genesis, the notion of being alone was never what God deemed as "good." Rather, God's ultimate good consists of humans being in peaceful relationships with the creation, each other, and their loving God.

The lack of God's obvious presence also sent the exiled Israelites into a deep lament (Isaiah 65). In response to God's seeming absence and the loss of Jerusalem and the Temple, they began to beg God to return and stop delivering them into the "hand of our iniquity." Without the active warmth of the Divine-human relationship, God's people just couldn't go on. Their only hope was the appearance of a loving, reaching, restoring God.

3. Galatians 3:23–29. How much like a Jew does a Gentile need to be in order to be a legitimate Christian? To whose standard does a convert to Christ need to conform? What about "Gentiles"? This is an odd question to modern ears. The church has been so dominated by Gentiles since the late first century that the very term has almost fallen out of the Christian lexicon. In the middle of the first century, however, this was the big membership question that the church faced. God had made promises to Abraham and Abraham's heirs. Gentiles were not considered natural heirs. Exactly who are the "chosen"?

How do God's promises apply to non-heirs who in fact comprise most of humanity? Not by human inheritance, Paul insists, but by a *restored relationship* with the loving God. God's Christ is the one with whom God's people must have a forgiven and growing intimate spiritual fellowship. By faith in Jesus Christ, anyone can become an adopted child of God (vs. 3:26). Believers are baptized into Christ and belong to Christ (vs. 3:29). God deeply desires restored loving relationships with *all people* and has acted to make that possible.

The Galatians had received the Holy Spirit, carrier of the Christ relationship. Fulfillment, salvation, and destiny resided in that relationship. A life of faith and fresh relationship to God through Christ, not circumcision or an Abrahamic bloodline, is what makes believers true descendants of Abraham. It's not careful adherence to a correct creed. It's not membership in the proudest of Christian denominations. These are good, but not the heart of the matter.

We Christians tend to be lonely if not tied closely to our human roots, ethnic/tribal/family/denomination. Still, we must understand that we belong to a much larger family. We should hunger for this divine family relationship with the whole body of believers. We should relate lovingly with our fellow believers so that the church's ranks might be nurtured by love experienced and keep expanding.

D. Reflections of Leaders of the Wesleyan-Holiness Tradition

God actively reaches and relates because God is love. Those who gladly receive are God's redeemed children, first receivers and then grateful carriers of love. Love is the church's binding force and the very essence of holiness. Such holiness points back to the "apostolic" church and its "optimism of grace" that offers hope for the church of today.

Who then is a Christian, according to the light which God has given? He that, being "justified by faith, has peace with God through our Lord Jesus Christ." He that finds the love of God shed abroad in his heart by the Holy Ghost which is given unto him, and whom this love sweetly constrains to love his neighbor, every man, as himself.[2]

> Thy faithfulness, Lord, Each moment we find,
> So true to Thy word, So loving and kind!
> Thy mercy so tender to all the lost race,
> The vilest offender may turn and find grace.
>
> The mercy I feel to others I show,
> I set to my seal that Jesus is true:
> Ye all may find favor who come at his call,
> O come to my Savior, His grace is for all![3]

Love is necessary to the maintenance of holiness. The dimension of love, which is the practical dimension of holiness, cannot be neglected. Love is enlarged by use. That takes time and practice. It changes the whole perspective of life's values. It mellows, beautifies, and enriches the personality. Where love is lost, holiness is lost. Love is the adhesive power in human relations. It must increase or be forfeited. The test of holiness is love.[4]

The bias in Wesleyan and Pentecostal movements is that the apostolic church most faithfully reflected the kingdom of heaven in its life and mission. While by no means perfect, apostolic Christianity serves as a model to emulate. For many, the recovery of apostolic faith and love would also lead to recovery of apostolic power. The ultimate goal is not to return to the past but, by way of the early church, to anticipate the future kingdom of heaven.[5]

---

1. A recent Christian theology built around this reality is Barry L. Callen's *God As Loving Gace*. Special emphasis is placed on the dynamic nature of holiness in Thomas Oord and Michael Lodahl, *Relational Holiness*.
2. John Wesley, *God's Vineyard*.
3. Charles Wesley, "Sinners Turn, Why Will Ye Die?"
4. Mildred Wynkoop, in the *Wesleyan Theological Journal*, 1969.
5. Henry H. Knight, III, *Anticipating Heaven Below*.

WEEK 38

Christian Life #6

WHEN THERE ARE NO RULES

The Jewish tradition by the time of Jesus had evolved numerous rules of precisely how the faithful should act in many of life's circumstances. To be pleasing to God, all rules were to be followed carefully. Jesus loved his heritage but proceeded to transform it in significant ways. One was to dispense with many of the religious rules when good sense or human compassion suggested acting otherwise. He said that an adequate fulfilling of the law was always practicing the *law of love*.

Rules can be cold, impersonal, and improperly limiting; they also can give security by making clear in advance what's to be done when particular circumstances come up. That way, no decision needs to be made. Just follow the rule.

By contrast, love is a marvelous law for life, highly personal but lacking in any advance specificity what should be done until a particular setting is faced. Each circumstance must be evaluated separately and fresh guidance from God received and followed. Jesus was a master at love applications. He violated many standing rules in the process and paid a high price for doing so. It's demanding when there are no advance rules other than the law of love. It's also wonderful.

A. Prayer

Thank you, Lord, for your great love shown to me. Thank you for pouring your love into me so that I can live my life by knowing and sharing it. I confess, however, that the lack of advance rules for behavior is hard for me to deal with. Please keep your loving Spirit close to me so that I will be able to determine on a daily basis precisely what you would have me do as each new circumstance presents itself. How I want to be ruled by love, and how I struggle with the absence of fixed rules of behavior. While love is flexible and adaptive to every present need, it also too easily can be a license for doing whatever I wish while trying to avoid accountability. O how I need the comfort and guidance of God's Spirit in all this!

B. The Voice of Rabbi Jesus: Luke 9:59-62

> My friends, dropping everything and following me isn't easy. Living by love has its challenges and certainly its risks. If you don't believe enough in me and my Spirit to take the risks, you had better stay home. You can't know it all in advance, you just can't. Love often has to be flexible and experimental in application. My Spirit won't give you a book of fixed rules, only a divine presence who always is prepared to show you the way, one step at a time.

Trust is what I'm looking for when I call people to follow me, trust and a heart prepared to risk loving. When I first called, some responded with, "Yes, but there are some things I need to do first." Following me doesn't allow for "yes, buts." If you have trust, you will be confident that my Father will protect and provide, shelter and send you out with whatever you really need.

People don't know what's going to happen, of course, so they think they need to first cover all of the bases. One potential disciple said he needed to bury his father first; another needed to spend some extended time saying good-bye to her family. I don't encourage irresponsibility, of course, but I do expect trust and not excuses. People always can find more pressing matters than launching out in faith.

I'm honest with potential disciples. Let the dead bury the dead; get on with the work of the kingdom or stop talking about it. We're wilderness bound. There are crosses to be carried. Are you coming or not?

My Spirit is anxious to continue teaching you on my behalf. I'm providing you with select portions from the revealed Word of God and from a particular tradition of my church with wisdom you need. Read carefully and continue listening closely to my Spirit who will guide your minds and hearts to understand properly and apply effectively.

C. Light from the Revealed Word

1. Psalms 16. In moments of pain and confusion and questions, so much depends on the believer having available a powerful memory of God's past actions. Such memory gives the present assurance and guidance. What God wants of me now surely will be in line with what God has done in the past. In the stories of Elijah and Elisha, Jacob and Joseph, Moses and Aaron, one consistently central message is that we cannot manage alone. We need a community of faith to help us remember the promises of God. We need the church, the community of memory. We need the church to have and help understand the Bible, the rich source of the church's memories of God in action yesterday.

When we can think only of our pain and questions, companions in the faith can remind us of God's presence and promises. When we cannot sing, others can sing for us. When we cannot pray, others can carry the load on our behalf. The theme of this psalm lends itself to hymns such as "Great Is Thy Faithfulness," "Our God, Our Help in Ages Past," and "God of the Ages, Whose Almighty Hand."

But what about when there is no clear memory of what to do in a novel set of circumstances? What should happen when a decision must be made and there is no map, only wilderness and an open road with no GPS? The psalmist answers, "I bless the Lord who gives me counsel" (vs. 7). Beyond the church and Bible, especially when there are no guiding rules, we need the holy love and present ministry of God's Spirit.

2. 1 Kings 19:15–16, 19–21; 2 Kings 2:1–2, 6–14.
When they finally come to the Jordan River, Elijah again uses the mantle to allow a crossing of the parted water. As Walter Brueggemann notes, this transitions the travelers beyond the settled territory of the monarchy back to the wilderness where prophets find their renewal. There's something wonderful about being in the deep woods, the silence, the mystery, the beauty, separation from the chaos of human noise and struggle. There also is the great danger of getting distracted and lost. Every direction seems to lead to the same nowhere. How do we know what's the right way home when there are no maps or rules? The law of love always applies.

3. Galatians 5:1, 13–25. The Galatian believers in Jesus lived in a world where the things we now take for granted—Christian customs, rituals, worship, a calendar for community celebration, even a written Scripture, were brand new or didn't yet exist. As a pioneering first-century community, they lived with little or no tradition to ground their experience as Gentile Christians. It was like playing football with no sidelines to the field. It's difficult to know when you are out-of-bounds!

Authentic Christian discipleship requires both right beliefs and proper behaviors. If the Jewish law and the "traditions of the Elders" were no longer the safeguards against sin and the misuse of freedom, what was? Paul responds, "The Holy Spirit!" "Live by the Spirit, I say, and do not gratify the desires of the flesh." There is one law, that of love. The whole law is summed up in a single commandment, "You shall love your neighbor as yourself" (5:14).

While God calls disciples to freedom, Paul is constrained to announce caution. "Do not use your freedom as an opportunity for self-indulgence" (5:13b). Believers must know that *sanctification* is ultimately not asceticism (denying ourselves to death) or athleticism (working ourselves to death). It's acceptance—allowing God's Spirit to love us into new life, abundant life, and finally everlasting life. The Holy Spirit, once accepted, motivates believers to engage the world with the hope of returning it to holiness or, perhaps better, to a wholeness of life grounded in love.

D. Reflections of Leaders of the Wesleyan-Holiness Tradition

How wonderful to be freed from sin and committed to the law of love. Even so, the cloud of sin lingers and the call to become resurrection people is an ongoing process of being perfected in the love of Christ. Love fulfills the law. Impart to me then, O Christ, the love of God! Such imparting calls for regular attention to the "means of grace" provided and modeled by Rabbi Jesus.

Here is a picture of a holy believer. All the commandments of God he keeps, and that with all his might. His obedience is in proportion to his love, the source from whence it flows. Therefore, loving God with all his heart, he serves God with all his strength. He continually presents his soul and body a living sacrifice, without reserve devoting himself to God's glory.[1]

> That blessed law of Thine,
> Jesus, to me impart;
> The Spirit's law of life divine,
> O write it in my heart!
> Implant it deep within,
> Whence it may ne'er remove,
> The law of liberty from sin,
> The perfect law of love.[2]

The law-freedom struggle fills the pages of the New Testament. Paul heralded a new freedom in Christ and was criticized sharply by some as a worldly and dangerous libertine. He understood the gospel of Christ to be marked by freedom, gratitude, and joy. It's the life of "I want to do this because of Christ" rather than "I will do this because I must." Christians are to live as resurrection people with an infectious testimony of fresh joy and really good news for all people.[3]

Nothing is clearer from the Scriptures than that there is a perfection which may be attained in this life. This perfection consists solely in a life of perfect love, or loving God with all the heart, soul, mind, and strength. This state of perfect love is a consequence of the purification of the heart from all sin, with that love being the fulfilling of the law.[4]

Accept, O God, our thanksgiving for the gift of your law which you have written on our hearts anew in Christ, for it is perfect freedom, the freedom of servant love.[5]

John Wesley denounces empty ritualism, but most of us need habitual practices that daily open our hearts and minds to God's transforming love. Without regular reminders we tend to drift away from God's missional call to love and serve our neighbors. Wesley recognized five "means of grace," the Christian spiritual practices that form a process of "going on to perfection." They are prayer, searching the Scriptures, the Lord's Supper, fasting, and Christian conferencing.[6]

---

1. John Wesley, *The Character of a Methodist*.
2. Charles Wesley, "The Thing My Lord Doth Hate."
3. Barry L. Callen, *The Prayer of Holiness-Hungry People*.
4. H. Orton Wiley, *Christian Theology*, vol. 2.
5. Paul Chilcote, *Praying in the Wesleyan Spirit*.
6. Elaine A. Heath, *Five Means of Grace: Experience God's Love the Wesleyan Way*.

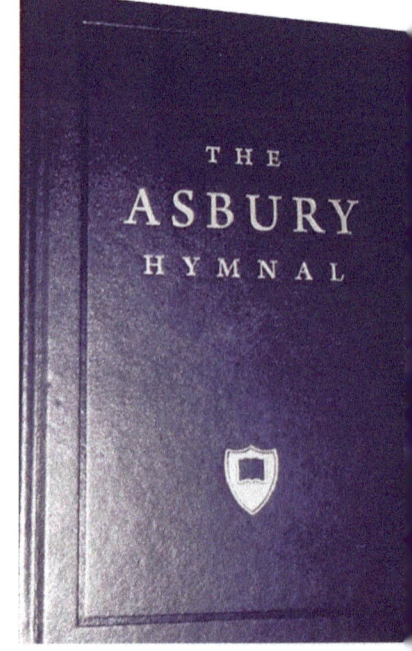

WEEK 39

Christian Life #7

NOBODIES CAN MAKE A BIG DIFFERENCE

Who's in charge? 2 Kings is about the paradoxes of power. Nearly every verse makes some reference to the issue of who has status and authority and who doesn't. Initial impressions are turned on their heads. The seemingly powerful end up dependent on the seemingly powerless. What about the limits of human power, the importance of humility, and the God whose power can be found exercised by the powerless?

Humility ranks high among biblical virtues (James. 4:10). Repeatedly, God sides with the powerless (1 Sam. 2:3-9; Ps. 113:7-9). The Bible tells story after story of bullies who lose and abused wimps who win. Never forget that the helpless baby in the Bethlehem barn was actually God with us! Listen to the wisdom of C. S. Lewis conveyed in novel form. Pride may be the greatest of temptations, a major danger to the holiness of a Christian believer.

Prince Caspian is a featured character in the *Chronicles of Narnia*. After the decisive battle, Aslan, the great Lion, reports surprisingly that the Prince now is able to assume his rightful kingship. But Caspian is uncertain about his readiness for such a large responsibility. He is grateful but humble. Aslan then offers this telling judgment. "It's for that very reason that I know you are!" Humility is a clear mark of Christian maturity, a holy readiness for major responsibility. Even a humble nobody can make a big difference!

A. Prayer

Help me grasp this difficult truth, my Lord. The world's nobodies are really somebodies in your divine kingdom. By your grace, we who have little can accomplish much. Indeed, little is much if God is in it. Let me hear well the witnesses of Aslan. His judgment certainly doesn't fit with the arrogance that marks the powerful of this world. Pride can be deadly and go just before a fall. I so want to stand, never bragging about myself, but glorifying your greatness, my God, and rejoicing in your generous love expressed to even me. In that humble spirit, Rabbi Jesus, enable me to make a holy difference in those around me.

B. The Voice of Rabbi Jesus: Luke 21:25–36

> When you go into the world in my name, dear disciples, go gently and humbly, although no less powerfully and confidently. After all, my Spirit will be going with you and staying just a little ahead of you. To be like me means that you will be meek but not weak. Go with assurance that what I will call you to do I also will equip you to get done. There are bullies on every hand who like to say that you are nobodies. That may be so by the world's standards. You now, however, are members of my Father's dearly loved family. So, stand tall and live by the standards and judgments of my Kingdom. The very design of the creation is on your side!

You are to go everywhere, beginning with a necessary caution. The fields of my Father's harvesting are not playgrounds of self-appointed spiritual entrepreneurs. You are not to chart your own courses and work in your own ways as if the outcome finally depends on our skills and efforts. You must never boast in your successes. It will be enough for you to rejoice in being numbered among God's people, whatever happens.

And there's another needed caution. "I am sending you out like lambs in the midst of wolves." Nonetheless, my little lambs, nobodies in the world's eyes, you can make a big difference. Dare to travel with modest provisions in your pockets. Risk rejection and welcome every new opportunity. Lean on me since it's my work you are about and the outcome is mine to define and judge.

My Spirit is anxious to continue teaching you on my behalf. I'm providing you with select portions from the revealed Word of God and from a particular tradition of my church with wisdom you need. Read carefully and continue listening closely to my Spirit who will guide your minds and hearts to understand properly and apply effectively.

C. Light from the Revealed Word

1. Psalms 30 and 66. We indeed will give you all the credit, our God. We know that the success of your mission in this world finally will be your doing, not ours. We know we are weak and seen as nobodies by this arrogant world. Eventually that will be their problem, certainly not yours. We call to all the saints to sing joyfully to the God who sets us on the road to life and keeps us out of the ditches of despair. When we were so down, Lord, you drew us up (vs. 30:1). We nobodies truly are somebodies in your sight. Praise the Lord!

As you did for your people long ago, we believe you will come through for us again, Holy Father. "We went through fire and water and yet you brought us to a spacious place, to full satisfaction" (vs. 66:12). That has made us ready for your service. We are unlikely people to be thought of as adequate servants of the Most High, as were those first disciples of Rabbi Jesus. Even so, with your help we will be adequate for whatever task we are assigned.

2. 2 Kings 5:1–14. Irony is everywhere in this story. The people who should know, like the king of Israel, appear clueless, while the marginalized, like the Israelite servant girl, perceive accurately what God is doing. Because of his arrogance, Naaman almost cheats himself of his healing. Fortunately, his servants persuade him to do as God's prophet was requiring, crazy and humiliating as it seemed. Yes, it was the servants who had the saving insight.

Knowledge of God, God's ways, and of the truth of our circumstances may come from quite unexpected sources and very unlikely people. Those with the big titles aren't always the ones with the big insights. Some nobodies turn out to be real somebodies because of God's gracious intervention and provision.

3. Galatians 6:1–16. "Bear one another's burdens and in this way you will fulfill the law of Christ. For if those who are nothing think they are something, they deceive themselves" (vss. 2-3). We in the church are profoundly connected to each other and have responsibility for each other. We are the family of God. We have different roles and gifts from God and must honor the roles and gifts given to others. We clearly are better together. We function best when all voices are willingly heard and when all divine gifts are allowed to be used freely for the good of all.

Wouldn't it be remarkable if the whole church of God revisited this ancient letter of Paul and then sat down and talked—listening carefully to each another—instead of each segment of the body proclaiming in isolation its version of the truth? We would extend that gentle patience that Paul encouraged. In the process, we would demonstrate to a fractured world what our Creator intends and enables, a unified church on loving mission together for the sake of the world.

It's finally not which of us disciples is to be in charge or whose version of the truth is to be mandated as the truth for all. There's wisdom even in the least of us. The seeming nobodies often have divine gifts of wisdom needed by the rest of us. Let's end the arrogance and instead highlight our mutual accountability as the people of God.

D. Reflections of Leaders of the Wesleyan-Holiness Tradition

We can have it all and still have nothing. We are not to be full of ourselves, but free of self-dominance and infused with God's freeing fullness. All of us are in equal need of God's anointing. The fact is that we are holy only when we are full of the Master!

Though I have the gift of prophecy, of foretelling those future events which no creature can foresee; and though I understand all the mysteries of nature, of providence, and the word of God; and though I have have all knowledge of things, divine or human, that any mortal ever attained to; and though I can explain the most mysterious passages of Daniel, Ezekiel, and the Revelation; yet if I have not humility, gentleness, love and resignation, I am nothing in the sight of God.[1]

> Clothe me with Thy holiness,
> Thy meek humility;
> Put on me my glorious dress,
> Endue my soul with Thee;
> Let Thine image be restored,
> Thy name and nature let me prove,
> With Thy fullness fill me, Lord.
> And perfect me in love.[2]

Oh, that God may anoint His people! Not the ministers only but every disciple. Do not suppose that pastors are the only laborers needing anointing. There is not a mother but needs it in her house to regulate her family, just as much as the minister needs it in the pulpit, or the Sunday school teacher in his or her class. We all need it together, and let us not rest day nor night until we possess it! If that is the uppermost thought in our hearts, God will give it to us, if we just hunger and thirst for it, and say, "God helping me, I will not rest until endued with power from on high."[3]

People have left the subject of holiness to the scholars and pastors to understand. It's been so warped and misunderstood that we stopped trying to understand it. In the process, the richness of its meaning became a shallow generic platitude that meant whatever folks wanted it to be—and usually it implied behaviors that were restrictive, as if somehow not doing certain things would help us achieve a super-spiritual holy state. But being holy is more than looking holy. In reality, holiness is nothing more than *living full of the Master* who is holy. It's Masterful living. Being masterful is not a matter of imposing a special set of behaviors with a special skill. A highly disciplined life is no more masterful apart from the Master than the Sistine Chapel is masterful apart from the artist.[4]

Here are lyrics from a nineteenth-century holiness pioneer who was humble indeed, and yet also knew something very important. He knew that, once filled with the fullness of God, the lowly in spirit can shine with the very fire of God!

> Fill me with Thy presence now,
> Lord, Thyself in me reveal,
> At Thy feet I humbly bow,
> to receive the holy seal.
> Come, O Spirit, seal me Thine,
> Come, Thy fullness now bestow,
> Let Thy glory shine in me,
> Let Thy fire within my glow![5]

---

1. John Wesley, in *The Arminian Magazine*.
2. Charles Wesley, "Wretched, Helpless, and Distressed."
3. A. M. Hills, Sermon: "Holiness and Power."
4. Kevin Mannoia, *Masterful Living*.
5. Daniel S. Warner, "Fill Me with Thy Spirit, Lord."

WEEK 40

Christian Life #8

THE CHURCH WALLS ARE CROOKED!

How terrible to watch a major building suddenly collapse and learn later that it was because of shoddy materials or poor design or irresponsible construction workers. A crooked wall can be unsightly at best and, at worst, the cause of coming disaster. Public buildings, yes, but what about the church of Rabbi Jesus and its structures? They are constructed of wood and stone and steel, of theological thinking and religious practices, and of human relationships inside and outside the physical boundaries where God's children gather to worship.

Unfortunately, a church may have a truly beautiful building that's perfectly built and still be crooked, in great danger of collapse in God's eyes. The people inside may be well-intentioned, at least on the surface, but have attitudes and take actions that hardly reflect the mind of Christ. Such waywardness constitute shoddy and risky construction.

Jesus was a tradesman, a builder who knew the importance of doing things right. The church, now his body, must maintain its Christ-like integrity by allowing the Spirit of God to draw the blueprints of the church and execute its ongoing construction and use.

A. Prayer

Help me, dear God, to avoid the temptations that plague me individually and even weaken your people generally. They include wasting time, doing things only half-way, and focusing on what will serve me best in the immediate instead of what's best for the church's long-term mission. If "orthodox" means "straight," let me not be a crooked disciple in a church proceeding in crooked ways. Allow me to zero in, Lord, on what's most important to you as you minister in this world through me and your whole church. Keep us properly focused. Straighten us out, Lord. Please start with me!

B. The Voice of Rabbi Jesus: Luke 10:25–37

> There's a long history of my people refusing to be faithful to my covenant with them, even while they were going through good-looking religious motions. Often they have been satisfied to specialize in religious rituals while being quite crooked in their hearts and actions. Don't ever look for discipleship loopholes or dare to take shortcuts in receiving, being changed by, and sharing my truth and love. Never try building my kingdom on your own by using human designs filled with little but religious platitudes and routines. That risks the finished product having your name over the door instead of mine. When that happens, regardless of the well-publicized headlines about great coming events inside, I won't be there!

You must not assume that the church walls are straight and only the world's crooked. Wanting to justify himself, a man once asked me, "And who is my neighbor?" The questioner thought he was justified in his actions because he followed the current reading of the Law, otherwise known as the church's stale status quo. Neither should you be too quick to turn the priest and Levite into bad guys. When they passed by the injured man, they were only standard religious leaders doing the standard religious thing at the time, avoiding contact with the presumably dead.

The lawyer's answer to my question was "right" (Greek *orthos* means "correct" or "straight"), but it was very wrong by being incomplete. One can be straight, technically correct, and still not be righteous. The church walls might be built out of the sturdiest concrete of right beliefs and yet be dangerously crooked if those beliefs are not acted out in loving actions in God's service. *"Do this*, and you will live."

My Spirit is anxious to continue teaching you on my behalf. I'm providing you with select portions from the revealed Word of God and from a particular tradition of my church with wisdom you need. Read carefully and continue listening closely to my Spirit who will guide your minds and hearts to understand properly and apply effectively.

C. Light from the Revealed Word

1. Psalm 25:1–10. This psalm lays waste "deities" lesser than the true God. It condemns the human tendency to accord such pretenders a status approaching the place of God. It makes painfully clear that God's justice never will be the chief purpose of the "gods" we create from our human obsessions. Our judgments will always be imperfect, as will be our god-like projections of ourselves. We always will mistake the popular or powerful for the deserving. Those in whom we wrongly invest our respect always will fall short of the standard of God's love and justice. They have neither knowledge nor understanding so, know it or not, they walk around in darkness.

"O, my God, in Thee I trust" (vs. 2). May I never forget that it was you who stretched out the heavens and laid the foundations of the earth (Isa. 51:16). You alone know straight from crooked. When we abandon loyalty to the only true God, we find our lives dominated by false gods of our own making—sometimes featuring ourselves as supposed divinities. When our loyalties stray from center, the very structure of our spiritual lives becomes crooked and dangerous. When our churches try to go it alone, go their own ways even with the best of religious rhetoric, their walls become poorly constructed and soon will crack and crumble.

2. Amos 7; Deuteronomy 30. Here's a picture of a complacent Israel and its serious predicament. In a time of relative peace and prosperity, a plumb line is stretched and reveals a fatal flaw in the community's structure. Israel had come out of being "true" with itself. The plumb line highlighted a serious gap between the uprightness of God's law and the missing harmony between God's people and just social relations. It warned of the coming of Israel's collapse. Faulty construction must be torn down and made right.

Amos decries the systemic exploitation of the powerless and the constant humiliation of society's lowly. He sees public religion masking rampant injustice and rages against the way official worship patterns were justifying social sin. God's people must start listening more carefully to God and acting accordingly. Nothing halfhearted will ever do. Crooked religion is never tolerable in God's eyes.

One of Martin Luther King's trademark lines came from the prophet Amos. King sometimes would clinch the power of an oration by proclaiming, "Let justice roll down like waters, and righteousness like an ever-flowing stream" (vs. 5: 24). We now live in a society schooled in the belief that we are accountable to no one except ourselves—what's right is what seems right to us. Who are others to judge me? We want to be left alone to live our lives as we see fit, according to our own rules, regardless to what happens to others. This is dangerously crooked business, the opposite of God's intended order.

3. Colossians 1:1–14. We so need "knowledge of God's will." Amos laid it out bluntly. The Psalmist points to the pitfalls. Paul now recalls Rabbi Jesus who is said to be the cosmic wisdom who holds all things together. What a claim that is! If true, Jesus is the ultimate in wisdom, the only sure foundation on which to build a "straight" life or church that will endure. With this huge truth claim comes an impassioned prayer for all God's saints (vss. 9-11). We must be strong, loving, patient, and full of the understanding that only the Spirit of Jesus gives.

Leaders of the early church understood that their future would not be easy. The walls of the world are crooked, and over time even some in the church would be less than ideal if not directed by the Spirit of God. May we always be "orthodox," straight and strong because we are willing to wait for the guidance and gifting of God's Spirit who alone knows how to build properly.

D. Reflections of Leaders of the Wesleyan-Holiness Tradition

Church members must guard their conversations with each other. Straightening crookedness in church life requires believing hearts that act courageously, in faith, and with justice. All must be structured by God's love. Otherwise, collapse awaits.

God being our helper, speak nothing harsh or unkind to each other. The sure way to avoid this is to say all the good we can, both of and to one another. In all our conversation, either with or concerning each other, we should use only the language of love, speaking with all softness and tenderness, with the most endearing expression which is consistent with truth and sincerity.[1]

> True and faithful as Thou art,
> To all Thy church and me,
> Give a new, believing heart,
> That knows and cleaves to Thee.
> Freely our backslidings heal,
> And, by Thy precious blood restored,
> Grant that every soul may feel,
> Thou art my pardoning Lord![2]

Only love can provide the proper dynamic of life, or constitute the cohering and balancing force which can mold faith, hope, zeal, knowledge, and all other graces and gifts into full-orbed Christian character. Love is the "bond of perfectness," wrote Paul. This is true for the individual and also for the church, and it is just as true for society. All social reform or cultural advance is stumbling and partial if not prompted and structured by Christian love.[3]

> How sweet this bond of perfectness,
> The wondrous love of Jesus!
> A pure foretaste of heaven's bliss,
> O fellowship so precious!

Beloved, how this perfect love,
Unites us all in Jesus,
One heart, and soul, and mind we prove,
The union heaven gave us.[4]

Any church with straight walls is tapping into the dynamism of the first-century Jesus movement through empowerment of the Holy Spirit. Some Christian groups become more concerned with maintaining their own separate movements within the church than aligning themselves with the ongoing Jesus movement. The church established by Jesus *is* a movement, *the* movement. Movements within the church come and go, but the Jesus movement is destined to continue to the end of time. For a movement to be part of the Jesus movement entails focusing all its energies and resources and relationships on discipling the nations and serving as dramatic signs of the present Kingdom of God.[5]

---

1. John Wesley, *Letter to a Roman Catholic.*
2. Charles Wesley, "Father, If Thou Must Reprove."
3. Richard Taylor, in the *Wesleyan Theological Journal,* 1967.
4. Daniel S. Warner, "The Bond of Perfectness."
5. Gilbert W. Stafford, *Theology for Disciples.*

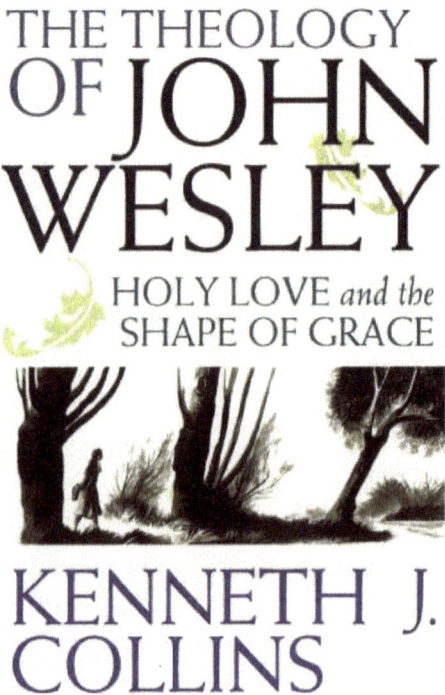

THE THEOLOGY OF JOHN WESLEY
HOLY LOVE and the SHAPE OF GRACE
KENNETH J. COLLINS

WEEK 41

Christian Life #9

DON'T GIVE UP ON WORDS

The Bible is full of words—all kinds of words. In the maze of kinds, we can get frustrated and confused and even stop reading. The New Testament has four Gospels, each telling the story of the same Jesus coming from the Father to be with us. They are similar in all essentials and yet quite different in the details included and audiences addressed. Sorry, but we need all four, and that's only the beginning the maze of multiples in the Bible.

The Bible was written by many different men and women in different languages, styles of expression, cultural settings, centuries, and often with differing concerns in mind. The composite "library" has been supervised ("inspired") by God's revealing Spirit. Even so, the Bible as we now have it must be read with considerable patience and care, allowing the Spirit of Rabbi Jesus to make clear the meaning for now of what was written so long ago.

Some biblical words said to be from God are hardly believable as written, and definitely when isolated from the whole. For instance, "Your wife Sarah will have a son." She laughed. Physical circumstances made conceiving quite impossible. The ancient Greeks allowed the insane to wander the streets talking their apparent nonsense. Why? Because it's hard to distinguish between nonsense and divine revelation that's clearly outside ordinary human thinking.

Believers have to learn to test the spirits. We must never give up on the words of the Bible, any of them, but we had better be open to the ongoing work of the Spirit. It's the Spirit, the original supervisor of the writing, who now is the best interpreter and applier. In their entirety and under the breath of God's interpreting Spirit, the Bible emerges as the written Word of God for all people and times.

A. Prayer

I admit, Lord, that I've tried several times to read through the entire Bible and have never made it. Some parts are so hard for me to understand. What I need is confidence that all of it is there for my good—if only I can figure it out. So what I ask is that your Spirit hover over my reading and bring alive my understanding. Unlock the mysteries I need to know and help me not worry about the others. Be my eyes as I read, Rabbi Jesus. Be my mind as I think. I'll never know it all, but do lead me at least to what's essential for my life and destiny.

B. The Voice of Rabbi Jesus: Luke 10:38–42

> Let me tell you again. Don't go out on my mission alone or try to read the inspired biblical pages alone, ignoring the interpretive wisdom of my Spirit, heard especially well in the community of faith. Individualism will be a future heresy. To read my Word properly, and especially to see the signs of the times and the best current applications, you'll need the eyes of the church and my Spirit. If you're going to be whole and mature disciples of mine in proper tune with my Father, you'll need the models of both Mary and Martha. Let me explain.

I have repeatedly stressed the necessity of both attending to my teaching and "doing" what must accompany the attending. My story of Martha and Mary balances well the two central aspects of discipleship—listening and doing. By themselves, Martha and Mary are each incomplete disciples, but together they embody the listening and service that I expect when sending you out on mission.

Martha's problem was that her "much serving" and "many tasks" were preventing her from seeing the bigger picture to which her service contributes. She saw only her parts and that restricted focus threatened to blind her and rupture the household. Something similar might also said about Mary. Her sitting and listening were insightful indeed, but she could have gone on forever without anything being activated. Martha and Mary's potential partnership would contain the two parts of the necessary whole.

Your hesitancy and weariness, even about the meaning of biblical words, is understandable. Despite the difficulty, you must both listen to my words and work hard at finding their meaning. You then also need the right words that will communicate my Father's Word for others in the here and now. Activism without contemplation ends in aimless "doing" that usually aggravates existing difficulties. Deep thought and worship without follow-up action is a worthy beginning to an aborted end.

When my church gets "worried and distracted by many things" (v. 41), inevitably it will dwell in the shallows of frantic potlucks, anxious stewardship campaigns, and events designed mostly to perpetuate the institutions of religion. This distraction must be avoided at all costs.

My Spirit is anxious to continue teaching you on my behalf. I'm providing you with select portions from the revealed Word of God and from a particular tradition of my church with wisdom you need. Read carefully and continue listening closely to my Spirit who will guide your minds and hearts to understand properly and apply effectively.

C. Light from the Revealed Word

1. Psalm 52. Some words are just evil, and here's a biblical blast against them. Some worldly leader lashes out at God's faithful with a deceitful tongue. He actually thinks he can plot successfully against God's loving plan. The bully is stupid in his arrogance, not realizing that he cannot win. His big ego soon will be his sharp downfall. His army and big bank accounts are doomed to defeat and bankruptcy.

The call is to abandon the world of evil words and enter the house of God where the words are ones of worship of God and not oneself. Focus in the church is to be on the word *hesed*, the dependable and loving kindness of God. If there is to be boasting, let it be like St. Paul's about the unchanging mercy of God (1 Cor. 1:31).

2. Amos 8:1–12. The prophet parades a series of bitter words that condemn. Most people think of fruit baskets as good things. Who doesn't love a juicy bite of freshly picked fruit? Amos's fruit basket, however, is horrifying. It leads to talk of wailing and corpses. Why is fruit connected with death? The Hebrew word for "summer fruit" (*qayits*) is remarkably similar to the word for "end" later in the verse (*qets*). This end word frequently carries deadly overtones (Gen. 6:13; Lam. 4:18; Ezek. 7:2–3). We must never quit on being careful about the subtle impact of our words on others.

Amos explains why divine punishment was drawing near. The people were oppressing the poor (vs. 8:4). They couldn't wait until the Sabbath was over—even though this day of rest served as a reminder that Israel was no longer under Pharaoh's merciless rule (vs. 8:5; Deut. 5:15). Meanwhile, business practices reeked of dishonesty. Sellers wanted to make smaller the "ephah," a unit used to measure goods like flour. They also wanted to make larger the "shekel," a weight and monetary unit often connected with silver (vs. 5). The text even alludes to purchasing slaves ("buying the poor . . . and the needy," vs. 6). Any people's fruit basket filled with such rottenness had no future. The prophet's words were especially blunt about this.

3. Colossians 1:15–28. Verses 1:15–20 are known as a "Christ hymn," one surely known by both author and readers of this Pauline let-ter. These were sacred words full of holy images and magnificent claims, like the more modern hymn "Holy, Holy, Holy." No biblical words carry more mystery and majesty. If you want to focus on sure words of divine revelation with massive meaning, here they are. Jesus is . . . "the image of the invisible God, the firstborn of all creation; for in him all things in heaven and on earth were created, things visible and invisible, whether thrones or dominions or rulers or powers—all things have been created through him and for him. He himself is before all things, and in him all things hold together."

God, this Colossians poem/hymn asserts, is Creator and Lord of all that is, and Rabbi Jesus is God's embodiment now come among us. Here are words that should cause one to fall down and worship. This cosmic Christ who is "head of the body, the church" intends that the church play a role in the redemption of creation! The church is God's idea—not ours—and it belongs to God and not us. Take to heart these amazing words if you can!

D. Reflections of Leaders of the Wesleyan-Holiness Tradition

The Bible stands at the center of Christian faith revealing the amazing reality of Rabbi Jesus. We must receive this divine mystery, while realizing that the Bible's intent is more "formational" than "informational." We search its pages not to become experts in religious knowledge but to be reshaped in the image of Christ.

I want to know one thing—the way to heaven; how to land safe on that happy shore. God Himself has condescended to teach the way: for this very end He came from heaven. He has written it down in a book. O give me that book! At any price, give me the book of God! I have it. Here is knowledge enough for me. Let me be a man of one book.[1]

> Jesus, in the sacred book
> Thou art everywhere concealed:
> There for Thee alone we look,
> By Thy Spirit's light revealed,
> Thee set forth before our eyes
> Faith in every page descries.[2]

Faith, the fruit of grace, becomes the seeing eye and the hearing ear that receives and embraces the divine mystery and presence. Again, it is the totality of the Christian life, in all its various dimensions, both public and private, heart and mind, personal and social, that attests to the truth of Scripture. The truth of Scripture must be actualized, operationalized in increasing Christlikeness in both personal life and in the broader community.³

My concern is to help people transition from an "informational" to a "formational" approach to reading Scripture. The Bible's text is not an object over which we have control. We don't come to master a body of information. Instead you will allow the text to become an instrument of God's grace in your life. The Bible stands close to the center of the whole process of being conformed to the image of Christ.⁴

---

1. John Wesley, *Preface to Sermons on Several Occasions.*
2. Charles Wesley, "When Thou Hast Disposed a Heart."
3. Kenneth J. Collins, *The Theology of John Wesley.*
4. M. Robert Mulholland, Jr., *Shaped by the Word.*

WEEK 42

Christian Life #10

WILL THE REAL GOD PLEASE STAND UP?

Life can be so paradoxical and confusing. The images in Hosea show a marriage disrupted by faithlessness and children named for estrangement. Then a psalm shifts to encouraging the assembly to sing in anticipation of the kiss between justice and peace and the marriage of heaven and earth. Hosea's images of a cheapened relationship give way to the psalm's images of mutuality and enduring partnership.

Preferring the partnership song helps us understand what it means to pray with this week's Gospel passage. It's that God's will be done "on earth as it is in heaven." But before that can happen, we must ask the real God to please stand up! Once he does and is known for who he truly is, then and only then can the faithful fulfill the wonderful image that ends Psalm 85. There we are told that God will gladly march ahead of us. He will show us the way forward by leaving footprints in the mud of our daily living.

When we walk in God's footprints, we are on our way to the holy land of our eternal home. However, do we recognize this pathway when we see it? Spotting and knowing the real God is the central task of our lives. That's what Easter Sunday morning is all about!

A. Prayer

Let me know who you really are, Lord, in order that I may be able to relate to you and others as I ought. I hear all the time about broken marriages and estranged children, reflections of the struggles of the prophet Hosea. What I long to hear and sing, however, are the lyrics of the psalmist. When will cheapened relationships yield to enduring partnerships? What's the answer? I think it's this. When I come to know the real Father of Rabbi Jesus, when his will starts getting done in my life, then I'm on my way to living where God dwells eternally. So, you need to stand up for me, God, so I can see who you really are. Isn't that what the coming of Jesus was all about? If so, I need to really know and follow my Rabbi Jesus!

B. THE Voice of Rabbi Jesus: Luke 11:1–13

> You asked me to teach you to pray. Try starting with, "Father, please stand up and show us who you really are." Be sure to know the Father who is in heaven, not merely the faulty concept of him in the back of your minds. Knowing my Father will assure you that sins will be forgiven, meals provided, and temptations survived. Pray to really know my Father. With that knowledge will come all else that you need. And consider this. My Father already has stood up for you in my coming. If you really see me, you are seeing my Father fully on his feet. In seeing my Cross, you see his heart. In seeing my resurrection, you can glimpse his power.[1]

After you come to know my Father, he will teach you how to live accordingly. The first thing is to honor my Father for who he really is. Prayer is important because it connects you with God, and he then connects you with your true life and calling.[2] The church of mine should not be known for how it's organized or by what plan it conducts its business. It should be known for how it prays, who it comes to know in prayer, and then whether its life and witness are conducted with the guidance of my Spirit.

My Spirit is anxious to continue teaching you on my behalf. I'm providing you with select portions from the revealed Word of God and from a particular tradition of my church with wisdom you need. Read carefully and continue listening closely to my Spirit who will guide your minds and hearts to understand properly and apply effectively.

C. Light from the Revealed Word

1. Psalm 85. This psalm moves the assembly to sing in anticipation of the kiss between justice and peace and the marriage of heaven and earth. We are being called away from any easy satisfaction with world conditions as they are, mostly created by our own faulty human character. We are being called to a longing for a better day made possible only by knowing and championing the true character and gracious intervention of God.

Here's a cascade of sung reminders of God's past faithfulness to the people. God is known best by knowing his past actions. He is remembered for having been gracious to the land, restored good fortune, forgiven iniquity, blotted out sins, withdrawn fury, and turned from wrath. The God of forgiving love, the Father of our Rabbi Jesus, has stood up to be known for who he really is and to make clear what is expected of his children. The final verses of the psalm look to the future fulfillment of God's promises, using vivid and beloved language of reunion, fruitfulness, and completion.

> The Lord has shown us what is good,
> in Him are joined truth and grace;
> Before Him righteousness always goes,
> and His steps our pathway shows.

2. Hosea 1:2-10. These words must be read carefully or they'll be misread. Is God promoting ministers marrying women who are known to be morally corrupt? Of course not. It's an object lesson helping us see the real God standing tall. The reference is to Israel, whose relationship with God had been corrupted, and what God longed to do about the corruption. When the true God stands up, we see that his very nature is loving faithfulness, social justice, and a longing to never give up on a wayward people.

For God, one word from his mouth can mean destruction of the faithless and corrupt. And yet, the most comprehensive word that comes is "restoration" (vs. 1:10). The God of standards and judgment is also, and overwhelmingly, the God of loving redemption. In the end, despite who we are and whatever we've done, God longs for our return and remains ready to welcome us home.

3. Colossians 2:6–19. Paul's Letter to the Colossians indicates that, unfortunately, an ugly church competition was alive and well. Some Jesus believers were pursuing intimacy with God in ways that were increasing a destructive competition in the church. Some claimed they had moved to a higher level religiously, beyond their simple confession of Jesus as Lord and Messiah. Those who supposedly had attained this new status were getting there by engaging in spiritual practices such as strict observance of a religious calendar and abstention from certain foods and drinks (vss. 16–19). Through these practices, this group at Colossae believed they would gain a mystical heavenly encounter in which they would join in worship with the heavenly angels.

Paul saw this spiritual elitism as both a distraction from commitment to Christ and an inappropriate judging and disqualifying of other Christians who didn't experience such spiritual ecstasy. The lesson? Our fundamental identity as Christians is not to be found in a preferred gender, age, vocation, spiritual practice, or supposed mystical status. It's not in our religiosity, education, or good deeds. The disciples of Rabbi Jesus are to be one as they kneel together at the foot of the Cross and stand amazed together at the mouth of an empty grave.

The focus of verses 9–15 is that "all of God's fullness dwells *in Christ*." There's where we believers also are to dwell. Our human traditions are not on the same level as our relationship with Christ. God's fullness does not dwell in our wisdom, politics, spiritual experiences, or church affiliations. Those of us who confess Jesus as Messiah and Lord are to be filled with God's fullness. How? By virtue of our union with Christ and our openness to his Spirit.

D. Reflections of Leaders of the Wesleyan-Holiness Tradition

One way to know if you're following the real God is if you are gladly doing the will of the Spirit of Jesus. Deeply knowing and being holy are ongoing processes. Determine to see Jesus only and you will find your eyes fixed on the real God. Look at the Cross and then the empty tomb of Jesus and you are looking right into the heart of the real God. In these two pivotal events, God has stood up to be seen clearly!

What is the best proof of our being led by the Spirit? It's a thorough change and renovation of mind and heart, and the leading of a new and holy life.[3]

> Thee, Jesus, Thee, the sinner's friend,
> I follow on to apprehend,
> Renew the glorious strife.
> Divinely confident and bold,
> With faith's strong arm on Thee lay hold,
> Thee my eternal life.[4]

This state of entire sanctification does not preclude further growth. It ends the warfare within and leaves the whole soul, with all its passions, to be led on in the path of holiness. It obtains clearer and higher views of human duty and destiny. The regenerated thus will press the whole soul on to know and enjoy more of God. When the embarrassments are removed out of the soul itself, progress will be more rapid, every virtue may increase in strength and brightness, and the will may become stronger and stronger in its determination in the direction of holiness.[5]

Ours is the holy God who issues a holy call for us to participate in a holy mission to create a holy newness. We come to know God as we respond in faith to God's call, move out in God's power on God's mission, and open ourselves continually to God's eternal newness. God is the dynamic one who shatters all rigidities. God is the moving one who defies all narrow conceptual confinements. God is the living one who abandons all dead religion.[6]

One particular Sunday morning is crucial to the very existence of the Christian faith. The disillusioned disciples of Jesus at first had thought of his cross experience as the tragic end. Shortly, however, came the resurrection morning and everything suddenly had to be rethought in its bright light. Heaven had been unleashed in the garden. The tomb was now empty! The holiest of truths had become apparent. The Cross had been the dramatic act of God's Self-revelation and provision of redeeming love. It made clear who God really is and is all about.[7]

---

1. A beloved song of the holiness tradition is Dale Oldham's "Let Me See Jesus Only." Why? Because "only He can satisfy!"
2. For detail on the Lord's Prayer, see Barry L. Callen, *The Prayer of Holiness-Hungry People*.
3. John Wesley, *A Further Appeal to Men of Reason and Religion*.
4. Charles Wesley, "Thee, Jesus, Thee the Sinner's Friend."
5. Luther Lee, *Elements of Theology*.
6. Gilbert W. Stafford, *Theology for Disciples*.
7. Barry L. Callen, *Catch Your Breath!*

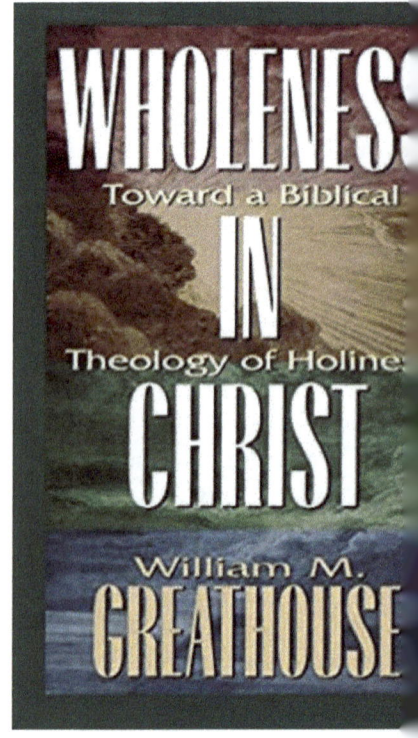

WEEK 43

Christian Life #11

KEEP YOUR BARNS UNDER CONTROL!

Farmers build barns to store their machinery, animals, and crops. We all have places where we keep things, sometimes even hoard things—under our beds, in secret closets, in bank accounts, stocks, bonds, etc. Planning is wise and saving can be a critical self-discipline of delayed gratification. But so many of us become very self-centered and decide that gratification cannot be delayed. Soon more barns must be built as we anxiously gather more and more, and there's never enough to satisfy.

Control can be lost and Christian faith become diverted into destructive channels of self-centeredness. We are warned by Rabbi Jesus that we could be called to full account by his Father at any time. We must be aware of falling into the pattern of building bigger and bigger barns to store our ever-growing piles of life's collectibles and selfish desires. To be a loyal disciple of Jesus, desires and possessions must be kept under control. All we need are modest barns for the few things really necessary.

A. Prayer

Why do we humans always tend to go to excess? It's our evil nature that always wants more and more. Even your first disciples, Rabbi Jesus, fussed over who could be seen as the greatest. They envied each other and each hoped to be the biggest and best in your eyes. I know that reaching for the highest mountaintop can so easily be a good way to collapse into the deepest valley. Like everybody else, I want to get ahead, but please save me from greed and the terrible assumption that having much makes me much. Shower me with humility and modesty, dear Jesus, so that I can represent you as I know you would want. Help me keep my barns under your control.

B. The Voice of Rabbi Jesus: Luke 12:13–21

> I'm now about to give you some critical wisdom and vision, so please listen carefully. All I'm telling you will be needed very soon. Never compete with each other for prominence or become greedy and think that will bring you security or my special attention. What you have is all a gift that easily can be removed. Yield to greed and pride and my Father may show up unexpectedly and you'll immediately realize the fool you've become. Life must never be defined by what you have or by who you are perceived to be, important as that tends to be in the world's eyes. My Father is not impressed by how large or attractive or numerous your barns happen to be!

My first disciples were ordinary people who were generally poor by world standards. I sent them out with little and encouraged them not to take much with them. They would have to trust me even for their daily needs. My farmer story is meant as a warning. Some of you may prosper, which is fine if your hearts aren't corrupted in the process. As a steward, the more you gain should lead to more that you gladly share with the needy.

Don't fuss about what's on your table, and certainly not about whether your clothes are the newest and most expensive and fashionable. If gaining more breeds in you an appetite for getting and storing more and more for your selfish personal use, then prospering ruins everything and will lead to severe judgment. Anything that takes over your life and distracts from my mission must be avoided. The cost in the long-run is more than you will want to pay. When the divine auditor arrives on your scene, a full accounting will be demanded. To avoid trouble then, stay modest now, prize unity among yourselves, and keep praising my Father rather than building bigger barns.

My Spirit is anxious to continue teaching you on my behalf. I'm providing you with select portions from the revealed Word of God and from a particular tradition of my church with wisdom you need. Read carefully and continue listening closely to my Spirit who will guide your minds and hearts to understand properly and apply effectively.

C. Light from the Revealed Word

1. Psalms 107. The Exile finally was over. The psalmist paints a series of word pictures of the struggle the people of God had to endure in order to get back home. It's summed up this way. "It's time you appreciated God's deep love" (vs. 43). If we wish to be wise, we should think on these word pictures, the experiences of God's people as they faced and survived many troubles, and received the instruction of verse 43. Focus attention on the *steadfast love of the Lord*. Celebrate God's amazing love.

The church of Rabbi Jesus has endured much over the centuries, with some of the negative well deserved. It's now being warned that what resources it may have are not its own. The only thing on which the church can depend is the grace of God that one day will bring it home to its full integrity and successful mission. Filling its barns with any other hope is the path of greed that will lead back to exile.

Here's the source of hope. If in the past God has worked successfully for the good of his people, gathering exiles from afar and guiding them through many trials, then the wise will conclude this. God never changes and will do such wonderful things again for those who remain faithful. Rather than build bigger barns, we are to fill our hearts with this memory and expectation.

2. Hosea 11:1–11. Distractions come easily in religious life and can be most destructive. God called his children out of slavery and they promptly ran off and left him. They were sucked into the ghettos of popular sex gods and began playing with religious toy gods that offered glitter and momentary excitement, and absolutely nothing else. God guided them into freedom and they stupidly volunteered to go back into slavery.

God's heart is broken by such self-destructive actions of his people, although he will not give up on them easily. Of course, should they persist in their waywardness, eventually they will have to pay the steep wages of their evil. One day, the God of love will roar like a lion, and how loudly will be that roar! When God the Judge encounters rows of overloaded barns built by his people, down they will come with the greatest of crashes!

3. Colossians 3:1–11. This divinely inspired letter of Paul picks up where Psalm 107 and Hosea 11 leave off. The word to Christians is that we must set our minds on things above. We are to put aside all earthly distractions and focus our expectations on the soon-arriving goodness of God. We are to be clothed in new selves not captured by selfishness, but are in the process of being renewed and changed into the image of God in Christ. We are to let the love of God make us lovers of others, even at real cost to ourselves. We are to put our treasures in heaven and not in bigger barns.

Our sin is said to be overcome in two ways. One is by the atoning sacrifice of Christ. The other is by our incorporation into a new reality, the body of Christ on sacrificial mission. We benefit from the first by repentance and from the second as we release ourselves into the hands of God and his people for selfless service together. This releasing demands that greed must go, ending our desire for what our culture tells us bestows status and privilege. We cannot serve God and also pursue such selfish gain (Matt. 6:24). What barns we have must be filled with righteous deeds on behalf of others. Those may be enlarged as much as possible.

D. Reflections of Leaders of the Wesleyan-Holiness Tradition

Gain all possible, if done fairly, and then give away as much as possible. Our desire must be to know and share the love of God. Being "perfect" in God's eyes is being fully engaged and responsible to Rabbi Jesus in the present stage of our spiritual journeys. We are to increase our freedom through subjection rather than enlarge our barns through selfishness. Increasing our joyous freedom requires our responding obediently to the gracious initiatives of God.

I gain all I can without hurting either my soul or body. I save all 1 can, not willingly wasting anything, not a sheet of paper, not a cup of water. I do not lay out anything, not a shilling, unless as a sacrifice to God. Yet by giving all I can, I am effectually secured from "laying up treasures upon earth." Yes, and I am secured from either desiring or endeavoring it, as long as I give all I can.[1]

> My one desire be this,
> Thy only love to know;
> To seek and taste no other bliss
> No other good below.[2]

The command "be perfect" does not express any well-known, definite act like the command "repent," nor any particular experience like being "born again." It has a greater latitude of meaning. It applies to a child of God in various stages of spiritual experience. A blade of corn may be said to be perfect in a dozen different stages of its growth. But if, before it's ripe, it stopped growing, it would not be perfect. So, at a certain period of spiritual experience, a person may be said to be a perfect Christian, and yet his attainments in piety be small in comparison with what they are after fifty years of toil and sorrow.[3]

The Christian community is composed of all those men and women who have subjected their own wills and lives to the direction and lordship of Christ. This subjection does not issue in bondage but brings the greatest liberty of all, freedom from the power and guilt of sin as well as the freedom to love God and neighbor, unfettered by excessive self-love. From the Bible's perspective, to be free from God is bondage; to be a servant of God is liberation. Discipleship, then, is the ongoing submission of our wills and lives to Jesus Christ.[4]

The life of God in the soul of a believer involves the continual inspiration of God's Holy Spirit—God's breathing into the soul and the soul breathing back what it first receives from God. God does not continue to act upon the soul unless the soul reacts to God. He will not continue to breathe into our souls unless our souls breathe toward him again.[5]

---

1. John Wesley, *The Desire of Riches.*
2. Charles Wesley, "When Shall Thy Love Constrain?"
3. B. T. Roberts, *Editorial Writings of the late Rev. Benjamin T. Roberts*, A. M., 1893.
4. Kenneth J. Collins, *Soul Care.*
5. John B. Cobb, Jr., *Grace and Responsibility.* See Barry L. Callen, *Catch Your Breath!*

WEEK 44

Christian Life #12

WHERE BANKRUPTCY IS IMPOSSIBLE

A run on the bank spells big trouble for investors who are too far back in line to get their money. Even banks can go bust. Thieves break in and steal. Computer hackers corrupt millions of accounts at once. To live in this kind of fragile world requires a courage based on faith that its real treasures are stored beyond the reach of nasty economic reverses in this world.

Who's really in charge and actually can control? Where can real assurance be found, if anywhere? In what is the church doing its investing? We cannot appease God with our misplaced attempts to earn divine respect nor can we avoid divine judgment when we invest our lives poorly. Avoiding bankruptcy is an urgent and often very uncertain business. If even banks can go bankrupt, is there anything that can't?

A. Prayer

Lord, I'm so afraid that things will go wrong for me. All of a sudden I might lose all I have, even if it's kept in the best of the local banks, invested in the best of national stocks, or supposedly protected by the best of anti-virus software. I do believe in the all-powerful Father of

Rabbi Jesus, but I admit to still being afraid to risk loss. How do I become a wise investor with a sturdy faith? Please reassure me of the positive outcome of my efforts for you, even if I don't see them in my brief lifetime. Help me to worship you for more than what I can get out of it for myself. Help me, Lord, to relax in your loving care.

B. The Voice of Rabbi Jesus: Luke 12:32–40

> Don't be afraid, my dear friends. My Father intends to give you all the benefits of his coming reign. These benefits are completely safe from all the dangers of this world. Be very careful where you do your spiritual banking, and choose well the identity of your service advisor. There is only one proper person to trust and one good place to keep your valuables away from thieves. That's my Father and his bankruptcy-proof bank above. Always keep your accounts with him up-to-date since you never know when he might suddenly show up to do a final audit.

What's presently seen isn't all there is. There's my Father, his good pleasure, and hopefully your treasures in heaven with him where they are beyond present sight and out of the reach of all bankruptcy possibility. Does fear of the future cause you to stash your goods wherever you can in a spirit of fear or greediness? Remember this. No matter how much you have, you can't take it with you when the day of final accounting comes. My Father is not one who originally created and now is sitting back passively to watch it all unfold as it will. Rather, he attends lovingly to the sparrows, the lilies of the fields, and even to the hairs on your head.

This divine superintendency of all things means that you don't need to hold tightly to what you have, always fearing loss. If fact, giving much of it away to those in need may be the best way to safeguard it for all eternity. Once you really believe in me, you will become increasingly free to be generous in my name. That way you will build a heavenly account that's never in any danger.

My Spirit is anxious to continue teaching you on my behalf. I'm providing you with select portions from the revealed Word of God and from a particular tradition of my church with wisdom you need. Read carefully and continue listening closely to my Spirit who will guide your minds and hearts to understand properly and apply effectively.

C. Light from the Revealed Word

1. Psalm 50. The fact is plain enough. God is sovereign and has available all options for action. Never forget this. This all-powerful God may be graciously *with us* but is hardly *like us*. His presence can be threatening when circumstances require—as they do right now. Your banks are loaded with many of the wrong things. Don't count on them to last.

Can you hear it? God is announcing that his people have become morally bankrupt. Long is the list of wrongs that is leading to impending disaster. God is saying, "I am passing judgment on you. Quit making worse than useless your animal offerings to me. All the animals in the world already are mine anyway. You are daring to mock the Most High with your greed, even though it's wrapped in lovely religious paper. If I don't deliver you, your fate is doomed."

2. Isaiah 1:1–20. This text lands like a loud gavel in the courtroom. The judge rules that the multitude of the church's sacrifices mean nothing. God doesn't delight in the blood of bulls. Bringing those kinds of offerings along with an evil heart is exhausting God's patience. When you stretch out hands seeking help, the eyes of God will be closed. Your way of doing church business is about over. When religious practices designed to increase the holiness of the people have soured into self-indulgence, the bank of God's grace quickly closes.

God forgives because God loves, not because God is ever bought off with anything humanly offered. Divine grace is not for sale and the banks of human waywardness are about to go bust. By contrast, God's loving faithfulness is a resource without limit. It's bankruptcy-proof. Its wonderful benefits, however, will not always flow to the faithless.

Is there hope? Of course. In this world, a run on any bank can trigger economic depression. And on the other hand, if we allow God to wash us clean, even the foulest of sinners can find themselves cleansed as white as snow and back in business!

3. Hebrews 11:1–16. It was *by faith* that Abraham believed and ventured forth. God is never ashamed of those who believe and dare to act accordingly, whatever the results. Here's what should be believed and acted on. The once-for-all sacrifice of Jesus should be sufficient to sustain faith and enable deeds of love that build treasures that are uncorruptable. Faith is a gift of God's unconditional grace. It also is the human response of gratitude, obedience, and hope.

Don't plan your worship services for what you can get out of them. Worship should focus on the love of and praise to God. Remember that Abraham trusted in the long-term promise of God. He died having left home in faith, but without knowing where he was going and without ever seeing the fulfillment of the promise. Faith in God's eventual tomorrow should fuel a faithful living today regardless of developments. The writer to the Hebrews encourages believers never to abandon hope even though faced with persecution and the unwelcome fact that Christ has not yet returned. Faith is the assurance of what is hoped for although it may not yet be seen.

D. Reflections of Leaders of the Wesleyan-Holiness Tradition

We must spend our resources as intended. There are a multitude of opportunities to go wrong, but there's only one bank that's totally secure. There are two ways to be wealthy. The only option that's eternally safe is the holy way, limiting our wants and living and loving like Rabbi Jesus. This way brings a deep inner assurance that God is with us now and will be always.

Why do you not deal your bread to the hungry and cover the naked with a garment? Did God entrust you with his (not your) goods for this end? Can any servant afford to lay out his master's money other than as his master has appointed him?[1]

> I sing of thy grace,
> From my earliest days,

> Ever near to allure and defend;
> Hitherto Thou hast been
> My preserver from sin,
> And I trust Thou wilt save to the end.
>
> O the infinite cares,
> And temptations, and snares,
> Thy hand hath conducted me through!
> O the blessings bestowed
> By a bountiful God,
> And the mercies eternally new![2]

There are two ways to be wealthy. One is in the abundance of your possessions and the other is in the fewness of your wants. In taking the latter way to be wealthy, you transfer to the inside of you the real wealth that cannot be taken away by depression or death. Keep your needs down to needs, not luxuries disguised as needs. The bank of human character will pay dividends through eternity. Invest all surpluses in that bank. If you have too much, then invest it in persons. Train at the feet of Jesus. This is the path walked by the holy.[3]

Apart from God, no one is holy. Holy people are set apart for God's purpose in the world. Empowered by the Holy Spirit, holy people live and love like Jesus Christ. Holiness is both gift and response, renewing and transforming, personal and communal, ethical and missional. The holy people of God follow Jesus Christ in engaging all the cultures of the world and drawing all peoples to God.[4]

God's greatest desire for me is for me to be happy and holy, and the only way to realize that dream for my life is to build it on a secure foundation. I could easily reduce religion to an external façade, simply trying to be good. But this falls far short of true religion, which is a living relationship with God through Jesus Christ. If my relationship with God is strong because of the indwelling Christ, then I will understand my place in the world as a pilgrim of love.[5]

The issue of assurance remains a vital part of the contemporary Wesleyan witness to the broader catholic church. The reception of salvific graces is marked by a twofold assurance that embraces the direct witness of the Holy Spirit that one is indeed forgiven as well as the indirect witness, the assurance of our own spirit to this same saving reality.[6]

---

1. John Wesley, *The Inefficiency of Christianity*.
2. Charles Wesley, "Away With Our Fears."
3. E. Stanley Jones, *Abundant Living*.
4. Kevin Mannoia, in *The Holiness Manifesto*.
5. Paul Chilcote, *Praying in the Wesleyan Spirit*.
6. Kenneth J. Collins and Jason E. Vickers, *The Sermons of John Wesley*.

Christian Life #13

LET'S START A FIRE!

It's a scene too awful to ever want to see. A couple goes shopping and comes home to observe flames shooting out of their upstairs windows. It's already too late to save anything! Given this frightening scene, we hesitate to encourage anyone to start a fire, unless in the most controlled of circumstances and for the best of reasons.

Even so, Jesus came to save and, so he said, also to start a fire (Lk. 3:16). The only sure way for beleaguered believers to survive and serve as expected is to experience this fire. We are to know firsthand the Pentecost fire of God's Spirit that cleanses the soul and inflames the faithful to a service that is both loving and courageous.

When proceeding with loving intentions, faithful disciples of Rabbi Jesus must risk causing divisions and conflicts in families and even nations. The fire of our baptisms is meant to cleanse and not destroy, although faithfulness sometimes stimulates reactions we wish would never happen. The holy ones of God must remain accountable to God regardless of any resulting conflict. We must manage any fires as peaceably as possible.

A. Prayer

There is so much wrong around me that the last thing I want to do is start another fight or set another fire. What I really need, Rabbi Jesus, is the fire of your Spirit to cleanse me so that I can enter conflicts as an agent of your holy peace. I also need to understand better what it means to serve a loving Lord who has standards and who, when they are blatantly violated, also is a God of judgment. How I personally need to be refined and not be a judge of others. Come to me, Lord. Mold me into an inflamed instrument of your cleansing Spirit, a loving reconciler, never serving my own ends.

B. The Voice of Rabbi Jesus: Luke 12:49-56

> I realize that these words of mine sound harsh. "I came to bring fire to the earth!" So be it. I may be the Prince of Peace, but I also came to bring judgment and, as necessary, even sow some unavoidable division. Grace and judgment are not mutually exclusive. Your role as my disciples is to assist people to understand both of these roles, and certainly to avoid the negatives of judgment whenever possible. My Father will finally do the needed judging. You are to concentrate on being instruments of holy cleansing and reconciling love, but only after being cleansed yourselves by the Spirit.

Luke begins his recounting of my life by saying that I would guide people into the ways of peace (1:79). He was correct, but there's the darker part reflected in the song popular among many of my disciples. The *Battle Hymn of the Republic* says, "hath loosed the lightening of his terrible swift sword." That's not the place for you to start, although one day my Father will have to end some things this way.

Begin here. Expose yourselves to an experience of the fiery Pentecost of my Spirit. That burning restores souls into holy new creations, inflaming them to great deeds of love and righteousness. I desire no division or loss. Even so, some people's response to my Father's coming reign will necessitate destructive fires. As my disciples, be holy but not harmless, and prepare yourself for anything.

My Spirit is anxious to continue teaching you about this on my behalf. I'm providing you with select portions from the revealed Word of God and from a particular tradition of my church with wisdom you need. Read carefully and continue listening closely to my Spirit who will guide your minds and hearts to understand properly and apply effectively.

C. Light from the Revealed Word

1. Psalm 80:1-19. This psalm is a community complaint. Why the complaining of God's people? Because the home place was in ashes, the walls broken down and vandals were sorting through the rubble. "Restore us, O Lord," was the complaint. "We had no insurance to cover all this destruction. Aren't we your special people? How can you be so distant from us when we need you most?"

The problem was that the destruction was the people's own fault. They had thrown into the fire God's known will for them and then turned around and tried to blame the result on God's inaction. They had no repentance for their selfish agendas, only complaint. We are warned about the consequences of making idols of our nations, group traditions, private desires, and even religious practices.

2. Isaiah 5:1–7. This parable of the vineyard tells story of Israel. God chose a people, planted, nourished, and protected them, and now expected the appropriate fruit in return. What happened was the yielding of rotten and bitter fruit. What more could God have done for his people? Since the answer was "nothing," devastation followed. The God who built now had to tear down. What had been tended so carefully now would be overgrown with briars and thorns. What an unnecessary waste, what a shame!

The vineyard was the house of Israel. God had expected justice and got only greed and bloodshed. He had planned on righteousness and heard only the cries of the abused. There was to be a "peaceable kingdom," a new order of things motivated by the loving kindness of God.

How sad if the only way to this desired goal was setting fire to the old that had failed and starting over.

3. Hebrews 11:29-12:2. God loved Israel, granted it freedom from Egyptian slavery, and enabled many great victories in its life. The walls of Jericho had fallen at the sound of the trumpets and voice of God. Now these veterans of the faith, graduated to their heavenly rewards, watch over current disciples of Rabbi Jesus and cheer them on. Given such amazing support, we had better never quit until we have yielded good fruit and finished our leg of the great race of faith.

We disciples of Rabbi Jesus need the courage to endure when we face hostility and ridicule. Earlier saints had to go on without fully reaching the grand goal, as likely will be true of us also. Jesus endured the Cross for the sake of a great joy, the potential of our salvation (12:2). He went through the fire for us so that we could be able to endure present fires. We are to seek ways to reconcile others with the power of love.

D. Reflections of Leaders of the Wesleyan-Holiness Tradition

God's cleansing fire will burn until his will is complete. Come, Lord, bring your refining fire to consume the selfishness of even your disciples. We must be fired and energized by a holy love and committed to a life of reconciliation.

We have strong reason to hope that the work God hath begun he will carry on unto the day of his Lord Jesus, that he will never end this blessed work of his Spirit until he has fulfilled all his promises, until he hath put a period to sin, misery, and death, and re-established universal holiness and happiness.[1]

> Come then, my God, mark out Thine heir,
> Of heaven a larger earnest give!
> With clearer light Thy witness bear,
> More sensibly within me live;
> Let all my powers Thine entrance feel,
> And deeper stamp Thyself the seal.[2]

Perishing sinners need our churches filled with men and women who are clothed with holiness and power. We shall not see such Christians till self is slain that Christ may reign. We are to be crucified, dead to self, and alive unto the righteousness of God. Only as the Spirit sanctifies us, and Christ lives in us, and works through us will we be clothed with power to lead the multitudes to him.[3]

John Wesley believed that for too many salvation had been "reduced" to a single notion of being declared right with God by faith at the cost of going on to a righteousness life. He was convinced that God implants righteousness in everyone to whom he has imputed it. Salvation involves more than a forensic declaration of now being right with God; salvation also involves a new life that is lived out in faith, energized by love (Gal. 5:6).[4]

I was speaking at a high-level meeting in South Africa when my emphasis on reconciliation was challenged as "too soft." I responded vigorously. Reconciliation is not soft and namby-pamby. It is rugged and tough. The revolutionary says, "The world is in trouble and I'm going to fix it. If you get in my way, I will kill you." The reconciler says, "The world is in bad shape and I'm going to work to change it. If you try to block me, I'm willing to lay down my life for the cause." I then asked, "Which of these two positions is soft and namby-pamby?"[5]

---

1. John Wesley, *The General Spread of the Gospel.*
2. Charles Wesley, *"Come, Holy Ghost, All Quickening Fire."*
3. A. B. Simpson, quoted in *A. M. Hills, Holiness and Power.*
4. Cliff Sanders, *The Optimism of Grace.*
5. Samuel G. Hines, *Beyond Rhetoric.*

WEEK 46

Christian Life #14

LEAD YOUR DONKEYS, I'LL LEAD MINE

Are some things right for some Christians and wrong for others? Are good things good only on six days each week, with separate rules for the Sabbath? Are we to follow the standing religious rules of our churches or the example of Jesus? Unfortunately, they aren't always the same. Is life in God's Spirit a fixed or fluid thing? It's hardly surprising that Jesus often was in trouble with his own people. He followed his Father's gracious will rather than always obeying the "traditions of the Elders." Love adapted to circumstance, while rules refused to do that.

Jesus knew that religious leaders in his day would routinely care for an animal's basic needs on the Sabbath but would not tolerate his lovingly transforming the life of a troubled woman. Jesus did as his gracious Father willed, not what his over-institutionalized people were insisting. What about today? The church is caught in the tension of adapting to the prevailing culture without being captured by that culture. The faith always will be the faith, although its styles of appearance and means of application will vary. Careful discernment is crucial. You lead your donkeys and I'll lead mine.

A. Prayer

Do rules in religion keep us on the *right* track or just on the *same* track, even if it's going the wrong way? I admit to having a tendency to want to control the actions of those around me in ways I think right. If I'm legislating the particulars of what it should mean to be holy in ways that don't really honor you, Rabbi Jesus, please forgive me and show me a better way. I know you often broke religious rules and thereby praised your Father more perfectly. Guide me daily by your Spirit so that I can do the same. Keep me and the church I attend from resting passively on any day when we should be doing some holy work that you desire.

B. The Voice of Rabbi Jesus: Luke 13:10-17

> All donkeys are worth caring for on any day, and certainly are especially needy people as well. Some religious leaders treat their animals better than they treat their desperate neighbors. Beware of setting rules that benefit yourself and demonize others. If you must step outside artificial rules to do the redeeming work of my Father, do it with love, but do it. When there is a cost, even from fellow disciples who don't understand, pay it gladly. Be my agents of relational love in action whatever the day or circumstance.

The Sabbath rules of my people were very fixed and clear, and on occasion I broke some of them. Technically, I was wrong and actually I was right. Leading their donkeys to water on the Sabbath was thought just fine, while healing a poor woman was totally out of bounds. You must come to know that human rules of what constitutes holy actions are fragile at best. Sometimes you will be held accountable by fellow believers to a standard not necessarily mine.

During my ministry the leaders of my people had chosen the rule of rest and no work on the Sabbath. The problem, of course, comes in how to define rest and work. I chose on occasion to engage in acts of mercy regardless of the day, the kind of work that is wonderfully restful in my Father's eyes. Being merciful is always honoring God. Books full of rules can shield disciples from the real work of God. If a donkey can be led out for a drink, know that a poor woman can be freed for new life within the allowable bounds of God's rules. Institutionalized religion can shape improperly your understanding of what actions constitute the good.

My Spirit is anxious to continue teaching you on my behalf. I'm providing you with select portions from the revealed Word of God and from a particular tradition of my church with wisdom you need. Read carefully and continue listening closely to my Spirit who will guide your minds and hearts to understand properly and apply effectively.

C. Light from the Revealed Word

1. Psalm 71:1–6. The call is for God to provide the needed rescue from the hands of the wicked and cruel. The Living God is imaged as two inanimate objects, a rock and a fortress, stressing God's unchanging nature and dependability. It's important not to misread the inanimate images, however. Theology too often is treated as a fixed set of ideas, even finished and mandatory statements of doctrine and definitions of how to act in every circumstance. Instead, true belief is rooted more in a flexible Divine-human relationship and proper life practices that are the loving fruit of that relationship.

Trust in God should arise from transformative experiences with God's Spirit and not be controlled by excessive obedience to local church regulations of acceptable conduct. New creations in Christ surely will generate acts of mercy in novel circumstances and on any day—including the Sabbath. God is a present, loving, and attentive reality, a gracious Father who responds to urgent need whenever and however it presents itself. God the Rock, anything but unfeeling, is eager for action—"there's no Rock like me" (Isa. 44:8). Sometimes donkeys need water and people need healing—both, now!

2. Jeremiah 1:4–10. God calls Jeremiah to be his prophet. The instruction is, "Go where I say and do whatever I inspire you to do." No wonder Jeremiah hesitated. True prophets often find themselves speaking the opposite of what most people think and acting in ways that generally are thought unacceptable, even offensive. God's encouragement is merely, "Now I have put words in your mouth. Speak these words even if some hold you accountable for breaking a local rule."

Clear rules of the road bring a certain kind of assurance—you need not think or struggle, just do whatever the rule says and move on. The servant of God, however, is to be an instrument of the Spirit, thinking and acting however the Spirit directs in each circumstance. Being such a divine instrument requires a discerning receptivity to divine guidance and the courage to follow regardless of resistance encountered. Not acceptable is just looking up the most relevant rule, maybe written in an earlier time and different culture, and mindlessly proceeding.

3. Hebrews 12:18–29. Can you remember a terrible thunderstorm? The writer to the Hebrews recalls past experiences of the most thunderous encounters with God, finally saying that Jesus was another such appearance and now is the Mediator of a new covenant. We are reverently to offer God acceptable worship, realizing that God is a consuming fire. Mere religion is a particular target of this fire. The Bible is not intended as a book of detailed instructions of exactly how to be holy in every time and place and circumstance. It's more an invitation to enter into an ongoing relationship and dialogue with God's Spirit about what God expects and requires from time to time.

Discipleship is less indoctrination into some set of intellectual particulars and more an ongoing walk with Rabbi Jesus, constantly learning in that relationship. What we learn is that God is beyond full comprehension, beyond being captured fully in any theological formula or fixed rules for what to do in each situation. God is rich in mercy and sacrificial love—as his people should be. Always relevant is Paul's statement: "The only thing that counts is faith working through love" (Gal. 5:6).

D. Reflections of Leaders of the Wesleyan-Holiness Tradition

There is a universal love of God that should define the character of a disciple of Rabbi Jesus. It should inspire a reaching lovingly to all people in all circumstances. We finally bow to Jesus alone, although we grow wise through certain practices and are accountable to each other. There is relational flexibility in the biblical instructions about loving our neighbor. Holy believers are freed to live in the immediacy of God's presence and leading on behalf of the needy world.

A Christian's heart is enlarged toward all mankind, those he knows and those he does not; he embraces with strong and cordial affection neighbors and strangers, friends and enemies. This is catholic or universal love. He that has this is of a catholic spirit. Love alone gives the title to this character.[1]

> Forth from the midst of Babel brought,
> Parties and sects I cast behind;
> Enlarge my heart, and free my thought.
> Where'er the latent truth I find,
> The latent truth with joy to own,
> And bow to Jesus' name alone.[2]

John Wesley understood the importance of sanctifying contexts. He knew people grew best when surrounded by others who embraced the same Story and sought the same goal. There is no holiness, but social holiness. "Holy solitaries,'" said Wesley, "is a phrase no more consistent with the gospel than holy adulterers." He structured the Methodist movement around a series of groups, each serving a different function beneath the one main purpose, restoration in the image of God. Wesley also recognized that sanctification was accomplished in part through the "means of grace," certain indispensable practices such as the Eucharist, prayer, Scripture reading, and Christian conference.[3]

Trying to master anything, including matters of faith, as objective entities apart from ourselves, is impossible. We cannot understand the biblical texts apart from ourselves and our reading community of faith. Unless our readings of Scripture allow those texts to come alive in responses of faithful and holy living, the Bible loses its character as holy Scripture.[4]

Just as Christ does not exist merely for himself, but extends himself for the sake of human beings, so Christian believers are truly human when they move outside their self-centeredness. This self-limiting vulnerability becomes evident in the life of Jesus. Through our holy self-limitation, we are set free to love others. We will be able to re-create the immediacy of God's presence for the sake of God's world.[5]

The heart of Christian faith sometimes involves conflict with civil and even religious authorities. It's the determination to live by faith and not just theorize about it behind sacred walls. Holiness is an exercise in receiving and then sharing hope with those living in the worst of circumstances.[6]

---

1. John Wesley, *The Catholic Spirit*.
2. Charles Wesley, "Forth from the Midst of Babel Brought."
3. Stephen Lennox, *Sanctifying Context*.
4. Richard P. Thompson, *Reading the Bible in Wesleyan Ways*.
5. Douglas M. Strong, in Callen-Thorsen, *Heart & Life*.
6. Barry L. Callen, *Catch Your Breath!*

WEEK 47

Christian Life #15

I'LL DO IT MY WAY!

We who claim to serve Rabbi Jesus have a subtle but fatal tendency. It's quietly replacing the prominence of God in church life with ourselves and our private agendas. We want to do God's things, yes, but in our own way. We put ourselves forward, subtly for the most part but sometimes even openly.

Such personal pride was thought acceptable for a prominent secular singer like Frank Sinatra. He crooned, "I've lived a life that's full, I've traveled each and every highway, And more, much more than this, *I did it my way*." That's Frank, and the world in general. But God says, "Frank thinks it's fine for him, but it isn't, and certainly not for my people."

Jesus is *the way*, truth, and life. For the Christian life, there is to be no *my way*. If God's people, on whom God has showered so much love and grace, insist on going their own way, their fate will be this. God sadly will allow them to do as they wish, and eventually pay the high price. Instead, Christians must be part of a disciplined community of faith determined to do things God's way.

A. Prayer

I admit it, my Lord. I like to do things as I wish. I want to be thought of as somebody special. I won't step on anyone to get ahead, at least not blatantly or obviously or often. But doesn't one have to take initiatives and make good impressions and throw around a little weight if necessary to get ahead, even in your special work? Still, I do hear Rabbi Jesus saying that the drive to get ahead personally, especially at the cost of others, is a cancer in church life. It's hardly a sign of the new creation Jesus came to make possible. So, Lord, bend my knees, make me new, fix my eyes only on you and your way of doing things. May the success of your kingdom be allI desire.

B. The Voice of Rabbi Jesus: Luke 14:1–14

> It's important who decides where you sit at the table. I was at one banquet and all eyes were on me. Reports were everywhere that I did things my own way, a way often upsetting to my fellow Jews but always my Father's way. Then it happened again. I healed a seriously ill man on this banquet evening. That wasn't thought acceptable protocol for the occasion, especially on the Sabbath. Eyes stared at me. I also noticed folks elbowing their way to the best couches. They were anxious to be noticed and honored and especially comfortable. I called them on it. Such selfishness must never be the way of my disciples. You belong at such banquets, but not always comfortably.

I'm sure I appeared to be a rude guest. No one else there that evening would have dared say aloud what I did. I'll also say it to you. If you ever walk around with our noses in the air, you'll finally fall on your face. If you'll do just about anything to get on the Temple's main stage instead of risking a Roman cross, you aren't going to be my disciples very long. "All who exalt themselves will be humbled, and those who humble themselves will be exalted" (vs. 11). Do it your own way and I assure you that it will be the wrong way.

Note carefully one of the more important passages in the New Testament. It's about my temptations in the desert. Why so important? The Gospel writers would have known nothing about this critical time in my early ministry if I hadn't made a point of reporting it to my first disciples. I did that because what happened out there is what will happen to all of you. Was I to carry on my ministry as my Father wished or in ways that would bring me comfort and applause? I determined that any way other than self-sacrifice would abort the mission--unacceptable! What was true for me is true for you also.

My Spirit is anxious to continue teaching you on my behalf. I'm providing you with select portions from the revealed Word of God and from a particular tradition of my church with wisdom you need. Read carefully and continue listening closely to my Spirit who will guide your minds and hearts to understand properly and apply effectively.

C. Light from the Revealed Word

1. Psalm 81:1–16. God is presented here as frustrated and even a little sarcastic. "My people didn't listen, paid no attention." So what does God do? He lets go of the reins of his people and tells them, "Run! Do it your own way. Crash and burn!" (vs. 12). What had the people done during their time of not listening to God? They'd gone after the latest in gods, opting for religious fashion instead of reality. That might have been stupid, but at least they had found it exciting for a short time. Then came the disaster.

The Father's thunder once rumbled over Mt. Sinai. Oddly, the people only wanted God to listen to their complaints. Instead, the heavenly thunder insisted on taking the floor. God announced that once he had shouldered the burdens of the people and set them free. They had taken advantage of that freedom. Now they would be left to the serious consequences of their selfish error. "I had set before you life and you chose your own way, death. Drink your fill of living your own way. The taste will be bitter indeed!"

2. Jeremiah 2:4–13. God's people made the mistake that Proverbs had warned against. Never push yourself into prominence because, if you do, the resulting demotion will be humiliating indeed (25:6-7). God wondered. "What fault did my people find in me that they drifted so far away, taking up with Sir Windbag and becoming windbags themselves?"

I brought my people to a lovely garden and they proceeded to pollute it. Now they must know that a bloated windbag requires only a little pin-prick to explode. I will react to their drifting by letting them blow away and eventually blow up. Any nation that trades God for no gods has traded my glory for a silly and short-lived shallowness. My way was junked for the way of no good future.

3. Hebrews 13:1–17. God is ultimate faithfulness and will never walk off and leave his people (vss. 5-6). Unfortunately, that doesn't stop God's people from leaving him. They easily get lured away with the latest speculations about who Jesus really is, even though "products named after Christ don't seem to do much for those who buy them" (vs. 9). Doing things our own way in defiance of God's revealed way is a poor manner of conducting one's life. Getting ahead our way will only be getting ourselves farther behind.

Some believers wouldn't consider defying God directly. Over time, however, they get weary and slack off from the strain of doing the Father's work. Disciples of Rabbi Jesus must persist in their faithfulness. They must pay attention to even the little things of living, like what God approves happening in the kitchen, in the bedroom, in the workplace, and on the streets. Stay alert to how life is going and continue working under God's careful supervision (vs. 17). May the God who put in place and holds all things together make you whole and full of joy as you live *in his way*.

D. Reflections of Leaders of the Wesleyan-Holiness Tradition

If we do not, God will not. All is to be done for the Lord and in the Lord's way. We must profit from membership in the community of God's people and learn to see things from the perspective of God's eternity. We must plan for and commit to maturity in Christ. Christian holiness is social in nature. Disciples of Rabbi Jesus are to mature and serve *together* and in God's revealed way.

If we do not love God who first loved us, if we will not hearken to his voice, if we turn our eyes away from him and will not attend to the light which he pours upon us, his Spirit will not always strive. He will gradually withdraw and leave us to the darkness of our own hearts. He will not continue to breathe into our souls unless our souls breathe toward him again, unless our love, and prayer, and thanksgiving return to him, a sacrifice wherewith he is well pleased.[1]

> Joyful thus my faith to show,
> I find his service my reward;
> Every work I do below,
> I do it to the Lord.[2]

We live in a time where people are desperate for community, belonging, hope, healing, and real transformation. The Methodist [Wesleyan-Holiness] theological tradition is ideally positioned to address these crucial needs. It's designed to help people connect with a God who is real and cares about them. We need each other. And we need to connect in deep, vulnerable, and authentic ways. In the age of disembodied and ever-present pseudo connections, I'm not sure there ever has been more of a hunger for community and connection in person.[3]

This Christian journey enables a person to be loving and bold, open and vulnerable. One becomes willing to put the whole of self on the line, being very concerned about the truth and meaning of biblical revelation, and being equally concerned with being involved personally in the implications of the faith. Being with Jesus and becoming like Jesus requires being part of the ongoing mission of Jesus Christ. God's grace understands our humanness, gives the space and time needed to grow and mature, and provides the passion to actually be the hands and feet of Jesus in this world.[4]

That people accept Christ as their personal Savior is *not* a sufficient goal for church life. The goal is that persons *mature in Christ*. The pastoral question—"How is it with your soul?"—is the most important question we as a church can learn to ask each other in the twenty-first century.[5]

Most Christians today are not and cannot be living as monks. Even so, many are looking for the experience of being part of some disciplined community of faith, maybe like the "Holy Club" or "class meeting" of early Methodism. There is today a fresh holiness movement springing up to serve busy modern Christians who long for more than regularly scheduled church services.[6]

Christians mature best in faith communities. To become *like Christ* must involve *being Christ* to others. Becoming mature in Christ is necessarily to be on mission for Christ, going arm-in-arm with fellow believers, being the church together.[7]

---

1. John Wesley, *The Great Privilege of Those That Are Born of God.*
2. Charles Wesley, "Lo, I Come with Joy."
3. Kevin Watson, *Perfect Love.*
4. Barry L. Callen, *John S. Pistole: Searching for Integrity and Faith.*
5. Gilbert W. Stafford, *Church of God: At the Crossroads.*
6. This fresh concern for holiness is seen clearly in and being assisted by the Wesleyan Holiness Connection (see Barry Callen's *The Holy River of God*).
7. Barry L. Callen, *Catch Your Breath!*

Christian Life #16

IT'S AN OPEN BOOK

Both things are the case. First, everything about us humans is known to God. That's not surprising or God wouldn't be God. Then comes the second thing that is surprising and truly wonderful. Because of the graciousness of God's *Self-revelation*, everything we need to know about God now is available to us humans!

We'll never know everything, of course, at least not in this life. What we can know about God, however, is *everything we need to know*—God has seen to that in the coming of his Son and now through the ministry of the Spirit of the Son. We are an open book to God--and God has opened the heart of his own book to us!

There is a related requirement, however. An open book is of little use if we can't read. Those who come to believe must discipline themselves, use all the "means of grace" that God provides to become skilled readers of the revealed Word of God. Once reading carefully, something begins to fill the believing heart. It is an "optimism of God's grace"!

A. Prayer

It makes me uncomfortable, Rabbi Jesus, to realize that you know me thoroughly, more than I even realize, and surely more than other people know. I'm trying to hide my worst parts from them. Still, I have some comfort in realizing that, given the negatives in my life, you love me still and are seeking my full restoration. How wonderful is your love, Lord! How grateful I am that your Father has come to inform me of his great heart. Keep me, Lord, from fearing your eyes that penetrate so deeply. Focus my attention on your desire to redeem and commission me to your work. Teach me to read well your open book of life. Fill me with an optimism about what you are offering your children and also a great desire to receive it!

B. The Voice of Rabbi Jesus Luke 14:25–33

> Planning is always good, the only reasonable way to go. Regarding life now and eternally, however, planning has its limits and must rely on the only architect who knows how to build tomorrow safely. You disciples can't know all things in advance, and you can't manage to take care of everything in the meantime. Come and follow me now, knowing who I am and becoming comfortable with living by faith. Turn your backs on the demand for certainty. My Father's book of all wisdom is open wide to me. Rely on that, trust me, and just come.

If you intend to be my disciples, not merely hangers-on and in-name-only people, you need to be aware of what you're getting into. Priorities need to be clarified and hard choices made. The challenges will be great and I expect no backing off, whatever the cost. Candidates for discipleship need to realize this in advance and really buy into the task—with all its joys and risks and costs.

Would a king go to battle without determining troop and weapon levels on both sides and deciding that victory is a reasonable possibility? No, and you need to know that I have checked the levels and know that life's battle *will be won*, not quickly or easily but absolutely! Rest in this knowledge and come with me. Do daily what it will take to really come to know me and my Father. The necessary grace will be given. Now discipline yourselves to actually receive.

My Spirit is anxious to continue teaching you on my behalf. I'm providing you with select portions from the revealed Word of God and from a particular tradition of my church with wisdom you need. Read carefully and continue listening closely to my Spirit who will guide your minds and hearts to understand properly and apply effectively.

C. Light from the Revealed Word

1. Psalm 1. The goal of God is one day being able to open his book of accounts and report the content of this psalm as being true about each of us as individuals, and about the people of God as a whole. Here's the hoped-for report.

We became thrilled with digging into the Word of God in order to learn more and more about how God graciously planted us in a fertile garden of life. We took advantage of this love-filled circumstance and bore lush fruit for the good of ourselves and our needy neighbors. We became well aware that the wicked are like helpless dust before a high wind. We chose to walk the right road charted for us carefully by our Maker. We came to rejoice that God had opened his book of wisdom, full of actual knowledge of God's very Self, and bid us to live by a wisdom far greater than our own.

2. Jeremiah 18:1-11. If my people claim to know me, then they should be aware of this about me. I'm planning a lot of negative against them because of my knowing what they're really all about these days. They had better learn quickly and start doing the right things. And there's one other thing to be known to fill out the picture. It brings a ray of hope. There's the marvelous metaphor of the potter and the clay that reveals a key element of God's very nature.

A vessel being shaped on the potter's wheel may be spoiled and the process started over. The substance of the clay, its clayness, had remained unchanged despite the spoiled attempt at a pot. It remained available for a reshaping that might work next time. So it is with God and his people. While we may sin and receive severe judgment, we remain the object of God's love and capable of being restored. God judges not to destroy but to save if people will allow. That's redeeming love!

3. Philemon 1–21. Paul writes to Philemon, knowing much about him and wanting him to know much about some important developments. Open books in church life can lead to rich fellowship that benefits all. Too many people live their lives with masks on, hiding their true selves in shame, embarrassment, and fear. But God already knows all and is prepared to forgive all. The church is to be a *masks-off* place. It's to be a testimony place where we tell each other about the goodness shown to us by God. Such stories help others consider removing their masks.

Paul knew about Philemon's faith and love and how they were enriching others. He prays that all the believers will allow their faces to shine with gratitude for the grace of God, allowing others to know the joy available through God in Christ for us all. Paul would hold nothing back from his dear friend, including the full story of Onesimus, a slave now become a treasured Christian brother. Here's a picture of a properly functioning faith community.

D. Reflections of Leaders of the Wesleyan-Holiness Tradition

God may now be Self-revealed, "music in the sinner's ears," but our awareness of that must be nurtured by all the "means of grace." The Bible is a book of experience and we now must develop the skill of reading it well, experiencing God's grace personally, and testifying to its restoring results. God is still at work and the story must be told. A child of God is always to be active and optimistic, always seeking to be more like Christ.

In using all means, seek God alone. In and through every outward thing, look only to the power of His Spirit and the merits of His Son. Beware that you do not get stuck in the work itself. If you do, it is all lost labor. Nothing short of God can satisfy your soul.[1]

> Jesus! the name that charms our fears,
> That bids our sorrows cease;
> 'Tis music in the sinner's ears,
> 'Tis life, and health, and peace.[2]

The Bible is a book of experience. Its events occurred in actual human history, among real people, with profoundly human involvements. The Bible was not given on golden plates but to people. Revelation was not given in a vacuum but concretely, in experience. Jesus was a Man who was seen, heard, touched, loved, and hated. He spoke to real persons enmeshed in the web of life and sickness and family concerns and labor and social involvements and death. The language of the Bible is the language of experience.[3]

The Bible is the norming norm that plays a central role in directing Christian wisdom. The Bible, however, does not play its central role in isolation from what inevitably impacts how the biblical text is read and interpreted. There are interactive aids to biblical understanding, graciously provided by God and ignored at the reader's peril. God's revelation, to be received and interpreted properly, necessarily includes a written apostolic witness (the Bible), a faithful remembering community (the Christian traditions), a process of existential appropriation (spiritual experience), a way to test for internal consistency (reason), and a commitment of readers to be open to the biblical text in this multiple and interactive manner.[4]

God, who is holy, has abundant and steadfast love for us. God's holy love is revealed to us in the life and teachings, death and resurrection of Jesus Christ, our Savior and Lord. God continues to work, giving life, hope and salvation through the indwelling of the Holy Spirit, drawing us into God's own holy, loving life. God transforms us, delivering us from sin, idolatry, bondage, and self-centeredness to love and serve God, others, and to be stewards of creation. Thus, we are renewed in the image of God as revealed in Jesus Christ.[5]

Wesleyan, Holiness, and Pentecostal movements are marked by an expectant faith rooted in an optimism of grace. Compared to most Protestant traditions, theirs is an expanded vision of what God has promised in this present age, coupled with an intense longing to receive it. What they envision and expect is *heaven below*. Women, lower class men, and African Americans all take on a new dignity bestowed by the love and calling given to them by God in Jesus Christ. This holiness enables them to envision renewed churches and a reformed social order in which God's will is done on earth as it is in heaven.[6]

According to 2 Peter 1:5, believers are to make every effort to "add knowledge." Of what? Of ourselves as known by God, of God as revealed in Jesus Christ, and then of what we are being enabled to become in light of Christ.

> More like Christ my heart is praying,
> More like Christ from day to day;
> All his graces rich displaying,
> While I tread my pilgrim way.[7]

---

1. John Wesley, *The Means of Grace*.
2. Charles Wesley, "O for a Thousand Tongues."
3. Mildred Wynkoop, in *The Preacher's Magazine*, 1958.
4. Barry Callen and Richard Thompson, *Bible Reading in Wesleyan Ways*. See the publications of Don Thorsen on the "Wesleyan Quadrilateral."
5. Kevin Mannoia, in *The Holiness Manifesto*.
6. Henry H. Knight, III, *Anticipating Heaven Below*. See Cliff Sanders, *The Optimism of Grace*.
7. Charles Wesley Naylor, "More Like Christ."

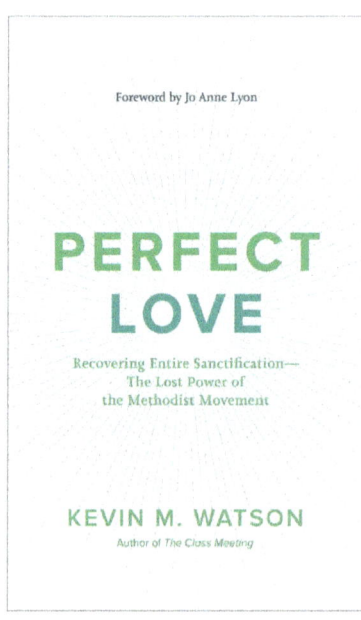

WEEK 49

Christian Life #17

WASH ME CLEAN, LORD

Today's world hopes for a free pass—no sin, no judgment, just its own ways through life on its own terms, and that's that. The Word of God, however, exists in a very different world of assumptions. God is, and thus the creation has an established order and definite standards built in. These standards naturally reflect God's character and will. Life is lived best when in line with these divine standards and expectations. We eventually will be judged in terms of the revealed order of things.

Great encouragement is found when prominent persons break God's laws, find themselves broken in the process, and then witness with overflowing gratitude to the rescuing love and mercy of a forgiving God. David and Paul are biblical examples recorded here. Countless others could share likewise if space permitted. They knew well the encrusted dirt that had come to clog their lives. They now could testify to having been washed clean by the living Lord!

A. Prayer

Hear my personal voice, my cleansing and saving God. It radiates with gratitude that one day you reached even me, touched me with a refining and forgiving fire, found another dirt-laden and lost one and made me clean and new. I may not have been the chief of sinners, but being one at any level is bad enough. I'm home now, in your loving care, and so thankful. May my experience and my voice be a faithful witness used for the encouragement of many others still somewhere on the outside and longing for home. You do seek and save the lost, precious Father. Help me now to be an instrument of your seeking. People all around me are lost and desperate. Give me your heart that bleeds for their plight. Give me a testimony that will encourage them to allow you to find them.

B. The Voice of Rabbi Jesus: Luke 15:1–10

> The professional religionists out to get me prompted me to tell these little stories. They never quite understood them, but you must. How far are you willing to go when a loved one is lost and desperate? Wouldn't you do anything possible because of your great love for them? I put these critical questions in terms of lost and valuable sheep and coins. My real story focus, of course, was on loved people who had strayed away from God, were in danger, and couldn't find their way home. Would my Father go all out for just one of them, determined to find, redeem, cleanse, and restore? Absolutely! Spread this good word as central to your own discipleship.

In all my stories there is a strong note of joy when the lost is found and the community of my children is made more whole. My parables point to the determination of my Father to "seek out and save the lost" (Lk. 19:10). I was on my way to Jerusalem when I told some of them. Heavy on my mind were the many lost of the world and what my Father through me was about to do to address their plight.

Surrounding me were some Pharisees and Scribes who were grumbling that it was shameful for me to be associating so closely with sinners. They didn't understand that my Father actually was focused on the sinners, as they should have been. It's the most ill who most need the doctor. God is so desirous of being hospitable, potentially healing and saving them all. That's why I came in the first place.

My Spirit is anxious to continue teaching you on my behalf. I'm providing you with select portions from the revealed Word of God and from a particular tradition of my church with wisdom you need. Read carefully and continue listening closely to my Spirit who will guide your minds and hearts to understand properly and apply effectively.

C. Light from the Revealed Word

1. Psalm 51:1–10. Only mentioning the names of Bathsheba and her murdered husband Uriah highlights the depth to which King David had fallen. When bottom had been reached, finally he cried out to God, a lost little lamb longing for his shepherd and the home fold. No more games, no more hiding. He admitted the awful truth. The cry was for God to soak him in a cleansing process until he came out truly clean again. "Don't throw me out with the trash or fail to breath holiness in me. Unbutton my lips, dear God, and I'll let loose with your praise." David was cleansed, unbuttoned, and let loose!

We all are to understand that God wants the sin-soaked truth recognized and removed. So, here's the whole truth. I now know my sin and I choose to rely on God's generous love, even though at this point I deserve nothing but severe judgment. I ask that God's loving kindness come from above and wipe me clean, scrubbing as necessary until, by undeserved grace alone, I can become white as the snow. What a possibility. What a God. My death sentence has been commuted and my tongue freed to praise the Lord!

2. Jeremiah 4:11–28. The tone of these verses is deep in despair. Jeremiah, the crying prophet, fears that God's people will never repent and thus will be lost and never found. They don't know me, laments God. Reflecting Genesis 1:2, God reports the sad truth. "I looked on the earth, and lo, it was waste and void" (vs. 23). In all this despair, however, there appears at least one small note of hope. "Yet I will not make a full end" (vs. 27). The creating God desires to re-create, bring home, make new. The hope is an undeserved patience of God.

Knowing God as revealed in the Bible, and especially in Rabbi Jesus, it's reasonable to assume that the days are coming when judgment will be overcome by restoration. In fact, Jeremiah later says on God's behalf, "I'll bring my people back, gather those who've gone blind and are lame and limping. Watch them come! They'll come weeping for joy as I take their hands and lead them." God actually was intending to make a new covenant with his people, and this time he would "write it on their hearts" (Jer. 31).

3. 1 Timothy 1:12–17. Paul decided to tell Timothy a story so that he would be fearless in his struggle to keep a firm grip on his faith. My record of actions against Rabbi Jesus, admitted Paul, was just awful. I was an arrogant leader of witch-hunts, a man who persecuted and even executed some followers of Jesus. My weak excuse was ignorance of who Jesus really was. Now, by his grace, I know him and I'm an apostle of his on special assignment to the large non-Jewish world. I'm proclaiming at the risk of my life that Rabbi Jesus came to save sinners—and I was one of the biggest.

What a change for Paul! Finally, he had yielded, cried out for mercy, admitted his fault and filth. Then the most amazing thing happened. "Grace mixed with faith and love poured over me and into me. And all because of Jesus" (vs. 14). He had been washed clean. Here's the testimony that now bursts from Paul's very soul (vs. 17):

> Deep honor and bright glory
> To the King of all time;
> One God, Immortal, Invisible,
> Ever and always. Oh, yes!

D. Reflections of Leaders of the Wesleyan-Holiness Tradition

Becoming really clean brings the "mystic joys" of the significant difference between *almost* and *altogether*. It's the thrill of being cleansed from all sin. To reach that point of spiritual maturity, however, we must become aware of the pervasive nature of our self-will and seek its cleansing. There's a deeper dirt level than the initial surrender to Christ for pardon. The goal is "All in all forever, Jesus will I sing."

May we all thus experience what it is to be not *almost*, but *altogether* Christians! May we be justified freely by God's grace, through the redemption that is in Jesus, knowing we have peace with God, being able to rejoice in hope of the glory of God, and having the love of God shed abroad in our hearts by the Holy Ghost given unto us![1]

> A pardon written with his blood,
> The favor and the peace of God;
> The seeing eye, the feeling sense,
> The mystic joys of penitence.[2]

Sanctification is that renewal of our fallen nature by the Holy Ghost, received through faith in Jesus Christ, whose blood of atonement has power to cleanse from all sin, whereby we are not only delivered from the guilt of sin, which is justification, but are washed entirely from its pollution, freed from its power, and are enabled, through grace, to love God with all our hearts, and to walk in his holy commandments blameless.[3]

By the increasing light of the Spirit, I had found there yet remained the root of pride, anger, self-will with many evils, the result of a fallen nature. From this snare I was mercifully preserved and led to believe that there was yet a greater work than that of pardon to be wrought in me. I retired to a secret place and said, "Lord *sanctify* my soul for Christ's sake." That very instant, as if lightning had darted through me, I sprang to my feet and cried, "The Lord has sanctified my soul!"[4]

To be truly sanctified demands moral decision. We must come to the crisis of self-abandonment to the will of God, a crisis that comes only after we have become painfully aware of our remaining self-centeredness and double-mindedness. Consecration moves on a deeper level than the initial surrender to Christ for pardon. Its motivation is a deepened conviction of the pervasive nature of self-will. It is the frank and contrite acknowledgment of one's pettiness, ambition, pride, and selfishness, and a conscious, willing commitment of the self in love to God.[5]

> Once it was the blessing, Now it is the Lord;
> Once it was the feeling, Now it is His Word.
> Once His gifts I wanted, Now the Giver own;
> Once I sought for healing, Now Himself alone.
> All in all forever, Jesus will I sing;
> Everything in Jesus, And Jesus everything.[6]

---

1. John Wesley, *The Almost Christian*.
2. Charles Wesley, "Sinners, Obey the Gospel Word."
3. Luther Lee, *Elements of Theology*.
4. Jarena Lee, *Religious Journal and Experience of Mrs. Jarena Lee*.
5. William Greathouse, *Love Made Perfect*.
6. A. B. Simpson, "Himself."

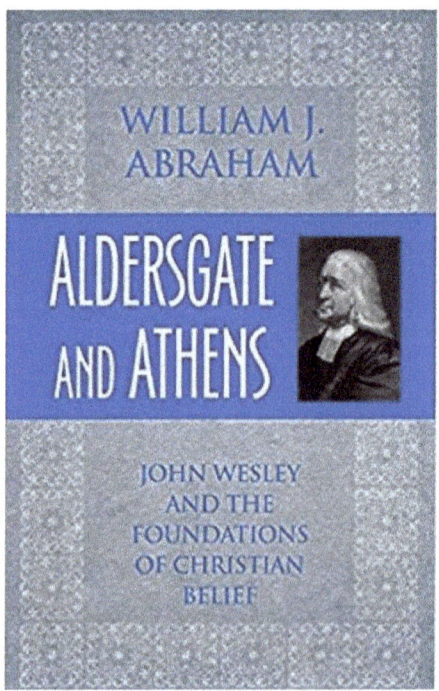

WEEK 50

Christian Life #18

LEARN FROM THE CROOKS?

If ever there has been need in the church for the integrity that comes from experiencing the holiness of God, it surely is now. How else can people of Rabbi Jesus go into this world believably representing the new creation intended in Christ? There's no other way, although there is a key lesson to be learned. All people in this world have access to some light from God and some opportunity to follow it if they choose. So, Christians blessed with so much light can still learn from others with less, even from crooks!

There are smart secular people on every mission field, non-Christian people capable of out-thinking and out-witting representatives of Rabbi Jesus. We disciples often are relatively naïve and inexperienced in the ways of the world. We must learn "street smarts" as we go, including learning from people far from God—the very ones to whom we're being sent. The needed lessons don't include how to mimic selfish motivations, of course. We must focus on the creativity and imagination expressed by even the most ardent opponents of Jesus. Disciples somehow must become worldly-wise without being "worldly."

A. Prayer

This whole thing scares me, Lord. You are sending me as one of your little lambs into a world of waiting wolves. How can I get the needed thick skin and yet retain the needed warm heart? How can I meet the selfish folks and not learn from them more than they learn from me? I so need to be wholly yours, Rabbi Jesus, or shortly I fear I'll be mostly theirs. Somehow, I need for you to get me on the path to true holiness or I'll be on the road to destruction, even while trying to be in your service. Help me out-think, out-live, and out-last those to whom I'm sent. Keep me humble in the process. This won't be easy; in fact, it's impossible without your wisdom and grace.

B. The Voice of Rabbi Jesus: Luke 16:1–13

> My parable is about a man caught and fired for his crookedness. This will sound strange, I know, so listen closely. I want you to be like that man, at least in some ways. I'm sending you to the streets and back alleys of this world and you need to become streetwise. You need to cultivate your imaginations and creativity in order to avoid being eaten up by the perverse worlds you'll encounter. When you are on the streets you must know the streets. Yes, there's risk in being involved closely with sinners. The problem Is that not being with them and knowing them well limits greatly your ability to win them for my kingdom.

A rich man caught his manager cheating their clients for his own gain. I condemned that manager, of course. I also commended him in certain ways valuable for you to know as you learn to be my disciples. The man was clever as well as evil. He figured out ways to pull off his twisted scheme. He was wrong but smart. You also must be smart without using your quick wits for wrong purposes. The man in the story always was looking for an edge. You also must keep your eyes wide open, looking for opportunities, not to cheat but to bless. You won't always succeed, but you can often enough.

On many occasions my opponents tried to corner me and I managed to maneuver and silence them, at least temporarily. People will throw up personal defense mechanisms and argue that there is no God. There is only getting ahead as much as possible. To counter all this, I call you to be holy persuaders, wise as snakes and innocent as doves (Matt. 10:16).[1]

My Spirit is anxious to continue teaching you on my behalf. I'm providing you with select portions from the revealed Word of God and from a particular tradition of my church with wisdom you need. Read carefully and continue listening closely to my Spirit who will guide your minds and hearts to understand properly and apply effectively.

C. Light from the Revealed Word

1. Psalm 79:1–9. Unfortunately, the history of God's people is littered with instances of enemies invading. Alien and arrogant outsiders have mocked the chosen and tricked them into complicity with evil agendas. God's people will find themselves being used as instruments of the state for purposes that sicken God. Words like slavery, holocaust, and crusades bring shame right to church altars. Barbarians have made God's servants carrion for the birds of prey.

The psalmist asks God how long he will put up with such abuse of his people. A reasonable question, of course. Here's another. How long will God's people so easily permit anti-God forces to draw them into complicity with outright evil? Those representing God in this world must be shrewd themselves by finding ways to maintain their integrity in the face of opposition. When disciples of Rabbi Jesus aren't smart enough or committed enough, they always will be outmaneuvered by the streetwise of the world. Beyond becoming complicit in the evil, they also won't be in any position to deliver the good news of God's love to those who need it so desperately.

2. Amos 8:4–7. The true prophet tells things exactly as they are. Amos was especially good at this, being particularly blunt and never pulling a punch. God was sick of his people's failures. Granted, their environment had been a tough one to deal with. The enemies they knew were shrewd, scheming, enticing, and the chosen people fell for it and caved in. The Jewish neighbors manipulated things quite well for their own advantage, walking over the weak and treating the poor as though they were nothing. Unfortunately, it had become much the same among God's people. Those in charge of Jewish society now also knew how to give little, take much, and work society's system so they stayed comfortably on top.

Why was Amos being so hard on God's people in these tough circumstances? Why was God's judgment surely coming for them? Precisely because they had allowed themselves to become a big part of the problem when they clearly should have known better. Those supposed to represent God somehow must engage the world without being captured by it and then merely mirroring it. Avoiding cultural captivity is never easy, nor is it an acceptable option.

3. 1 Timothy 2:1–7. Paul reports that he endured some rough times in Philippi, but that shouldn't discourage the rest of us from serving in such places. He found ways around the opposition and kept going. While we disciples of the Lord never are out for crowd approval, we always need to manage a threatening crowd in the most productive ways possible. We never are to manipulate people by throwing our weight around, nor are we to stand passively by and turn into compliant copies of others. There's a fine line between managing and manipulating a situation, serving without abusing people in the process.

No hidden agendas are appropriate for agents of Christ on mission. After all, we are trying to spread the good news of God in Christ and dare not attempt to do that by acting like representatives of more bad news in this troubled world. We must not use smoke screens and dirty tricks as ways of turning people in Christ's direction. Wrong methods usually lead to wrong results even when employed for good purposes. Still, you'll have to be creative and smart in dealing with conspiring opposition or your message will never get the hearing it deserves.

D. Reflections of Leaders of the Wesleyan-Holiness Tradition

We inevitably influence each other for good or bad. Even the crooks retain some semblance of God's image within. Disciples of Rabbi Jesus should be motivated by the life-giving Spirit within who is "a fountain of power." Whatever the obstacles, we can be overcomers, always reaching out in love to all.

Everyone has some measure of divine light, some faint glimmering ray which, sooner or later, more or less, enlightens every man that cometh into the world. And everyone, unless he be one of the small number whose conscience is seared with a hot iron, feels more or less uneasy when he acts contrary to the light of his own conscience. So that no man sins because he has not grace, but because he does not use the grace which he hath.[2]

> Jesus descended from above,
> Our loss of Eden to retrieve,
> Great God of universal love,
>
> If all the world through Thee may live,
> In us a quickening Spirit be,
> And witness Thou hast died for me![3]

Strangely enough, most evangelicals today do not have the Wesleyan heritage of a disciplined life as a Spirit-filled response to the extremes of legalism and antinomianism. For the good of the awakening, and as a witness before the world, holiness people themselves should be leading with the discipline of perfection in the business of life.[4]

Christian behavior, according to truly Wesleyan parameters, must be a response to the love of Christ, not a way to Christ. We receive God's grace, not earn it. Thus, the absolutism of the Christian's ethic is an absolute giving over of the Christian to responding to the love of God in Christ. It is not merely an absolutism of assigned duties. True life lies in the discovery of the real order of the universe which, says the

Wesleyan, is not a "what" but a "Who," and a Who who cares enough to submit to the natural order and die, that He might transform it by a resurrection.[5]

God wants us to live positively, to be on the offensive, to be victorious. Our openhearted God is a fountain of power. He would have our hearts open to receive his power. By believing this, and acting as though we believe it, we will be overcomers. We will rid ourselves of many of life's question marks. Some of them will remain to eternity, but many of them need trouble us no longer.[6]

We are to be a responsive church aglow with the Spirit, touched by the needs of the world, and reaching out in love to all regardless of who they are. We are to be willing to enter into discourse with all regardless of their religious life or truth claims.[7]

The holiness of the church is in its reflecting the activity of God in Christ. This is expressed in the inclusion and reconciliation of diverse peoples and cultures, the empowerment of diverse gifts and ministries, the abandonment of division and enmity, and demonstration of those spiritual fruits that produce love within the community.[8]

---

1. See Os Guinness, *Fool's Talk: Recovering the Art of Christian Persuasion.*
2. John Wesley, *On Working Out Our Own Salvation.*
3. Charles Wesley, "Would Jesus Have the Sinner Die?"
4. David McKenna, *New Shoes for Beautiful Feet.*
5. Paul Merritt Bassett, in the *Wesleyan Theological Journal,* 1973.
6. Charles Wesley Naylor, *The Secret of the Singing Heart.*
7. Gilbert W. Stafford, *Theology for Disciples.*
8. Theodore W. Jennings, Jr., *Loyalty to God.*

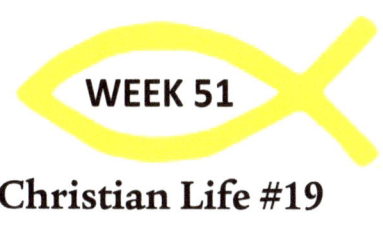

Week 51

Christian Life #19

LOVE ALL THE SAINTS

There must be strong connections maintained in the church, some of them transcending time and space. Current Christians must recall with profit the faithfulness of earlier generations of believers. Only then can the faithful today be at their best in passing on the faith to each other and eventually to many yet unborn. There's so much to be learned from yesterday, whatever its limitations. Our forebears ran the whole race of faith and now are waiting with valuable stories to share.

We are saints of God at our best only if we are in touch with that great cloud of witnesses anxious to instruct and encourage. Spiritual biographies and autobiographies are important sources of Christian inspiration. The Bible itself is the foremost example. It chronicles the big story of God's people across the centuries and in circumstances similar to our own. We are called to listen carefully to all the saints, not just to the few we happen know personally at the moment, and not only to those of your own culture, tradition, or gender.

A. Prayer

So many have walked the paths of faith before me. Thank you, God, for your faithfulness to them. I finally realizing that I must manage today in part by the enrichment of those who have gone before. Save me from the stupid assumption that the church of today has outgrown the wisdom of yesterday. I need to champion those who laid down their lives so that I might live. Let me know and celebrate the pioneers of my faith. Keep the martyrs fresh in my memory. Help me to so believe and live that those yet unborn one day will be able to look back to memories of me. May those memories cause them to rejoice in what I believed and accomplished on their behalf and by your enabling grace. Make me a time-transcending and "big-picture" follower of Rabbi Jesus.

B. The Voice of Rabbi Jesus: Luke 6:20-31

> Luke's presentation of my "Sermon on the Plain," as people sometimes call it, gives you my vivid picture of life as it should be lived under the reign of my Father. To be pitied are they who are self-satisfied, at ease in their wealth, happily gaining from the present order of things that fills their pockets on the backs of the poor. You must learn the art of giving away and how to love even when faced with enemies. Your faith must dare to be counter-cultural. I know this isn't a comfortable way to exist. it's just my way, really the only way.

The so-called "Golden Rule" is so simple to say and so demanding to live. It involves laying down your very lives for others, like I did. Love the poor, feed the hungry, grant all people the sense of worth they deserve. There will come a day when my Father will serve a lavish banquet for those now discriminated against so terribly. Meanwhile, place yourselves at the service of others. My disciples are to serve out of love and not for rewards. The proper sequence is this. You are saved by grace. Why? So you then can do good works (Eph. 2:8-10). Although the works don't do the saving, they surely show that you have been saved.

There should be an occasional "All Saints" celebration in my church. True saints move away from self-absorption to a holy simplicity, humility, and love of others, even enemies. Such living honors the great cloud of witnesses (Heb. 12:1), those who already have run the race with me and remained faithful to the end. Their names are in large print in the Lamb's Book of Life. One day I trust that you will join in their victory parade, singing with great joy, "Oh, when the saints go marching in!"

My Spirit is anxious to continue teaching you on my behalf. I'm providing you with select portions from the revealed Word of God and from a particular tradition of my church with wisdom you need. Read carefully and continue listening closely to my Spirit who will guide your minds and hearts to understand properly and apply effectively.

C. Light from the Revealed Word

1. Psalm 149. Part of this psalm is disturbing because of its outright call to vengeance. The psalmist allows humanness to erupt briefly, knowing that God will understand. Faithfulness to God puts us at dangerous odds with worldly powers and sometimes brings our worst to the surface. Jesus later would clarify that his disciples are to love their enemies and treat others as we ourselves prefer to be treated.

The central message of this psalm is not vengeance but a call for the "faithful" (vss. 1, 5, 9) to embody the reign of God celebrated in verses 1-4. "Faithful" can be translated "saints." Saints of God are those aware of God's past faithfulness and are anxious to praise the Lord in all present circumstances.

The saints of God are to sing a new song because the rule of God opens the possibility of new things still to come. We must be courageous disciples in the present, followers of Rabbi Jesus who grasp the big picture and see the long view. The battle today may mean the suffering of the saints. Even so, like the story of Jesus, resurrection will follow even crucifixion. We are to rejoice with and learn from all those who already have suffered and gone on to obtain the prize of life eternal.

2. Daniel 7:1-18. Today's world is riddled with political corruption, pandemics, rampant pollution, and mis-readings of biblical prophesies. Anti-saints like Jim Jones and David Koresh have twisted biblical intent and caused disasters among God's faithful. One lesson for us surely is this. We must be aware that "apocalyptic" biblical materials, like the books of Daniel and Revelation, are commonly misunderstood and used for private purposes.

Chapters 7-12 of Daniel share four visions dramatically picturing the coming collapse of the present evil order and God's coming rule. Verses 7:4-12 explain how to understand the four "great beasts" (presumably the Babylonians, Medes, Persians, and Greeks). In their midst emerges the "Ancient One" who establishes the rule of God, a reign never to be destroyed. The 'holy ones" will exercise authority in this coming kingdom.

God's faithful always have faced dark and beastly clouds that bring personal insecurity and even global uncertainty. God's people have endured before and will in the future. Therefore, we are to remember yesterday, hold steady today, and rejoice in the coming tomorrow. The saints of God are destined to rule alongside the "Ancient One" from the throne-room of heaven. Many saints already are doing the dance of joy—and soon we will be joining them! Meanwhile, we are to stand firm and break barriers that divide and demean our fellow humans, paying whatever price comes along.

3. Ephesians 1:11-23. We disciples of Rabbi Jesus are not alone in this sometimes difficult journey of faith, nor do we need to proceed only with our own resources. We are blessed that "in Christ we have obtained an inheritance" (vs. 11) which enables us "to live for the praise of God's glory" (vs. 12). We are privileged to be children of God (Gal. 4:7) who are provided with divine riches not earned but inherited. We have become members of the household of the Father. This membership inheritance requires us to express love "toward all the saints" (vs. 15). Love calls for the saints of today to learn from those of generations past. We must be aware that, if faithful, we ourselves one day will become lessons from which future generations can learn.

Jesus prayed for the church's unity so that it could have integrity as a community of the Spirit. The church is an enriching linkage with the saints of all times and places. Knowing the full range of "the riches of the inheritance among the saints" (vs. 18) brings heightened ability to have hope now and to be able to go on to the finish of our race of faith. There is a rich inheritance to be received, including especially the gifts and seal of the Spirit of God.

D. Reflections of Leaders of the Wesleyan-Holiness Tradition

The big picture is that the church of today is to be one with all its current members and also with those already "to glory gone." All have major contributions to make to us in the present. Holy love is key to the needed unity of the church of all ages, and cannot be known when a believer is disconnected from other Christians. This great cloud of witnesses includes our many holiness foremothers. We forget at our own peril.

I believe that Christ has gathered unto himself a church, to which he has continually added such as shall be saved. This catholic (universal) church, extending to all nations and all ages, is holy in all its members who have fellowship with God the Father, Son, and Holy Ghost. They have fellowship with the holy angels and with all the living members of Christ on earth, as well as with all who are departed in His faith and fear.[1]

> Come, let us join our hands above
>   who have obtained the prize,
> And on eagle wings of love
>   to joys celestial rise.
> Let saints on earth unite to sing
>   with those to glory gone,
> For all the servants of our King
>   in earth and heaven are one.[2]

We are strengthened by the Roman Catholic affirmation of the City of God. We are all benefactors of the Lutheran emphasis upon justification by faith. We rejoice in the possibilities of Christian freedom so insisted upon by the Anabaptists. The Pentecostals have insisted that the Holy

Spirit return to the stage of the church's life as a living, vibrant Person. The ecumenical church likewise needs the Wesleyan emphasis upon the realizability of holiness in the midst of the life of the world. The holy life is one entered into by an event in grace, sustained by burning devotion and unswerving discipline, and manifested in both personal fruits and corporate reforms.³

One cannot know holy love disconnected from other Christians. It is only by the work and grace of God within Christian community that holiness of heart and life is realized and actualized. The maintenance of holy life and love *in* the church requires deliberate and persistent cultivation *by* the church.⁴

The Wesleyan-Holiness movement has sought to model the early church by affirming a prophetic leadership which based its authority on the Holy Spirit. It has documented the role of women in primitive Christianity and sought to restore to women the prominent place they once filled. For a detailed addressing of the New Testament teaching on women and church leadership, see Sharon Pearson in the *Wesleyan Theological Journal* (1996).⁵

---

1. John Wesley, *Letter to a Roman Catholic.*
2. Charles Wesley, "Come, Let Us Join Our Friends Above."
3. Frank Bateman Stanger, in the *Asbury Journal of Theology*, 1983.
4. Jonathan A. Powers, in *The Asbury Journal* (2019).
5. Susie C. Stanley, in Thorsen-Callen, *Heart & Life.*

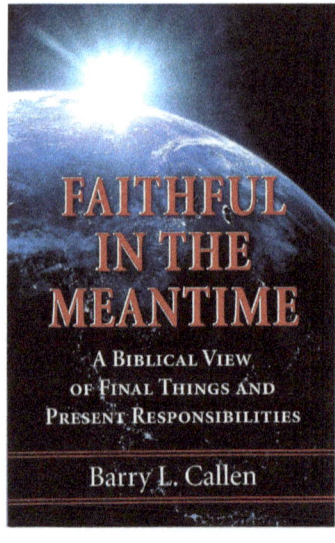

WEEK 52

Christ the King

THE DYING GOD IS ETERNAL

It's said that power corrupts and absolute power corrupts absolutely. The power of God is absolute, but in this one case not corrupted. Therefore, it's crucial to know the heart and intentions of God in order to avoid misunderstanding his use of such unlimited power. God's power is not just the ultimate expansion of our human will to power. God's reigning comes from his great heart of love. That love redefines political power in important ways that contrast sharply with how humans usually understand and employ it.

For what purpose is God's power directed? How does God choose to use power? What role does the church have today in resisting bad political policies and holding accountable arrogant leaders with improperly used power? How should the church go about its business? How is "power" to be involved in that business? Answers rely on understanding properly the eternal God who came to us as a "suffering servant."

What will stand eternally? What will be undying is God's love demonstrated so dramatically on the Cross of Rabbi Jesus. God's power, glimpsed in the resurrection of Jesus, is to be understood in relation to the purpose of the sacrifice made on that Cross. John's Gospel puts the ever-living truth this way: "The Life-Light blazed out of the darkness; the darkness couldn't put it out!" (1:5). Divine power is that Light that's able to clarify truth for us and willing to sacrifice that we, the undeserving, might live.

A. Prayer

Who you really are, God, surely controls how you act, how I can relate to you, and how I should relate to others as your representative. If you are the big policeman in the sky with a club in your hands ready to punish any misstep I make, I can manage to fear you, possibly respect you, but hardly love you. The presence of Rabbi Jesus makes all the difference for me. If you are exactly like him in nature and how you exercise unlimited power, then I *can and will love you!* Keep me from the twisted tales about who you are. Help me to live comfortably with the many unanswered questions. Keep my eyes on you so that I will understand properly and come to live fully and lovingly and eternally. Let me be a reflection of your Light of love shining on others. May the world never put me out as long as I'm faithful to you.

B. The Voice of Rabbi Jesus: Luke 23:33-43

> I realize that seeing me on the Cross was devastating to your faith. How could the true Messiah be so humiliated by this world? It would take my resurrection for you to realize that what you saw on the Cross was not the triumph of this world's power. It was an unexpected presentation of the amazing power of the love of my Father for all of lost humankind. That awful death of mine was completely voluntary and totally for you! When all else is gone, that sacrificial love will stand for all eternity. Receive God's gift and be that holy love yourselves, holy light in action in your time!

Even though I lived humbly and loved without limit, I was charged as a political threat to those in power. I was so feared that a murderous political insurrectionist was released instead of me. The nature of the reign of my Father is unlike this world and wasn't understood, only feared. I am the Messiah who would save others by not saving himself (vs. 35). Only in the powerlessness of the Cross would the true power of my Father's saving love be revealed.

Your faith as my disciples must be based on the amazing power of self-giving and saving love. It defies all human displays of power gone wrong, like discrimination, retaliation, and self-preservation. I save and rule not by pulling myself off the Cross but by dying on it willingly for others. That's where you finally glimpse a King like no other. My authority—and yours--is exercised by pardoning love. My chosen throne is the Cross. It points to an upside-down kingdom that gently puts all things right-side up.

My Spirit is anxious to continue teaching you on my behalf. I'm providing you with select portions from the revealed Word of God and from a particular tradition of my church with wisdom you need. Read carefully and continue listening closely to my Spirit who will guide your minds and hearts to understand properly and apply effectively.

C. Light from the Revealed Word

1. Jeremiah 23:1-6. Judah's rulers are denounced. Their bad decisions had brought only havoc to the people of God. Selfish kings had grabbed benefit for themselves instead of providing it to the people. These wayward monarchs were "shepherds who destroy and scatter the sheep of God's pasture." God promises a different future. One day he will be their Good Shepherd. The scattered will be regathered (vs. 31:10). There will be righteousness and justice in the land. God is our never-dying Monarch who promises and enables eternal righteousness.

The history of human rulers fills libraries with one sad tale after another. Only God's gracious intervention will save us from ourselves and the havoc imposed by wayward and powerful leaders. One day Jesus would ascend the Cross, a loving if cruel throne of God on earth. He would demonstrate there how the God of all power rules through forgiving grace and everlasting resurrection life. Rabbi Jesus one day will emerge as the Good Shepherd who liberates all those caught in the webs of present circumstances (Jn. 10).

2. Colossians 1:11-20. God is Jesus-with-us and now also the Spirit-with-us. Is God absolute power behind all creation and head of the church? Yes. All this power and headship is for what purpose? "To reconcile to himself all things by making peace through the blood of the Cross." God is the One who exercises the initiative to reunite, restore, and resurrect to new life. God expresses his great power in the form of Self-sacrifice for the benefit of all others. Through Christ, God has liberated humankind from the grip of darkness and granted an inheritance of light to all the saints. Amazing!

The strength needed to endure the injustices of the present time is graciously transferred in Christ from Creator to creature. The One who died and lives forevermore invites us "to be made strong with all the strength that comes from his glorious power" (vs. 11). The power reigning over heaven and earth is the power of love that was demonstrated so dramatically in the life, death, and resurrection of Rabbi Jesus, in whom all the fullness of God was pleased to dwell" (vs. 19).

3. Revelation 22:1-5. In a typical novel, the best is saved for last. The many threads of the story suddenly fit together, the lingering questions get resolved, and the reader is left with the overarching message the writer intended. While anything but a novel, the final book of the biblical library does all of these things. It ends with, "Come, Master Jesus!" By this point the insightful biblical reader has fallen in love with God because God first had loved the reader. The disciple of Rabbi Jesus has become anxious for the full and final presence of the gracious God behind the whole story. That coming is promised.

Love and celebration are the bottom lines of the revelation of God. God becomes known not as a dark cloud always threatening but the Bright Morning Star of hope always being the source of endless possibilities. God is the Fountain of Life who keeps planting and nourishing the future. Rabbi Jesus gave up all so that we might have all from the Father's hand.

We are blessed to be receiving the stamp of the divine image in ourselves. The holy God has planted, nourished, and now is harvesting a holy people.[1] We who have believed in faith soon will be privileged to rule *with God* from age to age to age. God's absolute power has been employed not to overpower but to love, save, and partner with us for the redemption of others. God is the One who came to die in order that we might live alongside the Ever-living One. Oh God, for all of this, we love you!!

D. Reflections of Leaders of the Wesleyan-Holiness Tradition

The amazing love of God is almost too good to be true! We now can boldly approach the eternal throne. God has provided foundations, impulses, intents, and assurances for the future. Since we know *Who* holds the future, we can relax in the confidence that the unknown whats, whens, and hows will take care of themselves.

Christian faith is not only an assent to the whole gospel of Christ, but also a full reliance on the blood of Christ, a trust in the merits of His life, death, and resurrection. In consequence of this, cleaving to Him as our wisdom and righteousness and sanctification and redemption is our salvation.[2]

> And can it be, that I should gain
> An interest in the Savior's blood?
> Died he for me, who caused his pain?
> For me, who him to death pursued?
> Amazing love! How can it be
> That Thou, my God, shouldst die for me?
>
> No condemnation now I dread,
> Jesus, and all in him, is mine!
> Alive in him, my living Head,
> And clothed in righteousness divine.
> Bold I approach the eternal throne,
> And claim the crown, through Christ my own.[3]

The ultimate future? The Bible provides divine foundations, impulses, intents, and assurances, but not calendars and grand political schemes with contemporary nametags. I have seen too many preachers with inflated confidence in their biblical interpretations. They, in fact, were skating on thin ice as they proceeded to build elaborate systems of future expectations and call the end result "exactly what the Bible says."[4]

We who truly believe do not know many of the whats, whens, or hows related to the final resolution of life's big questions and the evils of this world, but by faith we do know *Who*. That which finally will be is shaped by and in control of Rabbi Jesus, the One who already has come and is known. The best faith-abiding, therefore, is the posture of *Christ-celebrating*. Be sure of *Who* and the whats, whens, and hows of tomorrow will take care of themselves.[5]

---

1. See Barry Callen and Hubert Harriman, *Color Me Holy: Holy God, Holy People*.
2. John Wesley, *Justification by Faith*.
3. Charles Wesley, "And Can It Be That I Should Gain?"
4. James Earl Massey, quoted in Barry Callen, *Heart of the Matter*.
5. Barry L. Callen, *Authentic Spirituality*.

APPENDIX A

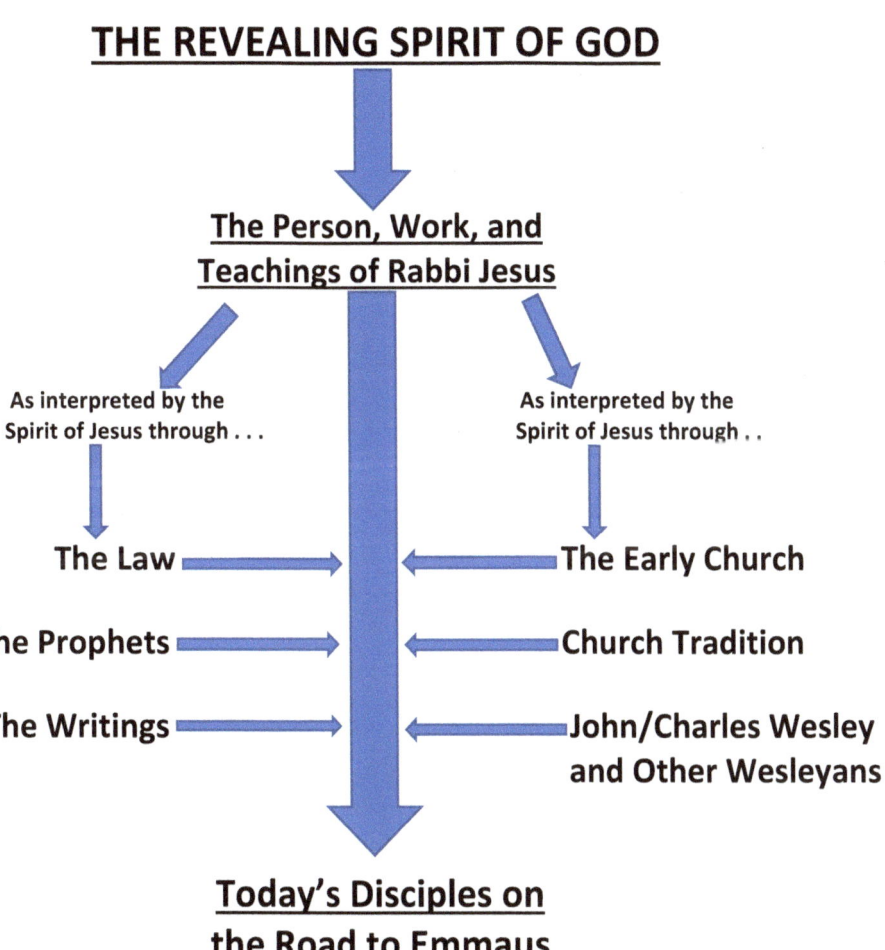

APPENDIX B

The annual cycle of the Christian Year is how Christians should learn to tell time. The clockwise movement is from Advent to Christmas, Lent, Easter, Pentecost, Ordinary time, back to Advent. This cycle follows the life of Rabbi Jesus, birth, death, resurrection, presence in the Spirit, and coming again.

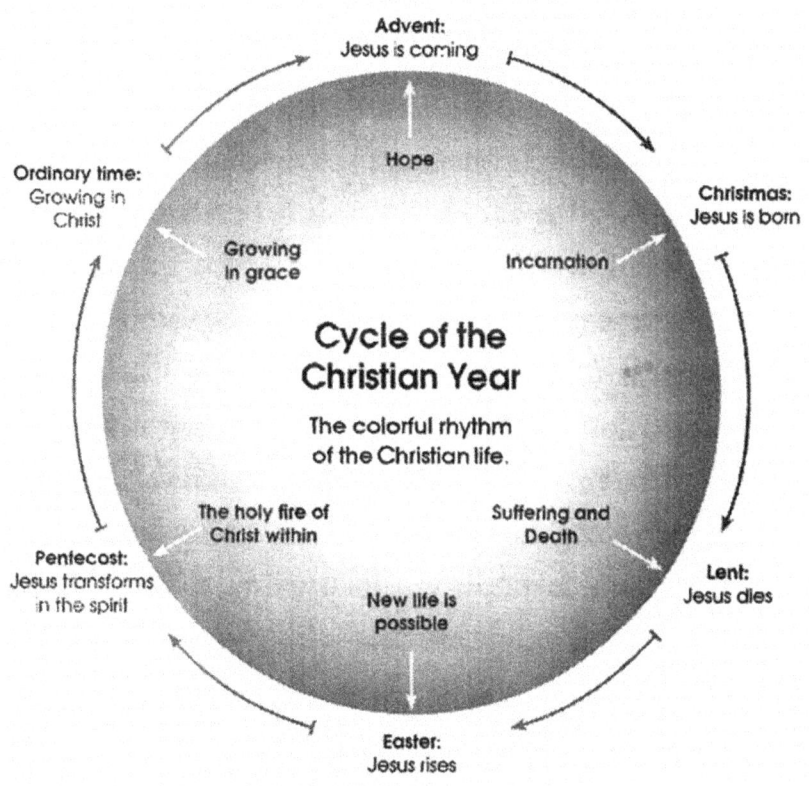

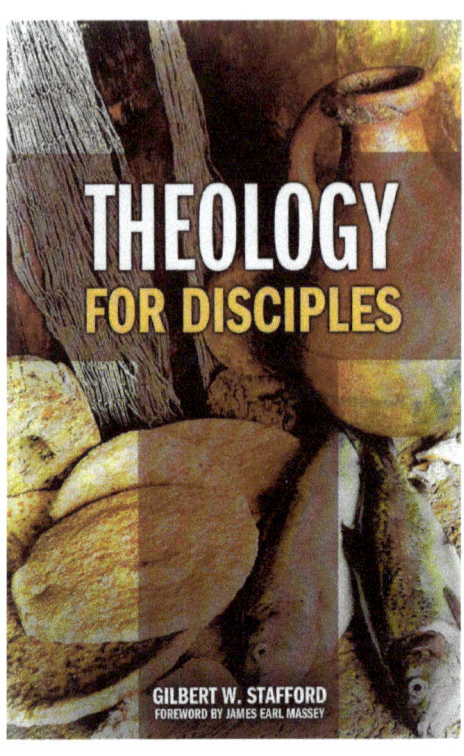

THEOLOGY FOR DISCIPLES

GILBERT W. STAFFORD
FOREWORD BY JAMES EARL MASSEY

Responsible Grace

JOHN WESLEY'S PRACTICAL THEOLOGY

Randy L. Maddox

GRACE FAITH & HOLINESS

H. RAY DUNNING

The Origin of the Wesleyan Theological Vision for Christian Globalization and the Pursuit of Pentecost in Early Pietist Revivalism,

Including a Translation of

The Pentecost Addresses
Johann Adam Steinmetz
(1689–1762)

J. Steven O'Malley

APPENDIX C

CONTRIBUTORS

Main contributors to this volume, of course, are the two authors-editors, Barry Callen and Steven Hoskins. They have been supplemented frequently by theological observations and hymn lyrics of the brothers John and Charles Wesley. The primary voice throughout, however, is Rabbi Jesus himself who appears everywhere with ultimate spiritual wisdom for his disciples. His voice is supported at every turn by numerous authors and editors of the biblical material.

Beyond all these, the Wesleyan-Holiness tradition of Christianity has provided a wide range of wise contributing saints. They come from the insightful men and women affiliated with the numerous denominational bodies comprising this significant tradition of the faith of Jesus. For their contributions, this volume is in debt to . . .

William J. Abraham
B. Acheson
Milton Agnew
Christlane Albertson
William Arthur
Paul M. Bassett
Catherine Booth
Christopher Bounds
Samuel Logan Brengle
Phineas F. Bresee
Esther Bridgers
Cheryl Bridges Johns
David Bundy
Barry L. Callen
Paul Chilcote
Leslie Church
John B. Cobb, Jr.
Kenneth J. Collins
Warren Cornell
David L. Cubie
Donald W. Dayton
Curtiss Paul DeYoung

Keith Drury
H. Ray Dunning
Bill and Gloria Gaither
William B. Godbey
William Greathouse
Roger Green
Georgia Harkness
Hubert P. Harriman
Elaine A. Heath
D. Michael Henderson
A. M. Hills
Samuel G. Hines
Steve Hoskins
Theodore W. Jennings, Jr.
E. Stanley Jones
Kenneth Cain Kinghorn
Dennis F. Kinlaw
Martin Wells Knapp
Henry H. Knight III
William Kostlevy
Diane Leclerc
Jarena Lee

Luther Lee
Stephen Lennox
Harald Lindström
Michael Lodahl
Jo Anne Lyon
David L. McKenna
Frank Macchia
Randy L. Maddox
Kevin Mannoia
James Earl Massey
Philip R. Meadows
Lucy Rider Meyer
T. Crichton Mitchell
M. Robert, Mulholland, Jr.
Charles Wesley Naylor
Thomas Oden
Dale Oldham
J. Steven O'Malley
Thomas Jay Oord
Phoebe Palmer
Sharon Pearson
Clark H. Pinnock
Christine D. Pohl
Priscilla Pope-Levison
Sam Powell

Jonathan A. Powers
Jonathan S. Raymond
Benjamin F. Reid
B. T. Roberts
A. B. Simpson
Hannah Whitall Smith
Howard A. Snyder
Gilbert W. Stafford
Frank Bateman Stanger
Susie C. Stanley
R. Eugene Sterner
Douglas M. Strong
Julie Tennent
Timothy Tennent
Richard P. Thompson
Don Thorsen
John Tyson
Bernie A. Van De Walle
Jason E. Vickers
Daniel S. Warner
Kevin Watson
George Whitefield
H. Orton Wiley
Laurence W. Wood
Mildred Wynkoop

APPENDIX D

SUPPLEMENTAL

Readers are encouraged to go to the following works for a deeper look into the theological foundations and current applications of the teachings of the Master, Rabbi Jesus. The covers of many of these outstanding works are featured in the pages of this volume.

Abraham, Wiliam J. *Aldersgate and Athens: John Wesley and the Foundations of Christian Faith* (Baylor University Press, 2010).

Brengle, Samuel Logan, *Love Slaves* (Salvation Army Supplies and Purchasing, 1923).

Callen, Barry L., *Authentic Spirituality* (Emeth Press, 2006).

_____, *Catch Your Breath! Exhaling Death and Inhaling Life* (Aldersgate Press, 2014).

_____, *Faithful in the Meantime* (Wipf & Stock, 2018).

_____, *God As Loving Grace* (Wipf & Stock, 2018).

_____, *Heart of the Matter* (Emeth Press, rev. ed., 2016).

_____, *The Prayer of Holiness-Hungry People* (Francis Asbury Press, 2011).

_____, *Radical Christianity* (Evangel Publishing, 1999).

_____, *The Holy River of God* (Aldersgate Press, 2016).

_____, *The Jagged Journey* (Cascade Books, 2018).

Chilcote, Paul, *Praying in the Wesleyan Spirit* (Upper Room Books, 2001).

_____, with Steve Harper, *Living Hope* (Cascade, 2020).

Cobb, John B., Jr., *Grace and Responsibility* (Abingdon Press, 1995).

Collins, Kenneth J., *Soul Care* (First Fruits Press, 2014).

_____, with Jason Vickers, *The Sermons of John Wesley* (Abingdon Press, 2013).

Dayton, Don, with Douglas Strong, *Rediscovering an Evangelical Heritage* (Baker, 2014).

Drury, Keith, *Holiness for Ordinary People* (Wesley Press, 1983).

Dunning, H. Ray, *Biblical Heights for Today's Valleys* (Aldersgate Press, 2015).

_____, *Grace, Faith, and Holiness* (Beacon Hill Press of K.C., 1988).

_____, *Reflecting the Divine Image* (WIPF & Stock, 2003).

Greathouse, William, *Love Made Perfect* (Beacon Hill Press of Kansas City, 1997).

Heath, Elaine A., *Five Means of Grace: Experience God's Love the Wesleyan Way* (Abingdon Press, 2017).

Harriman, Hubert P. and Barry L. Callen, *Color Me Holy: Holy God, Holy People* (Aldersgate Press, 2013).
Henderson, D. Michael, *John Wesley's Class Meeting* (Evangel Publishing, 1997).
Hines, Samuel G., and Curtiss Paul DeYoung, *Reconciliation as a Way of Life* (Judson Press and Wipf & Stock, 2000)
Hoskins, Steven, and Barry Callen, *The Wesleyan Theological Society* (Emeth Press, 2015).
Jennings, Theodore W., Jr., *Loyalty to God: The Apostles' Creed in Life and Liturgy* (Abingdon Press, 1992).
Kinghorn, Kenneth Cain, *The Heritage of American Methodism* (Lexington: Emeth Press, 2009).
Kinlaw, Dennis F., *This Day with the Master* (Francis Asbury Press, 2002).
Knight, Henry H., III, *Anticipating Heaven Below* (Cascade Books, 2014).
Kostlevy, William, and Barry Callen, *Heart of the Heritage* (Schmul, 2001).
Leclerc, Diane, *Discovering Christian Holiness* (Kanas City: Beacon Hill Press of Kansas City, 2013).
Lyon, Jo Anne, *The Ultimate Blessing* (Wesleyan Publishing House, 2003).
McKenna, David L., *What a Time to Be Wesleyan!* (Beacon Hill Press of K.C., 1999).
Macchia, Frank, "Justification through New Creation," in *Theology Today* (2001).
Maddox, Randy L., *Responsible Grace* (Kingswood Books, 1994).
Mannoia, Kevin, and Don Thorsen, eds., *The Holiness Manifesto* (Eerdmans, 2008).
_____, *Masterful Living* (WHC and Emeth Press, 2012).
Massey, James Earl, *Views from the Mountain* (Aldersgate Press, 2018).
_____, *Sundays in the Tuskegee Chapel* (Abingdon Press, 2000).
Meadows, Philip R., *Remembering Our Baptism* (Discipleship Resources, 2018).
Mitchell, T. Crichton, *Charles Wesley: Man with the Dancing Heart* (Beacon Hill Press of Kansas City, 1994).
Mulholland, M. Robert Jr., *Shaped by the Word* (Upper Room Books, 2000).
Oord, Thomas Jay, and Michael Lodahl, Relational Holiness (Beacon Hill Press of K.C., 2005).
_____, *The Uncontrolling Love of God* (InterVarsity Press, 2015).
Pneuma, official publication of the Society for Pentecostal Studies.
Pinnock, Clark H., *Flame of Love* (InterVarsity Press, 1996).
Pohl, Christine D., *Making Room: Recovering Hospitality as a Christian Tradition* (Eerdmans, 1999).
Pope-Levison, Priscilla, *Models of Evangelism* (Baker Academic, 2020).
Raymond, Jonathan S., *Social Holiness: The Company We Keep* (Aldersgate Press and Crest Books, 2018).
_____, *Higher Higher Education* (Aldersgate Press, 2015).
Sanders, Cliff, *The Optimism of Grace* (MACU Press, 2016).
Snyder, Howard A., *The Radical Wesley* (Seedbed, 2014).

Stafford, Gilbert W., *Theology for Disciples* (Warner Press, 2012).
Tennent, Timothy and Julie, *A Meditative Journey through the Psalms* (Seedbed, 2017).
_____. *For the Body* (Seedbed, 2020).
Thompson, Richard P., and Barry Callen, *Reading the Bible in Wesleyan Ways (Beacon Hill Press of K.C., 2004)*.
Thorsen, Don, and Barry L. Callen, *Heart & Life: Rediscovering Holy* Living (Aldersgate Press, 2012).
_____, *Calvin vs Wesley* (Abingdon Press, 2013).
Van De Walle, Bernie, *Rethinking Holiness* (Baker Academic, 2017).
Vickers, Jason E., *Minding the Good Ground* (Baylor University Press, 2011).
_____, with Kenneth Collins, *The Sermons of John Wesley* (Abingdon Press, 2013).
Wesleyan Theological Journal, official publication of the Wesleyan Theological Society.
Watson, Kevin M., *Perfect Love* (Seedbed, 2021).
Wood, Laurence W., *Pentecost and Sanctification in the Writings of John and Charles Wesley* (Emeth Press, 2018).

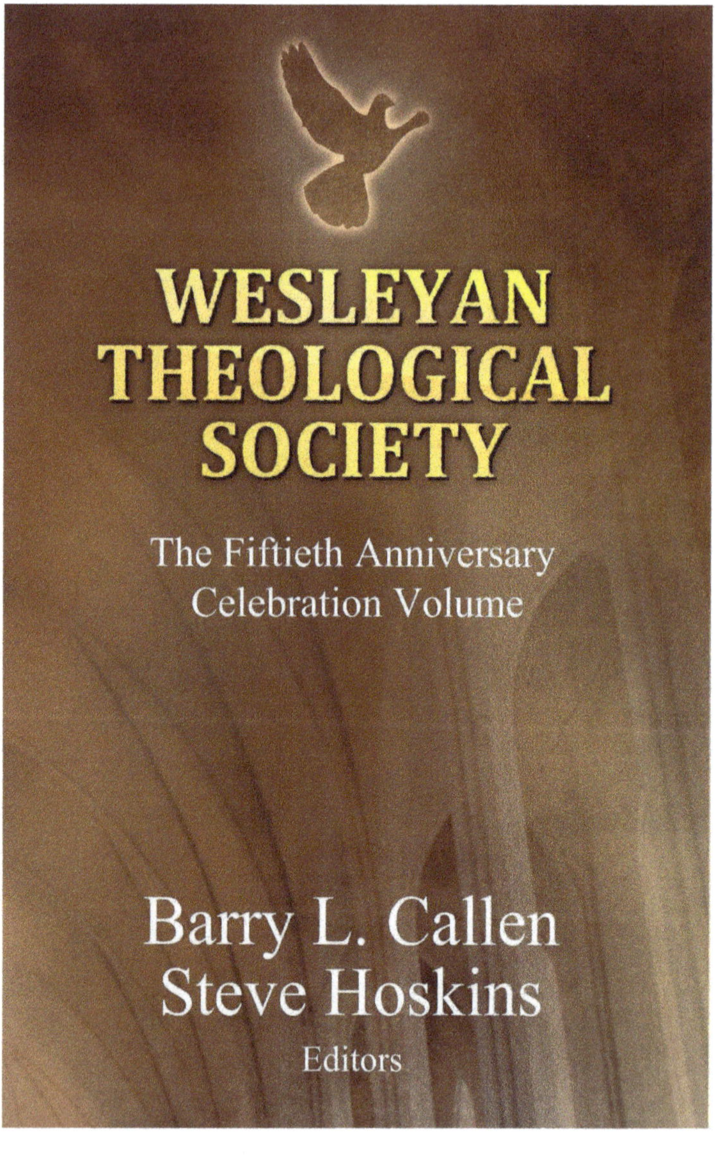

WESLEYAN THEOLOGICAL SOCIETY

The Fiftieth Anniversary
Celebration Volume

Barry L. Callen
Steve Hoskins
Editors

www.ingramcontent.com/pod-product-compliance
Lightning Source LLC
Chambersburg PA
CBHW040744020526
44114CB00048B/2909